ABOUT THE AU

Alice Hart-Davis is an award-winni..g author. For nearly 20 years she has been reporting on the aesthetic cosmetic procedures colloquially known as tweakments, and has trialled countless procedures in order to review them.

Alice has won many awards for her work, though none for services as a cosmetic guinea pig. She attends aesthetics conferences around the world and spends a lot of time catching up with the doctors, surgeons, dentists, nurses, and the companies behind the technology in this fast-expanding field, the better to understand the tweakments on offer.

Over the years Alice has seen – and experienced first-hand – plenty of bad treatments, and understands the many problems that beset the aesthetics industry, from the lack of regulation to the rising incidence of body dysmorphia among cosmetic patients and practitioners.

Despite this, she remains an advocate of good, understated cosmetic work – the sort which goes undetected and unremarked, because it doesn't lead to weird-looking hamster cheeks or frozen foreheads. She is also still enthusiastic about the potential of tweakments for making people look that bit better, which in turn makes them feel better about themselves and better able to get on with the rest of their lives.

She lives in London, a short bicycle ride from Harley Street, with her husband and a lively Jack Russell terrier. Her three young adult children take a dim view of tweakments, but accept that these are something she does for work (and are too kind to use the word 'vanity').

The Tweakments Guide: Fresher Face

Everything you've ever wanted to know about non-surgical cosmetic procedures — by the woman who has tried them all

Alice Hart-Davis

Editor and Typesetter: Guy Hart-Davis

Research Assistant: Karen Heath

Cover Image: John Godwin

Cover Concept: Vicky Evans

Cover Artwork: SilverWood Books

Published in 2019 by Tweakments Guide Limited

1st Edition Printing: February 2019

ISBN 978-1-9993596-0-7 (paperback)

ISBN 978-1-9993596-1-4 (ebook)

Printed on responsibly sourced paper

DISCLAIMER

Before engaging with any of the procedures mentioned in this book, you should obtain professional or specialist advice (such as from an accredited doctor who is properly trained in the procedure you wish to try) and make your own enquiries about the practitioner you want to engage. This book is intended for reference and information only. The author is not a medical practitioner. The information given here is based on the author's experience and is for your consideration when considering non-surgical cosmetic procedures and other tweakments. It is not intended as medical advice on which you can rely. Any reliance placed by you on the reviews in the book is done by you at your own risk. The author cannot be held responsible for the performance of a practitioner who you may find through this book or any other loss arising from use of this book. If you suspect you have a medical problem, you should seek professional medical help.

DISCLOSURES

I have been writing about cosmetic treatments and non-surgical procedures for almost 20 years. During this time, I have been treated by many practitioners at many different clinics and given many different treatments, none of which I have paid for, because my visits are either so that I can write about the procedure, or just to educate me about a procedure, to understand better how it works.

Also, over the years, I have taken press trips with, or worked as a consultant for, or on projects with, many companies that supply either products or technology in this area, including Allergan, Cynosure, Galderma, Merz Aesthetics, Sinclair Pharma, and Zeltiq Aesthetics.

I have been sent products for review by hundreds of different companies over the past 20 years.

This has helped to give me a unique, in-depth understanding of the field. Does this make me biased towards certain clinics, practitioners, or products? I really don't think so. All the opinions in the book are my own, save for the case studies from other people, which are in their own words.

I have not been paid for recommendations, neither by practitioners for reviewing their treatments or seeking their opinions, nor by the suppliers of products and devices that are mentioned in this book.

Should you choose to visit a practitioner mentioned in this book or listed on the website, I receive no referral fees.

If you choose to buy skincare or devices on offer in the shop on the website, I will receive a small percentage of the cost as commission. If you disagree with this, you can buy the products through other channels.

ACKNOWLEDGEMENTS: A FEW 'THANK YOU'S

Firstly, huge thanks to all the doctors, nurses, surgeons, dentists, dermatologists, facialists and other aestheticians who have shown me their work over the past 20 years, done their best to educate me about the procedures they offer, and demonstrated their techniques on my face, often with the unhelpful addition of my selfie-stick or a newspaper photographer leaning over their shoulder. You know who you are.

And then I owe thanks to Karen Heath, who has not only tirelessly helped out in my office for the past six years but has willingly subjected herself to a raft of tweakments in that time. She has written some of them up in these pages. Many thanks to Karen, and also to Helen Nuttall, Sharon Walker, Victoria Fisher, Dawn Meggs, and Lisa Littlehales, who have given me permission to use their tweakments experiences in the reviews in here.

Next, massive thanks to my brother Guy Hart-Davis, one of the most patient, skilled, and tactful copy-editors you could ever find. He has the knack of nicking out idiocies and straightening jumbled thoughts in the kindest possible way ('I've had a go at unpacking the next sentence…'), and has not only plunged into the intricacies of the world of tweakments without flinching, but has taken the book the whole way through from raw copy to print-ready files.

Also, grateful thanks to my friends Elaine and Anne, who ploughed through the first draft and raised many salient points that I had blithely overlooked, and to the doctors who have advised me on technical points.

And particular thanks to my darling husband, Matthew Hindhaugh, who for 20 years has had to contend with me nipping out 'for a quick meeting', then coming home looking somewhat different after trying one or other of the tweakments in this book (and quite a few that haven't made the grade for inclusion). Mostly, he thinks it's funny, but sometimes he gets extremely cross when he finds I've been a guinea pig for an experimental new procedure that leaves me looking like I've been stung by a swarm of bees, or totally unable to move one side of my forehead. I think, if the day comes when I overreach myself and go one tweakment too far, and have to wear a paper bag on my head for the rest of my days, he will still put up with me. But I'll try not to put that to the test.

DEDICATION

This book is for my friend Ellie and everyone else who has looked in the mirror, had 'a horror moment', and wondered whether a tweakment might help – and if so, what are these things anyway, and where should she start?

I'm not saying anyone has to do anything to their faces.

This is just in case, like Ellie, you are curious.

CONTENTS AT A GLANCE

TABLE OF CONTENTS

TREATMENT REVIEWS

INTRODUCTION

Who This Book Is For and Why I Wrote It

A year ago, I opened my inbox to find an email from my friend Ellie. She had had what she called 'a horror moment' in the mirror that morning. 'I really need to see someone good who can do something clever for my face,' she wrote. 'I have no idea what this thing might be but I am open to suggestions. I am throwing myself on your mercy here. What I really need is a good recommendation of someone you trust…'

Ellie is approaching 50 and has spent the past 25 years concentrating on her family and her high-octane career rather than her face. For sure, she had heard a good deal about treatments such as Botox or face peels. She knew that famous faces get a lot of discreet help in this area with subtle 'tweakments' and, like so many people, she had wondered, 'Would these things work for me?' But like most people, she was baffled as to which procedures did what, where to start, and who to go to for the best results, so that she could be sure of ending up looking like a better version of herself, rather than just slightly weird.

I pointed her in the direction of some great cosmetic doctors, reassuring her that there was a lot she could do with skincare and what you might call advanced facials before she stepped up to more serious procedures.

Why had she asked me? Because I have been investigating and writing about these treatments and the people who do them for nearly 20 years. Ever since Botox started creeping out of the secrecy of Harley Street consulting rooms and into the popular consciousness − along with chemical peels, face-plumping fillers, and skin-smoothing lasers − I have been there, reporting on the phenomenon and trying out the latest procedures in order to write about the experience (ok, and also to see what these much-hyped 'tweakments' might do for my face).

My work as a beauty writer means that I have interviewed the practitioners who develop the treatments, toured factories around the world where the products are made, and talked to the doctors and nurses who use these treatments daily about what works best, and why. I have also, over the years, tried a great many of these procedures, so I know which ones work best and which ones hurt the most – and also which ones aren't worth the bother.

This book is for the many people – men as well as women, younger as well as older – who, like Ellie, have wondered what all these tweakments are, and which might be right for them.

WHAT ARE 'TWEAKMENTS'?

Over the past 20 years, non-surgical cosmetic procedures like Botox, light treatments, thread lifts, and fillers have changed the way we look at ageing faces – and the way we view beauty. These treatments are less costly, time-consuming, and invasive than cosmetic surgery, yet way more expensive and effective than pampering, beauty-salon treatments.

Referring to these treatments as 'non-surgical aesthetic cosmetic procedures' is a bit of a mouthful and sounds really off-putting, which is why I'm calling them *tweakments*, a word which has crept into the language in the past few years and which gets the idea across more easily. These procedures, these tweakments, are about having a little something – but nothing as serious as cosmetic surgery – done to your face.

Most of these tweakments are temporary. The results may last for up to 18 months, but they rarely make a permanent change to the way you look.

ARE YOU READY FOR A TWEAKMENT?

The number of cosmetic treatments carried out in the UK each year is rising fast and it's a huge business, reckoned to generate some £2.75 billion a year. Having any sort of aesthetic procedure is now more acceptable than ever, and according to recent research from Mintel, 43 per cent of UK adults would be interested in having a cosmetic tweakment. Even though many people still feel tweakments are a step too far, particularly if they involve needles, this more-positive attitude towards aesthetics has encouraged Superdrug to start offering Botox and fillers at a major branch in central London, at prices way below those found in Harley Street clinics.

What the research in this area also shows is that, at least in the UK and much of Europe, people feel conflicted about tweakments. That 43 per cent mentioned above are madly curious and would like to see what difference tweakments might make to their looks, but they fear being judged harshly if the work appears obvious, or if their friends think them vain or foolish for having something done. Research by the companies behind the leading ranges of facial fillers has found that women who are considering facial fillers will go on considering the issue for at least a year before booking in for consultation. (Also, alarmingly, research shows that, of the people who are considering facial injectables, only one in 10 actively do any research into the product before blithely booking in for treatment.)

Why the reluctance? It's partly the stigma that hangs around these treatments, and partly the fact that we have all seen what happens when tweakments go wrong: the awful pictures of celebs who have gone too far and been photographed with features that look frozen, or over-inflated, or just bizarre and out of proportion.

People also worry about how much treatments may hurt, and whether they will be left bruised, swollen, or red in the face after treatment, and how long this will last for. Then there are concerns about how to find a good practitioner – very valid concerns, given that there is so little legal regulation in this whole area – and how safe and well-tested the treatments on offer are. What happens if something goes wrong?

This book is here to answer all these questions, to help you work out which tweakments might be appropriate for you, and to guide you towards the right treatments and the right practitioner.

IF YOU'RE INTERESTED, WHERE DO YOU START?

If you don't know much about the complex and highly confusing world of tweakments, it is hard to know where to start. You might be lucky, and have a friend who knows about these things who you can ask for advice. If you're really lucky, you will find your way to a good, reputable clinic (there are many) and will be offered appropriate advice and allowed time to digest this before embarking on any sort of treatment.

But few clinics offer a full smorgasbord of non-surgical tweakments, so they will suggest treatment with the products and equipment that they have. They certainly won't suggest alternative treatments that their competitors might offer. How can you possibly know if these are the most appropriate treatments for getting to achieve the results you want? Especially if you don't really know what's on offer elsewhere.

> One thing it is essential that you remember is that tweakments should be seen as medical procedures rather than beauty treatments. Even if the lines between the two seem to be becoming blurred, and people are taking a more casual approach to them, you should view these procedures with the utmost seriousness.

ISN'T ALL THIS INFORMATION AVAILABLE ONLINE?

To be sure, you can find out anything you like about cosmetic treatments online – but online it is always hard to assess the quality of the advice or opinions you are getting. Many practitioners claim much more for their treatments than can be delivered. Which procedures are reliable? Which work best for what concern, and how long do they take, how much do they cost, and how much do they hurt? And which should you stay well clear of?

WHICH TWEAKMENTS WOULD WORK BEST FOR YOU?

That depends on what your main concerns are about your face. Reading this book will help you identify those concerns and determine what would work best for you. As in so many areas of life, when it comes to aesthetic medical procedures, knowledge is power. Once you have a better idea of how different tweakments work, what they involve, and how much they cost, you will be better equipped to have a proper discussion with your chosen practitioner about your concerns, rather than feeling caught like a rabbit in the headlights when deluged with detailed information about treatment options.

This book demystifies the whole area of cosmetic procedures, and explains their benefits and drawbacks, how they work, what it is like to have each procedure done – often with a case study to provide real-life experience of each treatment mentioned – how much they hurt (or not), what they cost, and where to find great practitioners.

IS THIS BOOK FOR YOU?

This book is for:

- Anyone who is curious about what they might do to help keep their face looking as fresh and youthful as they'd like it to look.
- Anyone who has looked in the mirror and had, like Ellie, one of those 'horror moments', where you realise your face needs more help than you can give it through skincare, diet, and getting more sleep.
- Anyone who doesn't know where to start in this complicated and highly confusing area.
- Anyone who wants to know what all their options are when it comes to cosmetic treatments, and who wants unbiased advice to help them work out which procedures might work best for them.
- Anyone who wonders how all those celebs who never admit to having anything more than a sprinkling of laser light to get rid of sun damage have achieved what Dr Tracy Mountford, one of the best cosmetic doctors in the country, calls 'a state of aesthetic suspended animation', and managed to stay looking 35 for at least 15 years. (Spoiler: They're doing stuff like this – and probably doing quite a lot of it.)

WHAT THIS BOOK WILL TELL YOU

This book will tell you everything you need to know about the following topics:

- Why your skin and your face look the way they do as you get older.

- What you can do with skincare to help improve your complexion.
- Which tweakments – from high-tech facials to lasers, Botox, injectable fillers, and thread lifts – can help with which particular concerns, and how well they work.
- What it is like to experience one of these treatments, by someone who has tried it, and whether you will need any 'downtime' after a particular treatment.
- What the treatments cost, and where to find them.
- How to find a good practitioner.
- Why the UK is the 'Wild West' when it comes to tweakments, and why there is so little regulation in this area.
- How to avoid things going wrong – but what to do if they do.
- Which home-use devices can help and which ones work best.

To learn the answers to the most common myths about non-surgical treatments, and to read FAQs and the latest information about tweakments, visit this book's website, www.thetweakmentsguide.com.

HOW THIS BOOK IS ORGANISED – AND HOW TO USE IT

I've organised this book by describing the main concerns about the face, then explaining the ways that these can be improved – first with skincare, because it is always a good idea to start with skincare, and then with various different types of tweakments.

I explain the technology behind each tweakment as we come to it, to give you a better idea of how it works. I include treatment reviews of many of the tweakments, to give you an idea of what each procedure actually involves, what it feels like to have it done, and what sort of results it gives.

How This Book Is Organised

This book's chapters are organised by each concern, like this:

- **'Dynamic' lines and wrinkles.** These are the lines that appear on your forehead and around the eyes when you raise your eyebrows, frown, or scrunch up your eyes. They're called 'dynamic' because they are created by movement of the face muscles, though as time goes on they start to become entrenched.

- **Skin texture.** This is a bit of a catch-all, as lots of factors contribute towards the texture of the skin, leaving it feeling dry, rough to the touch, and covered in fine lines.
- **Uneven pigmentation.** That means the age spots that result from sun damage, and hormone-related pigmentation.
- **Thread veins, rosacea and redness, pores, and acne spots.** Those are all fairly self-explanatory, and all contribute to making the skin looking uneven in tone.
- **Loss of volume.** This chapter talks about the way the face starts to look a bit hollow with age, as the fat pads that provide volume start to shrink, and the bones of our skull start to shrink too, just for good measure.
- **Sagging skin.** We all know what this looks like, and it is what happens when slacker skin (from loss of collagen) is draped over a shrinking frame (as fat pads dwindle and bone recedes)

There are lots of different ways to treat each of those concerns, but there are one or two main ways that most practitioners will suggest for each of them, as follows:

- **Dynamic lines and wrinkles** – injections of wrinkle-relaxing toxins such as Botox.
- **Skin texture** – medical needling, laser resurfacing, under-the-skin moisturising injections.
- **Pigmentation** – laser and intense pulsed light treatment, skin peels.
- **Thread veins, pores, rosacea and redness, pores, and spots** – laser and intense pulsed light, microneedling.
- **Loss of Volume** – injectable fillers.
- **Sagging skin** – radiofrequency, ultrasound, laser, and heat-based skin tightening; thread lifts.

You might be thinking, 'But it's my eye bags I'm bothered about – which category does that come under?'

To work backwards to finding the appropriate concern, you need to think what it is about that area that is bothering you.

If it's baggy skin under your eyes or hollow-looking cheeks, those are both due to losing fat from the face, so go to the chapter on restoring volume to the face, though you could also consider treating the loose skin with skin-tightening tweakments.

If it's lines on your forehead, go to the chapter on dynamic lines and wrinkles. And so on.

To help you find the information you need, the website (thetweakmentsguide.com) includes a diagram where you can click on the relevant part of the face to see which tweakments could be used in that area. There are usually several options to consider.

For many of the tweakments, there are first-person reviews by someone (usually me) who has tried the treatment.

How to Use This Book

This book is stuffed with information about tweakments – and skincare, and skin-boosting supplements, and home-use devices. But how on earth do you go about putting all this information together into a practical treatment plan that will work with whatever budget you have available?

There's a list of the most commonly offered tweakments in 'The Recipe for a Fresher Face' on page 8 which can give you an idea of the sort of procedures a cosmetic practitioner might suggest, and in what order.

Still, it's hard to set any hard-and-fast rules. A lot of us fret about the same things when it comes to our faces, but everyone's concerns are different and specific.

This is where you might want to nip over to my website, www.thetweakmentsguide.com, and head for the Find a Tweakment section. Hover over the section of the face that is bothering you, and choose one of the 'concerns' for this area. Clicking one specific concern will take you through to a selection of tweakments that could be used on this part of the face. You can refine your search by cost, by whether you are happy to try treatments that involve needles, and by whether you need to avoid any downtime.

Once you have settled on a tweakment, you can follow on to the practitioner finder, which will help you identify a practitioner or clinic in your area. You can see whether a practitioner is a doctor, a nurse, a surgeon, or a dermatologist, and how many years' experience they have had.

And no, I don't get any kickback, financial or otherwise, if you choose any of them.

While you're considering your tweakment options, you might want to look at my suggestions for skincare products for particular skin concerns. There's an interactive tool on the website to take you through this, too, and you can find suggestions for my favourite home-use beauty devices and skin supplements, too. If you choose to buy any of these through the website, I will receive a small percentage of the cost as commission. If you disagree with this, you can buy the products through other channels.

PART 1: THE LOWDOWN

The world of beauty is always looking for a magic bullet to fix our perceived flaws – a pill, potion, or treatment to make us look as we used to, or as we'd like to.

There's only so much that a pill or a potion can do, but the treatment options for altering our faces have been expanding at a bewildering rate over the past two decades.

Between the world of skincare – which can smooth, condition, and firm the skin but which can't change the proportions of your face – and the world of cosmetic surgery – which can make dramatic and permanent alterations to your looks – lies a whole realm of non-surgical cosmetic procedures known as tweakments.

Tweakments occupy a strange space. They are minor medical procedures that ought to be carried out in an appropriately clinical setting. Yet they are often taken very lightly, offered in back rooms at hairdressers or at 'Botox parties'.

One of this book's main messages is that you need to take tweakments seriously. Another is that if you think you might like a tweakment, it is vital that you take time to educate yourself about what they are, how they work, and who can perform them. Knowledge, as always, is power – in this case, the power to make the right decision.

This first part of the book gives you the lowdown on what you need to know, starting with what happens to our faces as they age, and which tweakments can help to counteract this – and how.

There's a vital chapter on how to find a good, experienced practitioner – and you can follow this up by exploring the practitioner-finder on my website, www.thetweakmentsguide.com.

I talk about the trickle-down effect of tweakments, too; there's a chapter on what I call 'facials plus', which bridge the gap between pampering beauty salon facials and more effective but more daunting clinical tweakments, by adding, say, a little microneedling or laser treatment on to a traditional facial.

There's also a chapter on the home-use devices which offer watered-down versions of tweakment technology. These devices are not as powerful as in-clinic treatments, but if you use them as directed, they will definitely give results.

CHAPTER 1

Tweakments – What They Are and What They Aren't

I've mentioned already how tweakments are cosmetic procedures that can make significant, though usually temporary, improvements to the face. In this chapter, I'll discuss how tweakments aren't just about anti-ageing, how they're not just for women, and how they differ from cosmetic surgery. I'll also talk about whether tweakments are addictive, and why you need to keep a sense of perspective if and when you start trying them.

I'll then move on to laying out the basic recipe for creating a fresher face with tweakments, why collagen is such a vital component in our skin, and how most tweakments are aimed at stimulating collagen formation, before having a little rant about tweakments help celebs to look ageless and how cross it makes me that famous people so rarely admit how much 'help' they have in this area.

TWEAKMENTS AREN'T JUST ABOUT 'ANTI-AGEING'

There's a widespread misperception that tweakments are all about 'anti-ageing' – a phrase I have been deliberately avoiding. Yes, most tweakments will make you look a bit younger, given that they are softening wrinkles, smoothing away pigmentation marks, tightening up sagging skin, and giving back to the face some of the youthful softness and glow that it loses with the passing years.

And yes, this world of aesthetics used to be all about conquering ageing. But that was 15 years ago, when practitioners were keen to chase away all the lines on a face, and the TV programme 10 Years Younger was about to launch. But now, if you ask women why they are having these treatments, 'looking younger' comes way down their list of reasons, far behind 'looking more rested', 'looking fresher', and 'feeling more confident about myself'. It's not even about 'looking good for my age', which is the sort of phrase that makes the modern mid-lifer bristle. It's about looking good, full stop.

KEY TERMS DESCRIBING HOW WE WANT TO LOOK AS WE AGE

Here are explanations of five key terms I use in my descriptions of how the tweakments make your skin and your face look.

- **Fresher.** Your whole face looks less stressed and more awake. The back-from-holiday look.

- **Clearer.** Your skin has a more even, consistent tone, as if wearing tinted moisturiser.

- **Brighter.** Your skin has greater clarity and looks more radiant than before.

- **Plumper.** Plumping up your skin, with hydrating skincare, makes it look gently swollen – but in a good way, so skin looks healthy and wrinkles are less obvious. Plumping up the face with subtle amounts of injectable fillers makes an older face look less hollow and less deflated. So 'plumper' is good, whichever way you look at it.

- **Rested.** Your face looks as if you've had three good nights' sleep in a row.

Beyond the wrinkle-smoothing and face-plumping, tweakments are increasingly popular for making small but significant structural alterations to a face: raising the cheekbones a fraction, strengthening the jawline, adjusting asymmetry, making a curved or hooked nose appear straighter, redefining the lips – the sort of work which enhances a face whatever its age, and which is pulling in a whole new bunch of patients far too young to be thinking in terms of ageing.

This is particularly true when it comes to lips. You can blame social media influencers, especially Kylie Jenner – who had lip fillers aged 17, denied it, then later admitted it – for encouraging a generation of young women to see bigger lips as an easily-bought status symbol, or you could blame Instagram and other social media channels. But the fact remains that the unfeasibly plumped-up pout look isn't going away any time soon.

TWEAKMENTS ARE NOT JUST FOR WOMEN

Many of these tweakments are increasingly popular with men. Usually, men make up about 10 per cent of the patient group at a clinic, but some doctors find 40 per cent of their clientele is male. Non-surgical treatments often work better for men than facelifts, which frequently just look weird. Once men realise how swift, straightforward, and effective procedures like laser skin-freshening facials can be, or how quickly intense pulsed treatment can clear facial redness and thread veins, they become keen devotees.

If you ask men why they want the treatments, they'll might say they want to keep themselves looking sharp in a competitive office environment, or it could be because they're divorced and are dating again. If you ask me, men need practical information (like this book) about tweakments even more than women, not least because men rarely read magazines that talk about Botox and fillers and all the rest – and they certainly don't discuss it down the pub with their mates.

TWEAKMENTS V SURGERY

Just in case you're wondering, tweakments are not cosmetic surgery; they are all non-surgical procedures. Some tweakments are minimally invasive, but most are non-invasive. I mention this because lots of people refer to any treatment more challenging than a facial as 'a form of cosmetic surgery'.

Cosmetic surgery is serious stuff; it involves scalpels, anaesthesia, time spent in hospital, and a fair amount of recovery time afterwards. Tweakments are different. I'm using the term to cover procedures such as Botox, cosmetic laser work, facial fillers, skin peels, and thread lifts, the sort of treatments that might take an hour and after which you should be able to carry on with life as normal, though you may be a bit red in the face and not feeling like going out in the evening.

UNDERSTANDING 'NON-SURGICAL', 'MINIMALLY INVASIVE', AND 'NON-INVASIVE'

Here are the meanings of three key terms you'll see in the main text:

- **Non-surgical:** Procedures involving no scalpels and no general anaesthetics. All tweakments are non-surgical.

- **Minimally invasive:** Procedures which may involve needles, which obviously pierce the skin, but don't go deep; for example, facial fillers and wrinkle-relaxing injections.

- **Non-invasive:** Procedures involving nothing that breaks the skin. Tweakments that don't involve needles, like skin peels and laser treatment.

IF YOU START ON TWEAKMENTS – IS IT A SLIPPERY SLOPE?

The other question that pops up when people start considering cosmetic work is: just how much of a slippery slope is it? If you start doing a spot of wrinkle-softening, do you get addicted to it? Once you try fillers, do you have to keep them up forever – and if you stop, will your face collapse like an overdone soufflé, or look even older than before?

I think it very much depends on the sort of person that you are and, without sounding pretentious, your personal relationship with your looks and whether you can manage to keep your perspective. A cosmetic doctor I was working with recently, when asked the slippery-slope question by a potential patient, almost shouted 'Yes! It is!' And she wasn't joking, even though she is 20 years younger than me. I can see that keeping her own face looking as lovely as possible is vital for being a good advertisement for her business, and I know she does a good deal to her own features and clearly enjoys experimenting with new treatments, but she looks great, as in normal. The key, as ever with treatments, is knowing when to stop. It's when you start thinking that more is more that things start going wrong.

And if you stop having treatments altogether, your face will just go back to looking like it was before. It certainly won't look older than before. Having a tweakment or two is a bit like pressing 'pause' on the ageing clock.

ARE THESE TWEAKMENTS ADDICTIVE?

No. But what I find *is* rather addictive is the possibility of looking rather better, fresher, and more youthful. I have had a great many procedures over the past 15 years and seem to constantly be having top-ups of Botox and fillers and skin-tightening or pigment-clearing treatments – it's like painting the Forth Bridge, a never-ending job.

But Botox and fillers are temporary treatments. They only last so long, and I like to let their effects wear off before I jump in asking for more, to remind myself of what I look like without them, to help me keep a sense of perspective.

WHY YOU DON'T NEED TO BE SCARED OF TWEAKMENTS

I would strongly argue that cosmetic procedures are an empowering option that put women – and increasingly men – in control of choosing how they will look as they age.

Many people are fearful that as soon as they step into a cosmetic clinic, things will be 'done' to their face that they will hate. Don't forget that, to a good practitioner, you are a new and potentially valuable new patient. They want you to be happy. They would like you to be so delighted with your treatment and with the way you look that you will not only come back and spend more money with them, but that you will tell your friends about the brilliant work that they do, and bring in more customers. So they are not out to turn you into a freak. They're hoping to make you into an even better version of your current self, to subtly enhance your innate beauty, not wreck it.

KEEP YOUR EXPECTATIONS REALISTIC

Procedures can do a great deal to make your skin smoother and less pigmented. They can soften frown lines, tighten the skin, and restore lost volume to the face. *But only up to a point.* They will not make you look 10 years younger overnight – though they could turn back the clock if you did a good many of them, and supported them with great skincare and a healthy lifestyle, and kept doing them for several years.

A good practitioner with long experience will have a pretty good idea of the sort of result you may get from any particular treatment – but no practitioner can predict with total certainty the exact results that any procedure will give you. We all respond slightly differently to treatments, and there is always a small percentage of people who just don't respond in the expected way.

If you are a good candidate for treatment – something which your practitioner will advise you on – then you may well get great results from treatment. But while these tweakments can smooth, clear, lift, and tighten skin and give noticeable results, they are not going to change the fundamental proportions of your face. If you don't already have a strong jaw and a wide mouth like Angelina Jolie, you can't expect your lips to ever look like hers, and adding more filler won't make it happen. Nor can tweakments change your bone structure. They won't make you look like Gisele, or Helen Mirren, or Kylie Jenner, or David Gandy for that matter. They won't help solve any ongoing issues in your life, either, but they can certainly make you look like a fresher version of yourself – you on a really good day.

THE RECIPE FOR A FRESHER FACE

If there is a standard list, or recipe, for how to freshen an ageing face, it goes something like this:

- Soften deep frown lines and crow's feet with wrinkle-relaxing toxins (such as Botox).
- Replace lost volume in cheeks, lips, and temples, and adjust facial asymmetry with fillers.
- Make the skin's texture smoother with medical needling, or lasers, or radiofrequency devices, and moisturising injections.
- Reduce pigmentation marks with laser or light treatments, or with chemical peels.

- Clear thread veins, improve the look of large pores, and reduce skin blemishes.
- Improve skin firmness with radiofrequency devices, lasers, or needling, all of which can stimulate collagen growth.
- Tighten slack skin with radiofrequency devices that 'shrink-wrap' the collagen or with focussed ultrasound that tightens the muscular layer within the skin; or tighten the skin directly with a thread lift, which passes barbed threads through the skin and lifts it upwards into a more youthful position.

And then you will need to support the improvements in the skin quality with zealous use of effective skincare, and protect your skin year-round with broad-spectrum sunscreen.

Yes, that's a fairly extensive list of procedures, and no one is suggesting that you race off and have all of it done as quickly as possible. And yes, none of these procedures is cheap.

But this list gives you an idea of the various aspects of cosmetic medicine and how tweakments can be used to soften the effects of ageing. Your practitioner should work through all the possibilities with you, and draw up a treatment plan of the various options, so that you can consider which ones offer the best value and will bring about the difference that you are hoping for.

Which procedures you choose will likely depend first on how much change you're looking to make. Are you hoping to end up looking like a slightly fresher version of your current self – or are you looking for a major transformation? The procedures you choose to effect this change will depend on how much money you have to spend, and whether you can face the idea of procedures that demand a day or two of 'downtime'.

The great majority of good cosmetic practitioners in the UK prefer to take a 'less is more' approach. As they will point out, you can always have more done, but once it's done, you can't reduce it: you just have to wait for the effects of the treatment to wear off, which will take some time.

But there are many different ways of tackling each of these steps, and many different machines, or products, or techniques, for achieving the results. As you can see from the list at the beginning of this section, there are plenty of different ways to make the skin smoother or to stimulate collagen formation. Which one should you go for? I'll explain the benefits and potential of each particular method as we come to it.

TWEAKMENTS AND SKIN TONES

Most tweakments can be used on most skin tones, from pale to dark. Lasers used to be a no-no for darker skin, because they strike pigment in the surface of the skin, but now, lasers which reach deeper into the skin can work to improve pigmentation on darker skins. Radiofrequency and focussed ultrasound energy, which work beneath the surface, are usually fine on any skin colour. But always, always ask your practitioner whether the tweakment you are considering is advisable for your particular skin tone.

WHY COLLAGEN IS SO IMPORTANT

The majority of these treatments aim to improve and renew collagen in the skin. Why is collagen such a big deal? It's a protein that gives our skin its structure and firmness and that forms the scaffolding of the skin. Our skin makes its own collagen in cells called fibroblasts, and this process of producing and renewing collagen goes on very efficiently until we hit 30, when the production line starts to slow down. That means our skin doesn't repair itself as fast or as well as it did before, so that it is less resilient. Then, the expression lines that show up when we crinkle our eyes, smile, or frown start becoming embedded.

Collagen production keeps on ticking over in our 40s, but for women, the tipping point comes with the menopause. One surgeon told me that if you're looking at a graph showing collagen production and how it declines with age, that line slopes downwards fairly gently – until the point of menopause, at which point it more or less stops. 'Imagine a car hitting a brick wall,' he said.

(It's not so bad for men. In male skin, collagen production just continues to decline gradually with age.)

Worse, our lifestyle choices don't always help preserve our collagen supplies. UV light – that's good old daylight, not just bright strong sunlight – gradually wears down your collagen if you don't protect your skin with sunscreen. Smoking accelerates collagen breakdown, and so do free radicals, the unstable molecules that are created in the body by the effects of pollution, smoking, and ultraviolet light. Collagen breakdown matters because when the skin loses its collagen-based structure, it starts to look frail and collapses more easily into folds.

So collagen is fundamental to the look and the quality of the skin, which is why so many treatments focus on building it up. Anything that causes damage or injury to the skin will create a 'wound-healing response', as part of which the skin will start to make new collagen. That's why so many of these treatments involve brutal-sounding measures like driving tiny needles deep into the skin, or zapping it with heat, laser beams, radio-frequency energy, or focussed ultrasound, to provoke the skin into making more of its own collagen to repair the damage.

DO YOU NEED AGGRESSIVE TREATMENTS TO MAKE MORE COLLAGEN?

If you are keen to avoid those sorts of treatments, the good news is that there are gentler ways of kick-starting ageing fibroblasts into producing more collagen. Red light therapy, which involves nothing more troublesome than lying down under a screen or moulded face mask studded with tiny LED lights that give off a red glow, is increasingly popular with cosmetic doctors as well as in beauty salons. The red light has a healing effect on the skin and promotes the growth of collagen.

Skincare can also help here: creams with retinol or retinoic acid will wake up dozy, ageing fibroblasts, as will well-formulated vitamin C serums.

Or you could start talking a special kind of vitamin C supplement which has been proven to help your skin and its fibroblasts to produce a whole lot more collagen. I know it works, as I've tried it; I've explained more about this and how it works on page 119. And while we're on the topic, a number of the 'beauty pills' that promise to boost collagen levels in the skin do actually work, and have the data to prove it.

Why would you go for the painful options if you could just lie back under a red light mask or gulp down a supplement? Well, that's a good question. With LED light, you have to lie under it quite a lot – for 20 minutes, three times a week – so it depends on how easy it is for you to get to the salon or clinic with that light, and how much it will cost you each time. With the vitamin C, there's no downside, apart from the fact that this brand, the one with the data to show that it works, costs around £100 a month. Same with the collagen pills. The doctors would tell you that their needling, or laser resurfacing, or radiofrequency skin tightening has a more direct and immediate effect, and people who choose these treatments are usually using effective skincare already and want to see what else they can try.

I feel it's all a question of marginal gains. If and when you find one more thing that makes an appreciable difference to the way your skin looks and feels by improving its collagen levels, why would you not just add it into the mix, along with great skincare and a healthy lifestyle?

WHAT ARE 'BABY' TREATMENTS AND MICRODOSING?

In the same way that they have started talking about procedures as 'tweakments', many practitioners now talk of offering 'baby' treatments (eg 'baby Botox') or 'microdosing'.

What they mean is that they will give you a really light version of a treatment – maybe a tiny spot of filler, or wrinkle-relaxing toxins, or laser. It all sounds much more user-friendly, particularly if you are new to cosmetic procedures and a little anxious about how the whole thing will go, what the results will look like, and whether your friends will judge you for it. If that appeals to you, then for sure, give it a go. But bear in mind that, obviously, anything that is a 'baby' or 'micro' version of a normal treatment won't show as great a result nor last as long as a regular dose of the same treatment.

WHAT KIND OF RESULTS CAN TWEAKMENTS DELIVER?

You can get impressive results with non-surgical treatments. Take a look at some of the before-and-after shots that most clinics offer on their websites. Some of these changes are major transformations. Deep lines on the face can be softened, under-eye bags or hollows can more or less be made to vanish, and deflated cheeks can be softly re-plumped, while jowls and double chins can be greatly reduced.

All these things *can* be done – the real question is, will they work for you? Will you get the sort of results that you see in those before-and-after shots? Maybe. It all depends on what your face looks like before treatment, what sort of condition your skin is in, and also how old you are. Skin-tightening treatments, for example, are obviously going to work better on people with mild-to-moderate skin slackening than they will on older skin which has lost its firmness and elasticity and which really needs a surgical lift.

One of your practitioner's key skills is in offering appropriate treatment, or a selection of appropriate treatments, to get the desired results. Your practitioner also will know, from experience, whether you are a suitable candidate for particular procedures. And a good practitioner will tell you when a procedure isn't going to deliver for you.

It's like asking how long and difficult a journey is going to be. It depends on where you are going and where you are starting from. If you are only looking for a tiny bit of facial enhancement, and your skin is healthy, then it will be quicker and easier than if you want to make a good deal of change and your face is more lined and saggy.

When you're looking at before-and-afters on a clinic website, they will show you the very best results that they have been able to achieve. It's worth asking the date of the before-and-afters – if the pictures are old, you might wonder why there are no newer examples of better work.

DO TWEAKMENTS MAKE EVERYONE LOOK THE SAME?

No, but there is definitely a 'done' look, and it's not a great one. If you were to start attending aesthetic-industry conferences, you'd see a lot of it: the foreheads that are too smooth and immobile, the eyebrows that sit a little too high and make a face look permanently surprised, the cheeks that are surprisingly full, the lips that are stuffed to bursting point and stick out forwards too much…

But no one has to look like that. All our faces have plenty of individual character, and a good, sympathetic cosmetic practitioner will work with you to enhance your own features without blanking them out into some kind of idealised template or trying to change anything fundamental about the way you look. Most UK practitioners are aiming to achieve gentle improvement. They don't want to scare you away.

CELEBS, TWEAKMENTS, AND AGELESS BEAUTY

The changes that take place in a face as it ages – the encroaching lines and wrinkles, the drier skin texture, the sagging – happen to everyone: to me, to you, to your friends, colleagues, and relatives. They're also happening to all the actors and celebs and public figures who look surprisingly good for their years. Did those people just win the genetic lottery? Perhaps, but genes will only help you so far. They won't help prevent collagen breakdown, fat loss, and bone resorption – that's the gradual breakdown of bone tissue that nibbles away at the jawline and makes eye sockets larger with age.

So how do all the beautiful, preternaturally young-looking older people look that way? Have they perhaps had a little help? For most of them, however much they deny it, the answer is a resounding 'Yes'. Sometimes that help is a bit overenthusiastic and too obvious – the plastic-looking foreheads, over-surprised eyebrows, chipmunk cheeks, and trout-pout lips.

But increasingly, cosmetic doctors are getting so good at what they do that their work is hard to spot, and they would be mortified to think that the variety of tweakments they carry out for their famous patients is obvious.

The Tweakment Deniers

But this help goes unacknowledged, and the way that celebs and the well-known consistently pretend they don't get this subtle work is really unhelpful for the vast majority of people who despair of the toll that life is taking on their ageing faces. I've sat opposite famous interviewees who've declared, while looking me straight in the eye, that they would never do anything like Botox – because they tried it once and it 'looked weird', or because it is against their principles. 'Look at how my forehead moves!' they'll say, and I'll feel it isn't my place to say, 'Yes! You can twitch your eyebrows – just – but you can't actually frown, can you?'

I'm sure they'd say it's just a little white lie, and anyway, it's none of my business. But it is downright deceitful. Yes, these people also benefit from having great stylists and make-up artists, and flattering lighting on screen and in photo-shoots, and possibly just a smidgen of retouching in their photographs – but that won't account for their fuller lips, tighter skin, higher cheekbones, and remarkably smooth foreheads.

I love watching well-known people on TV chat shows, particularly when there is someone in the line-up, maybe an older British character actor or musician, who has clearly had nothing done to their face, and comparing and contrasting that face, with its natural range of movement, to the others next to it. Have the people with the extra-smooth, barely-moving faces had stuff done? What do you think? In an un-tweaked face, the eyebrows can lift right up, wrinkling the forehead, or pull together, creating the '11' tram-lines between them. Eyes can be scrunched up or opened wide. Smiles crease up the whole face, and light up the eyes. It's a useful reality check.

Is Glossy the New Normal?

Glossy-looking celebs may have come to represent a new 'normal' by the standards we now seem to expect of famous faces, but if you took these people and put them in a line-up with their old school friends, they would stick out a mile. Is that just luck, or maybe the result of a clean diet and exercise programme and the sort of sheen that comes with being well known and having access to make-up artists and all that? Or is it thanks to the sort of stealthy, continual 'tweakments' that help soften expression lines, pad out sagging cheeks, and freshen the complexion? I think you know the answer.

It would be so great if people in general and celebs in particular were a little more honest about the tweakments they have had done. It would make the whole discussion around trying procedures and what works and what doesn't more open. It would remove much of the stigma that still hangs around the whole idea of getting treatment.

I do appreciate that cosmetic treatments aren't for everyone and that most people will never regard them in any way as normal, but for those people who are interested in procedures, greater openness from celebs would reduce the fear and shame around trying them.

WHAT ABOUT THE SO-CALLED 'BOTOX BACKLASH'?

In the past few years, there has been a great deal of nonsense talked about the so-called 'Botox backlash', the idea that people who had been doing Botox have gone off it and turned to other means of softening the onward creep of ageing – because that is what you will read in almost every interview where a celeb has been asked about cosmetic work.

I spend a good deal of time visiting and talking to doctors, dermatologists, and cosmetic surgeons, and I like to ask them whether they're doing less Botox these days. They always look at me oddly – am I not aware, they ask, that Botox is one of the top two procedures they offer at their clinic? (Along with facial fillers, it's the bread and butter of almost every clinic in the UK.) 'Just checking,' I say, 'because of this so-called Botox backlash you must have heard about – apparently all the celebs have stopped doing it!' And then the penny drops, they get the joke, and we have a bit of a laugh about it. But believe me, no practitioner in the UK is doing fewer Botox treatments now than five years ago. They're just getting better at doing subtle work that makes a face look great.

HOW TWEAKMENTS ARE CHANGING THE FACE OF MODERN BEAUTY

The key thing that non-surgical treatments do is provide options for those who are interested. Options about how you age, which is a big deal. It's your choice whether you engage with them, and it's your choice as to how far you take it. But how fabulous is it that we even *have* that choice?

For the first time in history, the way your face looks is not simply at the mercy of your genes and your lifestyle. Well, ok, cosmetic surgery has been there as an option for many years, but that is drastic and irreversible. The key thing about the huge majority of today's non-surgical cosmetic procedures is that they are all about taking small steps in the direction of softening the effects of ageing, or improving on what nature gave you.

CHAPTER 2

What Sort of Changes
Do You Want to Make?

You may be reading this book because, like my friend Ellie, you've reached that stage where you look in the mirror and wonder whether your face needs a bit more help than skincare, sleep, or diet can provide.

We all have days like this, particularly after a late night, or too many drinks, or when stress has got the better of us, or we aren't sleeping well. But when those horror-moments in the mirror become an everyday occurrence, you might feel you need to take action.

The good news is that there is a lot that you can do, from making your complexion look fresher, to softening frown lines and reducing sagginess in the face.

What you need to do to achieve such changes very much depends on what your concerns are, what sort of difference you are hoping to make to your face, and the current state of your face and skin.

There's also the question of how far you are prepared to go to achieve results. I know that what we really all want is a painless magic wand of a treatment that will make us look miles better in one swift session, but the reality is that the treatments that are quick and comfortable are usually ones that produce minimal results, and which need to be repeated multiple times to give the best effect.

Are you up for using the sort of highly active skincare that will mean, for six weeks, you will have a sore, peeling, super-sensitive face, but after which you will look transformed? How do you feel about treatments that require a spot of downtime, as in a day or three when you really won't want to show your face to your nearest and dearest, let alone your colleagues? Do you feel comfortable with the idea of lasers? Or treatments that involve needles? Many procedures involve one or the other, though they needn't be painful (honestly). The trend in aesthetics is for small, subtle tweakments rather the old-style, 10-years-younger-in-a-fortnight type of work.

If those sorts of things are already giving you pause for thought, don't worry – there are masses of treatments that involve almost no downtime, though you may have to have repeated sessions of them in order to get the maximum results. But then 'maximum' results may not be your aim. Maybe, like most of us, you just want to look that bit fresher, rather than vastly different.

The first step that you need to take to bridge the gap between looking in the mirror and feeling dispirited about what you see, and actually doing something about it, is working out what is most bothering you.

WHAT IS BOTHERING YOU ABOUT YOUR FACE?

When you go to see a cosmetic doctor, the first thing they should do is give you a hand mirror and ask you to look at your face and tell them what your main concerns are. So it is really helpful if you have had a think about this beforehand. Even if your main aim is just to look more relaxed and fresh-faced, it helps the practitioner no end if you can be a bit more specific about the changes you're looking for.

Is it your frown lines that are troubling you? Or a general sagging and crumpling of your face? Or is it the way the corners of your mouth are starting to turn down? Very often, it's not so much these things as the tone and texture of the skin that are the real concern; skin that is becoming drier, rougher, and more leathery or – which is possibly more annoying – drier and rougher but spotty at the same time.

Your practitioner is bound to have some private views about your face, but if they are good and thoughtful, they will listen to you rather than wading in with their own opinions. Most of them can tell you a story of what happens when they forget this, like the eminent cosmetic doctor, now retired, who told me how he once cheerfully greeted his last patient of the day, saying, 'Well, Mrs X, we can certainly do something about that big hairy mole on your cheek,' only for Mrs X to look appalled and ask him what mole he was talking about, because she had come about her frown lines, she didn't have any moles, did she?

So how do you narrow down the things about your face that are bothering you?

WHAT HAPPENS TO THE FACE AS IT AGES?

Here's a list of what happens to the face as it ages, to help you identify what your main concerns might be. We all know what an older face looks like when we see one. That's because a combination of the following things are going on, usually – unkindly – all at once.

- Lines and wrinkles become more obvious on the face – even when the face is still.

- The skin becomes less firm and springy as production of collagen (which keeps it strong) and elastin (which keeps it bouncy and pliable) decreases. This decrease starts in your thirties, picks up speed in your forties, and becomes unavoidably obvious in your fifties or around the menopause (whichever comes sooner), when the drop in hormone levels mean collagen production tails right off. What this reduction in collagen and elastin production means is that skin doesn't bounce back so easily from being pulled into expressions, and becomes wrinkled more easily.

- Pigmentation marks – a freckling of age spots, little broken thread veins, or a general sort of light mottling – become more obvious.

- Skin looks a bit drier as it loses its ability to hang onto moisture. That makes the skin's texture rougher, and it doesn't reflect the light so well.

- The fat pads that fill out the face and give it its youthful contours start to shrink with age, so the face starts to look gaunt.

- Robbed of the supporting fat, which gave the face the volume that was keeping it plumped up, skin starts to sag.

- The bone recedes around the eye sockets, the brow, the nose and the jaw. In men, this starts around the age of 65, but in women, very unfairly, these changes start earlier, from 40 onwards.

And that's all before you add in the undoubtedly ageing effects of stress, whether that's coming from your work or your personal life.

I've divided up the various tweakments that you might try into chapters based on each of these concerns – though as any practitioner will tell you, no one treatment is a magic bullet, and you usually get the best results by combining, say, treatments to soften wrinkles with ones that restore lost volume to the face. But more on that in a minute.

HOW MUCH DO YOU WANT TO CHANGE ABOUT THE WAY YOU LOOK?

Your next decision is how much you want to change, and how obvious you want this change to be. In the UK, we are cautious (and, yes, conflicted) about playing around with our looks. We want to look good, but we don't want any improvements to look obvious. In the USA, by contrast, people take a more proactive approach to treatment; many people feel that if you can't see a decent change in your face after treatment, what were you spending your money on?

CHANGE AS MUCH – OR AS LITTLE – AS YOU CHOOSE

Say you just want to be rid of the 'eleven' lines between your eyebrows so you don't look permanently irritable, but feel your laughter lines lend character to your face. That's easy to achieve with a few injections of wrinkle-relaxing toxin. Or perhaps you'd love to clear the redness from your complexion that makes you look not just older, but as if you might have a problem with alcohol. It can be done, with laser or Intense Pulsed Light treatment. If you want several tweakments – well, discuss with your chosen doctor where to start (see the section 'The Recipe for a Fresher Face' on page 8).

WHAT IF YOU HATE THE WHOLE WAY YOU LOOK?

If you hate the whole way you look, you should perhaps consider a chat with a psychologist about self-image and self-esteem before you rush off for treatment. Seriously. Body Dysmorphic Disorder (BDD) is rife among people who seek cosmetic procedures. Doctors and clinics are getting better at identifying BDD, and many clinics can put you in touch with a psychologist who specialises in this area.

Many people, me included, see cosmetic procedures as the logical next step in what you might call the sliding scale of beauty treatment options, which starts with skincare and make-up and moves on, via hair colouring and tooth-straightening and whitening, to high-tech facials and finally the lasers, ultrasound machines, and needle-tipped syringes found in a medi-spa or clinic. It's a question of what you are comfortable with and where you draw the line.

WHERE A GOOD COSMETIC PRACTITIONER CAN HELP

These days, of course, you don't have to be stuck with the face that nature or your lifestyle has given you. Coco Chanel may famously have said that by 50 a woman had the face she deserved, but today, it's more accurate to say that at 50, a woman has the face she can afford. Thanks to all the subtle changes that good cosmetic doctors can bring about in a face, you can improve on what nature gave you or has left you with. How far you want those improvements to go depends on your own personal aesthetic, ie what you consider to be beautiful and appropriate.

WHAT ABOUT AGEING GRACEFULLY?

Of course there's nothing wrong with doing nothing and, as the phrase has it, 'ageing gracefully' – except that I'm pretty sure, if you're reading this book, that you will share my opinion that there is little that is graceful about the natural process of ageing. It's Mother Nature having a laugh; a constant reminder that we have outlived our biological usefulness. But this is the 21st century, and with so many options for softening the onset of wrinkles and sagging skin, ageing gracefully is starting to sound like a concept from another era.

Besides, the Baby Boomer generation is now hitting retirement age. They have never stuck with their parents' principles, whether these were for no sex before marriage or putting your feet up when you get near retirement age, and many Boomers take the view that they're damned if they're going to let their faces go when there are things they can do to slow the process down.

GOOD GENES? GOOD LIFESTYLE? OR A GOOD DOCTOR?

There's no doubt that some people age better than other. And why might that be? Our usual inclination is to say it's all thanks to 'good genes'.

Where Genes Come In

Research into the genes that govern skin ageing is an area of intense interest for beauty brands at the moment. And there *are* genes – or rather there is genetic variation – which seem to confer youthful looks.

Procter & Gamble (aka P&G, the parent company of Olay skincare) has been researching genomics (the study of how our lifestyle and environment affect the way our genes express themselves) and how it relates to the skin for nearly 20 years. The company's scientists have identified a couple of key genetic variants which are common among 'exceptional agers' who look 10 years younger than they are. But if you don't have these genetic variations, there's no way to acquire them.

Do 'Gene Creams' Help?

And then there are the 'gene creams'. Already, several companies (like ALLÉL, Younom, GENEU, and iDDNA) will take a swab of saliva from the inside of your cheek and, from the DNA this contains, analyse how some of your key skin-related genes are functioning. Then they create a special cream for you with ingredients to compensate for the weaknesses in your skin-gene profile. This type of personalised product is widely predicted to be the future of skincare. But – there's always a 'but' – there are hundreds and hundreds of genes that relate to skin ageing, and these swab-tests only look at half a dozen of them, so although they're moving in the right direction, custom-made creams are not yet the answer to your skincare dreams.

Why Lifestyle Matters Most

More pertinent for now is other research conducted by P&G for Olay in 2017. This research has shown that what really makes a difference to the appearance of your skin is not your genes but your lifestyle. So eating a healthy diet, getting enough sleep and exercise, minimising your intake of sugar and alcohol and, crucially, using decent skincare and being scrupulous with daily use of sunscreen, will have a far bigger impact on your looks, long-term, than your genetic make-up.

SO WHAT IS CONSIDERED BEAUTIFUL THESE DAYS?

Society has always fetishized beauty. However much we like to think we're not influenced by looks, the bald statistics put out by researchers beg to differ. A preference for beauty is hard-wired into us from early on. If you give a baby the choice of looking at a plain face and a beautiful one, guess which it will choose to stare at? (Yes, the lovelier one.) Better-looking people are frequently paid more, and are more successful. There's a whole field of study on this area, called 'pulchronomics' – which translates roughly as the economic benefits of looking good. People with nice-looking teeth are presumed to have higher levels of education than those who don't. It's terrifying.

While we all have rather different ideas on exactly what we think is beautiful in a face, there are several generally accepted principles as to what makes a beautiful face, and most cosmetic practitioners can talk you through these.

The OO7 Beauty Formula

The most thorough explanation of these principles that I've ever heard comes from a brilliant Canadian cosmetic surgeon called Dr Arthur Swift, who has kindly allowed me to include his views in this chapter. He points out that our current beauty ideal has been remarkably consistent since the 1950s, and that if you analyse it, there's a formula to it, a formula he calls OO7 PHI (as in o-o-7 as opposed to zero-zero-seven)

FIRST, THE 'O'S

For Swift, the key markers of the beautiful face are that it is an oval shape (as he points out, every culture prefers its women to have an oval or heart-shaped face), and that the cheeks show an 'ogee curve', the almost-S-shaped double-bend that sways outwards as you trace the line of the cheekbones, then inwards and down towards the chin. That's the two 'O's.

THE MAGNIFICENT SEVEN

Swift then lists what he calls 'the magnificent seven' – the key features that we all take note of when we are assessing the beauty of a face:

1. The triangle of youth (see the nearby sidebar)
2. The height of the forehead (not too high, not too low)
3. The shape of the eyebrows (lightly arched)
4. The size and spacing of the eyes (pleasingly large, not too close together)
5. The shape of the nose (appropriate to the height of the face).
6. The width and height of the lips (generous, but again, appropriate to the face they are in).
7. How clear and smooth the skin is (the clearer the skin, the younger we judge a face to be).

If we find all these things to be pleasing – well, that's a beautiful face.

WHAT IS THE TRIANGLE OF YOUTH?

The widest point on a beautiful face is the measurement across its well-shaped cheeks, which taper down towards the chin and emphasise what is popularly known as the 'triangle of youth'. That means if you were to draw a triangle with its base up and superimpose it on the image of a lovely face, two of its points will be at the cheekbones, and the third will be at the chin.

As the face gets older, the cheeks lose volume, and the jowls start to sag, that triangle of youth gets lost. In fact, it ends up upside down, with the two widest points being the corners of the jaw, and the third point starting at the nose.

When a cosmetic practitioner is assessing a face, he or she is looking at all these features, too, to assess how that face is ageing and how they might make it look more lovely. Perhaps they could improve the facial contours, or make the face a little more symmetrical. Most of us have asymmetric faces, and although symmetry is something the human eye finds pleasing, if you analyse most very beautiful faces, it is their slight asymmetry that gives them their real attraction and stops them looking robotically perfect.

A doctor could maybe help restore the triangle of youth, or help make the skin look fresher and clearer with the tweakments at their disposal. While it might seem that there's not a lot that can be done about, say, a long face, because that's just the way it is built, judicious use of facial fillers in the cheeks and chin can alter the way light falls on that face, which can make it look shorter and better proportioned.

And Then There's Phi (*Warning: Maths!)

There's also a mathematical element to all this, in the form of the golden ratio or 'divine proportion'. That's the ratio of 1 to 1.618; this second number is known as Phi, after the Greek sculptor Phidias, who used this proportion in a lot of his work. This ratio sounds improbable and baffling until you see how pleasing things that have these proportions look to the human eye.

I say 'things' because this golden ratio crops up everywhere, from the structure of DNA to the proportions in a beautiful face

(Angelina Jolie's lips, for example, comply to this ratio – if her lips are the 1.618 bit, each side of her face beside the lips is 1), to the Apple logo…

If you're a particularly precise sort of cosmetic practitioner, you might even want to try applying the principles of golden ratio to your clients. Arthur Swift does, and has even had made a set of gold-coloured callipers that measure out this ratio, which he uses to demonstrate to clients his views on what looks good on a face, and how he might use the principles of Phi and divine proportion on their faces. Not to make them into some cookie-cutter version of themselves, but to move the proportions of their face closer to the ideals that are known to be pleasing.

It's Global, This Beauty Ideal

Here's another strange-but-true observation from the beauty world: good-looking people all over the world look more like each other than they look like ordinary-looking people of their own ethnicity. That may sound unlikely, but if you look closely at, say, top models or film stars from any country, you'll see that they tick most of the boxes on that OO7 list.

PRACTICAL ADVICE

Leaving aside the theory and moving on to practicalities, here are a few more factors that you need to bear in mind before booking in for a tweakment.

How Well Do These Tweakments Work?

Very well, by and large. These treatments give results, that is why they have become so hugely popular and are so widely available.

No one treatment is a magic bullet for suddenly looking like your own fabulous best self five years ago. You will get the best results if you find a great practitioner, discuss your aims for your face with them, and hatch a plan for a slow and steady course of treatment.

Part of the skill set of the best aesthetic doctors and other tweakment specialists lies in knowing which treatments will work best for which patients. Suitable treatments depend on a bunch of things, such as a patient's age; the quality of their skin; the extent of wrinkling, sagging or fat loss; and their lifestyle.

How to Track Improvements

Even with an expert practitioner, it is hard to predict the precise result you might get from any particular treatment. Clinics will show before-and-after photographs on their website, to demonstrate what treatments can do. Bear in mind that these will be the very best results that they have achieved with a particular treatment.

Your practitioner should take pictures of your bare face – from head on, with your head turned halfway to either side, and with your head turned fully to either side – before starting on any treatment, so you have a baseline for reference. Ideally, they will have a set place within a clinic for taking pictures, so that when you come to the 'after' pictures, you will have the same lighting conditions and be in the same positions. That way it is much easier to gauge changes.

If the clinic has a Visia machine or something similar, it is a great idea to have this done, too, even though you may wince at adding another £100 to the bill. Visia is an imaging system that takes detailed shots of your skin, so it can give you a precise reading for your skin smoothness, the extent of your wrinkles, how much damage from UV light you have notched up, how spotty or not your skin is, and so on. Visia compares your data to people of your age around the world. Yes, it makes for alarming reading, but it means that in future, you will be able to tell whether the procedures you have tried, or the skincare that the clinic has recommended you use, are having a measurable effect on the surface of your skin.

It is always a good idea to have before-and-after pictures taken, because we are all bad at assessing changes in our own face, particularly when those changes take place slowly, as they do if you have a treatment that rebuilds collagen in the skin over the course of several months. Then, if there is any difference of opinion between you and your practitioner as to the success or otherwise of the treatment, you will have the pictures to refer to.

Also, it is worth asking your practitioner about the proportion of people who don't see good results from a particular treatment.

Because whatever the treatment, there will always be some people for whom it doesn't work. The number of 'non-responders' for any treatment is usually small, but it is worth knowing about.

Do These Things Hurt?

Ok. Let's talk about pain. It's one of the factors that most puts people off even contemplating cosmetic procedures, and it shouldn't. Of course we don't like pain, we are programmed to go out of our way to avoid pain, and we fear pain – a lot – and don't want to deliberately inflict it on ourselves.

And admittedly most cosmetic procedures are not exactly pain free. But would you really expect them to be? When they involve the use of needles or intense light or heat to deliberately cause an injury to the skin in order to stimulate the wound-healing response that creates new collagen? I'm trying to avoid saying 'no pain, no gain', as it is not necessarily true (some treatments, such as LED light, deliver measurable benefits but don't hurt one bit), but there is an element of this to most procedures.

But It Doesn't Have to Hurt!

Many treatments sound immensely painful because they involve needles or, say, lasers, which burn. But they don't have to hurt that much, thanks to ingenious 21st-century methods of pain management.

No practitioner wants to inflict pain on you, their precious patient. They're not trying to scare you away. You'll notice practitioners don't talk about 'pain'; they are more likely to use words like 'discomfort', so I will do the same. They're hugely concerned with how to minimise discomfort, and they have a whole range of tricks up their sleeve to help them achieve this. They want to make each treatment as easy an experience as possible, so that you go away happy and, when you see the great results, you will not only want to come back for further treatment, but will also tell all your friends about it.

Ways to Manage Discomfort

To manage discomfort during treatment, clinics use a wide range of methods, such as the following.

- **Numbing the area to be treated** with cream containing a local anaesthetic, which takes around 20 minutes to take effect. This is good before a radiofrequency, heat, or laser treatment (unless it's one of the very gentle new types of laser treatment, in which case you won't need it). The standard numbing creams used are Emla (which is 5% anaesthetic: prilocaine and lidocaine) and LMX4 (4% lidocaine). Some clinics have their own, stronger creams made up to soften the impact of more intense treatments.

  Clinics will check whether you are allergic to these creams before using them and may require you to take a patch test of cream before they'll use it. But if you're unlucky, like a friend of mine who has eczema and whose skin can't tolerate numbing creams, you will have to find other ways of managing the discomfort.

- **Injecting a dental block** to deaden the nerve endings around the mouth. This used to be the most popular way to manage the pain – sorry, discomfort – of lip filler injections. The lips are particularly sensitive because they contain so many nerve endings. A dental block works a treat but it also can make the lip area swell, which makes it harder for the injector to judge the result.

- **Paracetamol or ibuprofen** – always an option, especially if you are having a 'sensitive' day (see the 'What Makes Tweakments Hurt More' sidebar on page 32).

- **Distraction therapy** – vibrating tools such as the NUEVIBE, which looks like a thick brass pen with a T-shaped head, are remarkably effective at distracting your nerve-endings from what is going on. I've had this used, just to the side of my lips, while they were being injected, and was fascinated by the way I just didn't feel the injections.

- **Diazepam** (Valium). If you're particularly anxious, or are facing up to a treatment like focussed ultrasound, some clinics will offer you diazepam, which I am sure helps the whole thing become a happier, more floaty experience. I have yet to try it, but people tell me it can really help.

- **Skin cooling.** Some lasers come with a built-in cooling device which supercools the skin before the laser strikes it with very hot light.

- **Ice.** Good old ice is remarkably effective at both numbing the skin enough to take the edge off an injection, and in calming down swelling after an injection or two. Most clinics have gel packs in the freezer to help with this. Some doctors like to fill a latex surgical glove with water and freeze that – it sets in a curved-hand sort of shape which can be surprisingly comforting to hold to a red, post-injection face.

- **Slow breathing.** I would always prefer to distract myself by chatting with the practitioner during a treatment, but that isn't usually an option, since it is vital to keep my face still while they work. Deliberate, slow breathing is what practitioners prefer, and it works nicely especially, I find, if you pair it with a spot of…

- **Visualisation.** To fight down the anxiety that is making my nerve endings buzz ('Ow! That zap hurt! How many more are there to go? Dozens? Help!') I like to imagine myself swaying in a shady hammock on some warm, distant beach, watching the waves crash on the shore and trying to work out which is the seventh wave and whether it really is bigger than the others… It might sound crazy, but believe me, it really helps.

How Much Each Tweakment Actually Hurts

For all of the treatments that I've mentioned in the following chapters, I have given an indication of how much they hurt, from mild, to moderate, to more-than-average. When I'm writing for newspapers or magazines, they often ask me to rate treatments on a 'pain scale' from 1–10, where a one is a something that you can barely feel, and a nine is such intolerable discomfort that, if you were at the dentist, you would raise a hand to make them stop RIGHT NOW.

I find this hard to do because I know that the same treatment can feel quite different on different days, depending on a variety of factors (see the 'What Makes Tweakments Hurt More' sidebar nearby). Also, whatever pain-rating I give, my editors invariably ramp up the pain factor because they think I am a tough old boot who has had a lot of these things and who has a high pain threshold. Even if I am as hardy as they think, I can't remember having any treatment that qualified as a nine, or even an 8.5/10 on the pain scale.

WHAT MAKES TWEAKMENTS HURT MORE

Some days, we have a higher tolerance of pain than on others. The following are things that can all make you feel more sensitive than otherwise.

- Lack of sleep

- The time of the month. During your period, the hormones that your body releases make the skin feel more sensitive than usual.

- Having had a glass or two of wine the night before.

- Your genes. Some people tolerate pain better than others, and some of this is genetic.

- Lack of understanding about the treatment. If you know what's coming, it's easier to manage your expectations and anxieties than if you feel something is being 'done' to you.

- When it's the first time. I presume this must be due to nerves and anxiety about the treatment, not knowing what it will be like and how much it may hurt, but I have always, always found the second round of any treatment I have ever tried to be easier and more comfortable than the first.

- Your own fear and reaction to the pain. As above, I find that if I can settle into a steady pattern of breathing and imagining myself to be somewhere else, I feel the jabs or zaps of the treatment far less than if I'm anxiously waiting for the next one.

Will You Need 'Downtime' After a Tweakment?

Downtime is the recovery time after a procedure when you might not be looking at your best. We all react to treatment differently: what will leave one person only a little pink, can leave another red and puffy-faced and really not fit to go back to the office or face curious family members.

The current trend is for light versions of popular procedures, whether peels or lasering or injections, which are far less likely to leave you needing to take any downtime. Old-style chemical peels would need a week off work to recover; today's versions leave no trace, and even the peeling is subtle.

Downtime is another thing to discuss with your practitioner – whether the procedure you are lining up for is going to need any time off afterwards, and if so, how long.

How Safe Is All This?

This is a really crucial question, and it's a hard one to answer.

All of the procedures and treatments that I talk about in this book are safe when administered by experienced, well-trained hands. Mostly, they are the best-accredited procedures and devices from the best-known companies in the field. But here are some factors that complicate the discussion around safety, to help you understand why this discussion isn't as straightforward as it might seem.

- Many of the products and procedures that I'm writing about – whether these are facial fillers or radiofrequency machines – are ones that been assessed or cleared by the Food and Drug Administration (FDA), the U.S. government body which polices medical devices (the category that both fillers and aesthetic equipment falls into). The FDA's assessments are lengthy and detailed, and require a considerable amount of evidence to show that a product or device lives up to its claims and does this safely.

- Unfortunately, there is no equivalent assessment standard in the UK. Most aesthetic machines and products such as fillers available in the UK are classified as 'medical devices' and are required to have a CE mark. The CE mark is a symbol applied to products to show that they conform with relevant European directives about safety standards, which gives a certain amount of reassurance that the product does what it claims to do, and does it safely. That said, CE marks are not hard to obtain – companies have to provide far less safety and efficacy data to obtain a CE mark than to achieve FDA clearance.

- The regulations around cosmetic medicine in the UK are lax to the point of invisibility, which means there are many more products and devices available in the UK and Europe than are legal in the USA.

- And here it gets complicated because some of these newer products, such as new types of fillers, may well be very good and may well be working their way through the lengthy process of FDA accreditation, and may be the go-to products of the future. But it can be hard to tell these apart from the many other fillers that are cheap or badly formulated products, or which have new ingredients with little data on their safety and efficacy and which are best avoided.

- Many products or tweakments are considered safe because they have been around for long enough, and have been used enough times, by many expert practitioners, for there to be some consensus that they are a good thing.

- Botox is a prescription medicine, so its use is more closely regulated than any other cosmetic procedures or tweakments. Only doctors, dentists, and nurse-prescribers can prescribe its use, and other people can inject it only directly under the prescriber's supervision. Because of its heritage as a nerve poison, Botox has been studied in considerably more depth than other cosmetic treatments. More than 2,600 peer-reviewed papers on Botox have been published in medical journals, and over 65 randomised, placebo-controlled clinical trials have been conducted on Botox.

- The doctors and nurses I mention throughout this book are the sort of top-class, responsible practitioners who will only use products and treatments that they know and trust, and with which they have long experience, so that patients can be confident of quite literally being in good hands and of being safely and appropriately treated.

- Training programmes for treatments such as cosmetic laser work and injectable fillers vary widely. While some industry bodies – such as the new Joint Council for Cosmetic Practitioners, JCCP (see page 42) – are regularising some aesthetic training programmes, it is possible, and perfectly legal, that practitioners have only done a weekend course to familiarise themselves with basic techniques before starting to practice.

So, all of the procedures and treatments that I mention are pretty safe. *But* (there's always a 'but', isn't there?) things can and do go wrong. So it helps to know what to avoid.

What to Avoid at All Costs

There are certain tweakments which you should steer well clear of. If any practitioner offers you any of the following, your answer should be a flat 'No'.

- Any non-surgical procedure that claims to be a permanent fix.
- Permanent fillers – such as silicone (see the section 'Permanent Fillers' on page 207).
- Products that have not been subjected to proper clinical trials – but bear in mind, as I mentioned a page or two back, that some of these products may be going through the lengthy process of FDA assessment and clearance.
- Any practitioner or clinic where you feel uncomfortable, or anyone who puts pressure on you to commit to a treatment you are unsure about, or anywhere that won't answer your questions. See page 39 for more on choosing a practitioner.

Do Some Medical Conditions Mean I Can't Have Tweakments?

Yes. Clinics can advise you on specific contra-indications for particular treatments, and you will be asked to complete a detailed medical questionnaire before having any treatment.

In general:

- Practitioners will not inject you with either Botox or fillers if you are pregnant or breastfeeding, as the effects on your baby are unknown.
- And they will be cautious of injecting you with anything if you are using an anti-coagulant medication such as Warfarin or Heparin. Just in case they nick a blood vessel.
- If you have chronic breathing difficulties, Botox may cause problems.

- Auto-immune diseases aren't necessarily a contra-indication for some tweakments such as fillers, but you should discuss the idea with your main doctor first before having a consultation with an aesthetic practitioner.

What Are the Potential Problems with Tweakments?

If you have spent any time looking into tweakments, you'll have seen that this area is plagued by problems. Before you go for any treatment, look it up online and see if there are any obvious stand-out problems associated with it. You probably won't find this on the websites of the clinics that offer the procedures – they are trying to lure you in, rather than put you off – but websites such as the following two are very enlightening:

- **RealSelf.com.** This is an American site where visitors can post questions about aesthetic and surgical treatments, and have these questions answered by top-level practitioners.

- **Consultingroom.com.** This is Britain's largest cosmetic-information website and provide masses of helpful information. As they very rightly say at the top of their site, 'an educated decision is the right decision'. Go on their site, choose your treatment, look at the 'Side Effects and Risks' section, and start educating yourself about possible issues.

In this book, I have discussed the potential problems that can crop up with particular treatments in the relevant chapters.

Ask Your Practitioner About Problems

You should always ask your practitioner, 'What can go wrong with this procedure?' Perhaps also ask, 'How often have you had things go wrong with this procedure?' When you have digested the answers to those questions, follow up with: 'If something does go wrong, what are you able to do about it?' See page 45 for other things to ask your practitioner.

Don't let your practitioner dismiss your questions with glib answers. A good practitioner will take your questions and concerns seriously. You won't be the first person to ask; and don't worry, there is no such thing as a stupid question. Besides, the practitioner is taking your money to work on your facial features, so you need to be very sure that you understand what is being done to you and any potential complications.

Read the Consent Form

Before you see your practitioner for any treatment, you will be asked to sign a consent form. This form will detail all the possible complications that might result from undergoing the treatment you are considering, from the fact that it might be uncomfortable, to the way that your skin might be red and swollen afterwards, or that there might be bruises from needles.

These lists of possible complications can tend to be as long as the lists of possible complications or reactions that you find inside boxes of prescription medicines, because these are all things that have been noted to occur after treatment over the course of years. It's enough to put you right off going any further but, as with the side-effects of prescription medicines, 99% of what is on that list is unlikely to be an issue for you. Even so, it is as well to read the list, rather than just skipping over it and signing.

NEEDLES AND BRUISES

I've met many people who boast proudly that their doctor is amazing, and 'never gives them a bruise'. Which is great, but ending up with a bruise doesn't mean you have seen a bad practitioner. There are so many tiny blood vessels in the face that, particularly if you are having a treatment that requires multiple injections, you will be lucky if you escape without any bruises, however skilled your injector.

Will I Bruise?

How your face will behave after injections is very hard to predict. My skin takes injections fairly well, without much swelling, and any bruises tend to be small and localised.

But if you are very fair or have delicate skin that bruises easily – well, you might bruise more. It's not the end of the world, it's just a bruise; but if it is on your face, it will show, and it will take up to two weeks to clear.

You can help to reduce swelling and bruising after injections by applying icepacks (wrapped in a clean cloth) to the area every few hours and by using arnica cream.

Don't drink alcohol after having injections. Not because it will affect the treatment in any way, but because it will dilate your blood vessels a little, which may mean you are more likely to get bruising or swelling. Your practitioner may recommend that you stop taking fish oil, vitamin E supplements, or aspirin for a few days before treatment; this is because these can slightly thin the blood and so increase the chances of bruising or bleeding.

Don't race off to the gym straight afterwards, either, just because forcing your blood to pump faster around your body can, again, make bruising worse.

If you do get bruising, you'll need a good concealer to cover things up, one with a good density of pigment. My secret weapon for concealing bruising is the Tattoo Secret Camouflage Kit (£33.50, www.tattoocoverup.co.uk), which you can mix to the skin-shade that you need and which is very effective at covering up both the purple and the yellow stages of bruising. It's good for fair and medium skin tones but doesn't come in anything darker than medium.

How Do I Know If It's a Bruise or the Start of Necrosis?

If, after injections of filler, you get a purplish swelling in the area, get back to your doctor immediately, or at least send them a picture of it. If they have accidentally injected the product not into your skin but into a blood vessel, the product will be blocking the blood vessel, and the blood will back up and cause all sorts of problems, such as ulceration and tissue necrosis (where the skin tissue dies). Yes, it's horrible, but it is also rare. But if you are in any doubt, ask for their expert advice, at once.

TREATMENT REVIEWS

Most of the treatment reviews in this book are by me. Where there are procedures I haven't tried, the reviews are from other people, and I have put their names in to make this clear.

CHAPTER 3

Finding the Best Practitioner for You

To get the results you're looking for from any tweakment, you must find the right practitioner for your needs. This chapter shows you how to do so.

Unfortunately, finding a good cosmetic practitioner isn't as straightforward as it ought to be, largely because of the lack of regulation in the whole aesthetics industry in the UK. Many industry bodies and organisations do their best to give credibility to the practitioners who belong to them (as discussed later in this chapter), but there is no central, Government-approved register of qualified practitioners. Nor is there any requirement for anyone who wants to give injectable treatments or use cosmetic lasers to acquire specific qualifications and be registered and approved as fit to practice.

While there are many brilliant doctors, dermatologists, and nurse-injectors in the UK, there are many who aren't so good, and plenty who are alarmingly bad. And because there are no legal restrictions on who can inject fillers or use lasers – terrifying but true – anyone (including you or I), could buy the equipment and products, take a short course, get a certificate of proficiency, and set themselves up in practice. And those training courses are sometimes only a couple of days long.

So to stay safe and get good results, you need to do your research, making sure that the person to whom you are entrusting your face and paying your money is not only properly qualified but is also good at what they do.

This chapter tells you what you need to know about the industry bodies and associations and the practitioners they represent. It also tells you how to find a good practitioner, and how to make sure that the practitioner is suitable for you; makes sure you know what happens when you go for a consultation; arms you with key questions to ask your practitioner; and advises you what to do if something goes wrong with a tweakment.

I recommend you use this book as a starting point in your search for the right practitioner for you. All the doctors, practitioners, and clinics that I mention in the treatment reviews are very good at what they do, and have the proper training and accreditation to carry out the various procedures they offer. To find a practitioner who offers a specific tweakment, in a particular area of the UK, you can use the search tools on my website, www.thetweakmentsguide.com, where you can also see what sort of accreditation each practitioner has.

WHO CAN GIVE WHICH TREATMENTS?

In many countries there are laws to make sure that cosmetic medical treatments can only be done by doctors with specific, relevant qualifications. There are no such laws in the UK, so almost anyone can offer almost any treatment. Here's what you need to know.

Botox

Botox is a prescription-only drug, so has to be supplied by a medical professional who is qualified to prescribe – a doctor, a surgeon, a dentist, or a nurse-prescriber (a qualified nurse who has taken a further course to become a non-medical prescriber). The injections can legally be given by someone working under the supervision of that qualified professional, though the prescriber is the one who takes responsibility for the treatment.

The makers of Botox, and the makers of other wrinkle-relaxing toxins such as BoCouture, Dysport, and Azzalure, are scrupulous about only supplying their products to medical professionals. Does that mean that the system is watertight? Unfortunately not. Unscrupulous practitioners find ways around the system.

Dermal Fillers

With injectable face fillers, the situation is even looser than with Botox. There are no restrictions on who can take a training course in dermal fillers, and some of these courses are only a day or two long. There are no requirements to show competence in injecting fillers before a practitioner sets up in business. So anyone can do it, and they can inject you with almost anything, because in the UK, fillers are not classed as prescription medical devices.

Lasers, Ultrasound, Radiofrequency, and Other Devices

The situation is the same with the machinery used in cosmetic procedures – the lasers, the ultrasound machines, the radio-frequency or 'plasma' generating devices. Anyone can use them and offer treatment with them.

HOW TO FIND A GOOD PRACTITIONER

If possible, get a personal recommendation from someone you know who has tried the treatment you are interested in and has had a good result.

Alternatively, look for a doctor, surgeon, dentist, or aesthetic nurse who is registered with one of the following associations:

- **British College of Aesthetic Medicine.** (www.bcam.ac.uk) The BCAM used to be called the British Association of Cosmetic Doctors, and its main aim is to encourage safe and ethical work in the cosmetic and aesthetic area. All members are registered with the General Medical Council (GMC), and many of them are GPs who have moved over to cosmetic practice. To keep up their membership, they have to attend regular educational and scientific meetings and need to get their membership revalidated every five years.

- **British Association of Aesthetic Plastic Surgeons.** (www.baaps.org.uk) BAAPS surgeons are all listed on the GMC's specialist register, and the organisation is dedicated to safety and education in cosmetic surgery. Why have I listed a surgeons' association in a book on non-surgical tweakments? Because many surgeons offer these tweakments alongside their surgical work.

- **British Association of Cosmetic Nurses.** (www.bacn.org.uk) The BACN represents nurses who do cosmetic treatments and promotes patient safety via a strict code of conduct. They're great campaigners for improving the regulation of cosmetic procedures

- **British Association of Dermatologists.** (www.bad.org.uk) There are relatively few consultant dermatologists in the UK. Most of them concentrate on skin conditions, but some are cosmetic dermatologists, who do aesthetic procedures.
- **British Association of Plastic, Reconstructive and Aesthetic Surgeons.** (www.bapras.org.uk) This organisation represents plastic and reconstructive and aesthetic surgeons.
- **British Association of Cosmetic Surgeons.** (www.b-a-c-s.co.uk) BACS is a smaller group, representing surgeons who do cosmetic surgery but who haven't necessarily done years of specialist cosmetic training in the UK. BACS surgeons are more likely to be working at private clinics and hospitals.
- **British Dental Association.** (https://bda.org) If your practitioner is a dentist, they should be registered with the BDA. Some people might wonder why you would go to a dentist for cosmetic procedures, but some dentists are brilliant at fillers and Botox.

If the practitioner is a doctor, check that they are registered with the General Medical Council, (GMC; www.gmc-uk.org).

If the practitioner is a nurse, check their registration with the Nursing and Midwifery Council (www.nmc.org.uk).

If the practitioner is a dentist, check with the General Dental Council (www.gdc-uk.org).

Beyond these professional associations, there are voluntary quality-assurance schemes such as Treatments You Can Trust, which has now become part of the Joint Council for Cosmetic Practitioners (www.jccp.org.uk). This provides information and advice about treatments, and has a list of accredited practitioners, all of whom have to meet the JCCP's entry requirements, pay the registration fee, and sign up to the code of conduct.

The JCCP is leading the way in quality control. Since last year, beauticians have not been allowed to join the register for administering injectable fillers (though, as the JCCP website points out, it is not illegal for beauticians to do these treatments.

Another voluntary register is Save Face (www.saveface.co.uk), which also lists practitioners who have met the organisation's standards and have paid the registration fee. This site is government-approved.

Which is all good, but as with previous schemes, these two have no teeth and cannot compel practitioners to register with them. It also means, confusingly, that some of my favourite – and very highly qualified – practitioners are not listed on either site.

You could also try one of the practitioners mentioned in this book. As well as the particular practitioners I've mentioned for particular treatments, there's a searchable directory of practitioners on my website, www.thetweakmentsguide.com.

FINDING A CLINIC

Allergan (the makers of Botox and Juvederm injectables) offer a 'clinic finder' tool on their website at www.thisisrealme.com. Galderma, makers of Restylane fillers, have a clinic-finder on www.restylane.co.uk. These websites only list clinics and practitioners that have been approved to use the products by the manufacturers.

The Consulting Room website (www.consultingroom.com) offers a mass of helpful information about cosmetic treatments, and also has a clinic-search tool. You can look up cosmetic doctors, their qualifications, and where they practice. There's a comprehensive list of every clinic in the UK that offers Botox and other botulinum toxin treatments, too.

GENERAL ADVICE

The General Medical Council (GMC) offers advice online on what patients should consider when thinking about cosmetic procedures at https://www.gmc-uk.org/-/media/ethical-guidance/related-pdf-items/cosmetic-interventions/cosmetic-procedures---what-do-i-need-to-consider.pdf.

There's some information on the NHS website (https://www.nhs.uk/conditions/cosmetic-treatments/), but it is limited.

If you are wondering whether cosmetic clinics need to be registered with the Care Quality Commission (the government's health regulator for England) – they used to, but the regulations were changed in 2010 and now only cover premises offering surgical procedures where instruments are inserted into the body. So premises that offer treatments involving a scalpel, or involving a liposuction cannula, need to be regulated, but anywhere that does cosmetic injections and laser treatments do not.

SO YOU'VE FOUND A GREAT PRACTITIONER... BUT ARE THEY RIGHT FOR YOU?

This is the bit where it is difficult to lay down hard-and-fast rules. Even if a practitioner ticks all the relevant boxes – appropriate qualifications, wide experience, and a mass of keen clients – you may feel, when you meet them, or even when you walk into their clinic, that they are not quite right for you.

Don't ignore that feeling. Finding the best practitioner for you may involve a bit of trial and error. If your gut instinct is telling you that the clinic is too laid back, and you would prefer somewhere more medical in its approach; or if strikes you that all the clinic staff look a bit too 'done'; or if they are unhelpful or try to give you the hard sell – in any of these cases, move on.

As we are all different, so are cosmetic practitioners. Some take a very proactive approach and favour the sort of treatments that will show marked changes; others tend towards more conservative tweakments. The trick is to find someone whose work chimes with your personal aesthetic and in whose clinic you feel comfortable and welcome.

Take a look at their company website and social media profiles – they are very likely to have before-and-after pictures on display to showcase their work. Do you like the sort of looks that they are creating? If not, move on.

DO YOUR RESEARCH BEFORE BOOKING A TREATMENT

Before you commit to treatment, make an appointment to visit a clinic you are interested in and meet the doctor or nurse who will be doing the treatment, for a consultation. Doctors may well charge for this, because you are taking up their valuable time. In the UK, where we are used to free healthcare on the NHS, this somehow offends us, but if you're a doctor and have 10 consultations scheduled for a day, and all pay nothing – well, it hardly makes sense from a business point of view, does it? Paying for a doctor's time is usually money well spent. You will also have the opportunity to ask them all the questions you can cram into your time-slot (see below for what to ask).

WHAT HAPPENS WHEN YOU GO FOR A CONSULTATION?

At the consultation, discuss your concerns and what you think you are looking for, and listen to the practitioner's suggestions as they explore the treatment options that are available. These may be different to what you think you need – for example, if you are bothered by nose-to-mouth lines, many practitioners will suggest adding a little volume in your cheeks, which lifts the cheeks and makes the lines vanish, rather than injecting filler directly into the lines that are bothering you.

Should you then go ahead and have treatment straight away? If you are really sure what you want, then, ok, go ahead and have it done. But don't be pressured into committing to any treatment immediately. If you have any hesitation, allow yourself time to think about it. A good practitioner should give you a 'cooling off' period to think about what you have discussed before you book for treatment. He or she will also tell you when you don't need treatment, and explain why. No reputable clinic should offer you a financial incentive for signing up on the spot.

KEY QUESTIONS TO ASK YOUR PRACTITIONER

Not sure what to ask? Here is a list of the key questions that you may want to put to your practitioner.

- Who will be doing my treatment? Ideally you will have your consultation with the practitioner you have chosen, and they will be the person who does your treatment. But it's worth asking in case they are planning to pass you on to an associate.
- Do you do this procedure a lot?
- How soon should I see results?
- What sort of results should I expect to see?
- Will I need anaesthetic or other pain relief?
- Can I see pictures of other people who have had this done?
- Can I talk to other patients who have had this done?
- How much does it cost?
- What do I need to do or avoid doing after treatment? Usually, you should avoid things like strenuous exercise or saunas for a day or two, and after some treatments, you may need to avoid direct sunlight.
- What will I look like immediately after the treatment? Will the treated area be swollen? Will there be redness? Or bruising? And if so, how long for?
- How soon can I wear makeup afterwards?
- What are the possible complications or side-effects of this treatment?
- Are you qualified to deal with any of these possible complications?
- How often does something go wrong with this particular treatment?
- What happens if something goes wrong? Don't let anyone get away with saying, 'Oh, we very rarely have a problem.' There should be a policy on complications, and the clinic should let you know what it is. You're a paying patient; your concerns should be fully addressed rather than dismissed.
- When should I come back for a review of the treatment?
- What if I don't like the results?

WHAT TO DO IF SOMETHING GOES WRONG

If you think something has gone wrong after your procedure, call the clinic immediately, explain the problem, and send them photographs. Speak to your practitioner and ask for advice.

If it is something minor, like an area that has been treated with filler swelling up a few days after treatment, it may simply require antihistamine and time to calm down. If there is any sort of infection, it may require antibiotics.

If it is filler that is going into lumps – again, see your practitioner as soon as possible to see what they can suggest. If the filler is a hyaluronic acid gel, it should be possible to dissolve it with an injection of Hyalase (hyaluronidase).

If your practitioner is unwilling or unable to help, you may need to seek help elsewhere.

Practitioners who are members of the organisations listed in the section 'How to Find a Good Practitioner' on page 41 may be able to help you. Many of the best cosmetic practitioners spend a distressing amount of time correcting other people's bad work.

If you need further support or redress after a treatment that has gone wrong, you can try the Safety in Beauty charity (www.safetyinbeauty.com). Or consult a firm of solicitors that specialises in cosmetic procedures, such as Hill Dickinson or Irwin Mitchell.

THOUGHTS ON PRICING: 1 – PRICE AND EXPERTISE

Tweakments are expensive. With the best doctors, or Harley Street practitioners who have expensive premises, they can be really expensive. So it is always tempting to look for a better deal. But if there is one area of life where it rarely pays to economise, it is with tweakments. What you are paying for is not just the product and the time the procedure takes; it's for the expertise and aesthetic judgement of your chosen practitioner, and that expertise can hugely affect the results you get. Besides, your face is on show every single day. You want it to be looking its best.

THOUGHTS ON PRICING: 2 – DON'T BE A GUINEA PIG

Use your head and don't be seduced by the offer of cut-price treatment, particularly not if you are going to be used as a training model. If someone says to you, 'Oh, you can get that treatment much more cheaply, I've got a friend who has just started doing it, they'll give you a discount...', stop and think. All practitioners admit that the more procedures they do, the better they get at them, so you do not want to be a human pincushion for them to practise on.

And I know that's fine advice coming from someone who has been a guinea-pig for many of these procedures when they were at an early stage – but please, do as I say, not as I have done.

THOUGHTS ON PRICING: 3 – PRICE AND LOCATION

Because I'm based in London, the majority of clinics I have reviewed in this book are also based in London, where the prices are higher than elsewhere in the country. So if you have a local clinic with a great practitioner, their prices are likely to be lower.

CHAPTER 4

Entry-Level Tweakments: 'Facials Plus'

Before we jump into the full detail of aesthetic treatments, this is an interlude, a transitional chapter if you like, for people who are curious but uncertain about tweakments. Is there a way to put a toe in the water and try a lightweight version of some tweakments? You bet there is. All you need is the right sort of facial – a 'facial with added extras'. I use the term 'facials plus' for such facials.

WHAT ARE 'FACIALS PLUS'?

Over the past few years, while non-surgical cosmetic procedures have become ever more popular and widely available, facials have been upping their game to keep pace. The result is a new generation of treatments which have moved into the space between the old-style pampering facials and the sort of tweakments that require needles, anaesthetic, and a fearless disposition.

That means, along with traditional cleansing and massage, these new 'facials plus' weave in tolerable doses of tweakments that will help regenerate the skin. A spot of lasering to tighten skin and clear pigmentation, perhaps, or a gentle peeling treatment for a fresher complexion. Or maybe radiofrequency that shrink-wraps the skin into better shape, or microcurrents to hoick saggy face muscles back where they belong.

The one thing you'll find tacked on to many treatments is LED light therapy, which is very gentle but also effective. It feels like it's not doing anything, but used at the right wavelength and intensity, it is well proven to help calm inflammation (red light), clear bacteria (blue light), and boost collagen production (red and near infra-red light), so it works with any and all other treatments. It even works on its own.

These 'facials plus' are perfect for people who want a treatment that is effective but not too challenging and which guarantees that they won't look frozen or pillow-faced, since there are no face-relaxing toxins or injectable fillers involved.

These in-between treatments are all very tolerable (read: almost painless), need no downtime (that's time off for recovery while any redness or puffiness from the treatment subsides), and give results that make you think paying £200 for another session is an eminently good use of funds.

Sometimes you'll find just one of these extras appended to a facial; sometimes there's a bunch of them piled together in the same treatment. Before you start fretting that, say, an acid peel plus laser plus light therapy is overkill, bear in mind that these treatments offer mini doses of powerful technologies, so they won't harm you. However, you will need repeated sessions to get the best results.

WHERE TO FIND THESE TWEAKMENTS

You'll find these 'facials plus' at beauty salons, where having something a bit more high-tech and offering more results helps make their treatment menu seem more impressive. You will also find that many of the best-known facialists offer treatments involving lasers, radiofrequency, or microneedling, as a way of taking their already popular facials to the next level. You'll also find these tweakments at aesthetic clinics and medi-spas, as the 'softer' end of the treatment spectrum, or to work in conjunction with other treatments like filler injections or Botox. Some of them might involve a few needles, but they're worth it.

Even if you don't regard these 'facials plus' as quite as serious as other procedures, please do take them seriously, and always have a chat with the salon or clinic before you book in. That way you will understand what you are booking in for, and what it will – and won't – do for your face.

THE TREATMENTS

There are so many 'facials plus' available that the few reviewed here are just the tip of the iceberg, to give you an idea of what you might find. I will be adding reviews of more of these facials on my website, www.thetweakmentsguide.com. For each category of these facials, I have explained the theory of what they do, then included a review from when I tried each treatment.

The In-Depth Exfoliating Facial

Normal cleansing will clear your skin of the dirt, oil, and loose skin cells that sit on its surface. But if you want to deep-clean your skin and perk it up with an infusion of hydrating serums, this treatment does a great job.

TREATMENT REVIEW: HYDRAFACIAL

A deep-cleansing, exfoliating facial that gives your skin a quick acid peel and plumps it with hydrating serums, all in the space of half an hour or so.

What It Is

The Hydrafacial uses a device that looks like an overgrown pen with a whirling vortex of water at its tip and a tube at the other end of it. Somehow, this water-vortex whirls in and out of the device without spraying everywhere and, by changing the tip of the device, it can be used to cleanse the skin and do a spot of lymph-draining massage, exfoliate the skin to get rid of old dead skin cells, then apply glycolic acid to soften blockages in the pores. The softened gunk is then vacuumed out, leaving the skin much smoother and more receptive to the dose of complexion-boosting vitamins, peptides, and moisturising hyaluronic acid that follows and plumps up wrinkles.

The final step is a few minutes of soothing red light that calms the skin and stimulates collagen formation. Depending on what your skin needs, you can have either some or all of the various steps.

What It's Like

Not pampering, so it's not relaxing, but it's extremely effective. It might sound a bit like putting your face through a high-speed car wash, but no, you don't end up being hosed down – that clever vortex tip sucks the water back up as fast as it delivers it, so you don't end up covered with water, serum, or exfoliating solution.

Comfort Level

Mostly comfortable. Can feel a bit rough during extractions.

Verdict

Quick and easy and gives great results. It's like a deep-cleansing 'reset' for the face. My skin was a bit pinked-up by the end but it also looked fresh and glowing, very clean and plumped up from the hyaluronic acid and peptide solution. I'd do this a day before a big event to give my skin time to calm right down afterwards. The glow lasted for several days and the super-clean, super-fresh feeling lasted for a week.

Cost and Location

Around £140, at many clinics around the country including cmedicalclinic.co.uk in Bristol and sthetics.co.uk in Buckinghamshire. For other locations, see hydrafacial.co.uk or my website, www.thetweakmentsguide.com.

The Oxygen Glow-Booster

A soothing, calming treatment that leaves your skin looking noticeably plumper and healthier.

TREATMENT REVIEW: INTRACEUTICALS

When treatments claim celebrity fans, you usually need to take the claim with a pinch of salt – maybe the celeb in question tried the treatment once, and never went back. But Intraceuticals points as evidence to the growing number of A-listers who have bought the (expensive) machines that deliver these treatments, so they can get that glow at home any time they want. At the last count, Madonna, who has been a fan of the system for over a decade, had six machines (one for each of her houses around the world).

What It Is

A gentle, deeply hydrating, and face-sculpting treatment which makes skin look so amazingly plumped up and glowing that it has become a pre-event staple for celebrity fans ranging from Kim Kardashian to Justin Bieber. You might think that it is almost too gentle for inclusion in this book, but I reckon it qualifies because of its spectacular results.

A slim wand of a device is used to blast pressurised oxygen mixed with skin-improving serums over the face. The main serum that is used is a low-molecular-weight hyaluronic acid serum; 'low molecular weight' means its molecules are really small, so that they can sink more readily into the skin, rather than sitting on the surface. Then you can have an acne-calming serum or a skin-brightening serum, or another hyaluronic acid with a larger molecular weight layered on top… The idea behind the jet of oxygen is that it is meant to push the serums more firmly into the skin and also delivers a face-sculpting lymphatic drainage massage at the same time.

What It's Like

Unusual but very comfortable. Having the oxygen-spray-jet worked steadily around my face is a strange but not unpleasant sensation. Once I realise it isn't going to hurt even in the slightest, it becomes quite hypnotic, and I drift off into a nap.

Comfort Level

Very comfortable.

Verdict

Wow. The improvement is immediate (well, it has taken 45 minutes) and obvious. My cheeks look more defined and a little lifted, and my skin has the most fabulous dewy glow to it, as if I'd been on a detox regime with early nights for a week. I can completely see why A-listers whose faces are under a lot of scrutiny would want these treatments regularly. My skin went on looking great for the best part of a week, but after that, alas, it was back to normal.

Cost and Location

From £85 – for clinics and salons, see intraceuticals.com.

The Electrical Skin Tighteners

Passing a low-level electrical current through muscles makes them contract and tighten, which helps to coax face muscles that are becoming stretched and floppy with age into a neater, tighter shape. It won't make a permanent change to your looks, but will give a temporary improvement.

TREATMENT REVIEW: CACI SYNERGY

CACI treatments have been around for such a long time and are so widely available in beauty salons that they don't sound very new – but the Synergy treatment is the latest update on their popular and well-proven technology, which combines face-lifting electrical microcurrents to tone and tighten the muscles that support the skin, with LED light therapy to reduce pigmentation and make the skin look brighter. The technology is called Simultaneous Photo Electrical Delivery, or SPED: not very catchy, but what you really need to know about it is that CACI with SPED has been clinically proven to give better results in a shorter time than the original CACI treatments.

What It Is

The treatment is done by a beautician wielding the various different treatment heads that are attached to the CACI machine itself. The main tools are long metal prongs with smooth tips, which are placed precisely on the face at either end of each particular muscle that is targeted for a workout. As the microcurrents move through the muscle, it contracts, and all this muscle activity improves blood flow in the skin, too. Then there's light treatment, involving both red light, which helps calm inflammation in the skin and stimulate collagen production, and blue light, to bring down levels of bacteria on the skin.

What It's Like

It feels 'electrical' rather than pampering. It's tingly, having electricity passed through my skin, but no worse than that. I had thought it might make my muscles spasm or twitch, but the treatment is much subtler than that. I get a metallic taste in my mouth, too, as the electricity is stirring up the metal in my fillings, which is strange but again, not too bad. After the prongs, the therapist uses a 'wrinkle comb' which helps to soften and relax the muscles that are making some frown lines set in. It's a thorough treatment, but at 90 minutes, it is very long. The light treatment at the end is – pun intended – light relief.

Comfort Level

Feels mildly electrical, but not actually uncomfortable, if that makes sense.

Verdict

A terrific result (thank goodness, after all that electrical tingling). All those tiny microcurrents have achieved a noticeable effect, lifting and smoothing my face, and my skin looks impressively smooth and glowing, which must be from the combination of improved circulation and the light therapy. And I'm told if I did a course of treatment, as is recommended, I'd see longer-lasting results. As it is, my face is definitely better than usual for a week afterwards.

Cost and Location

From £90, at salons nationwide, www.caci-international.co.uk.

TREATMENT REVIEW: THE FACE GYM SIGNATURE ELECTRICAL WORKOUT

Face Gym is a company that offers facials, but styles them as 'workouts', the idea being that they really put your face muscles through their paces.

What It Is

Deep, firm, wonderful facial massage, with added electrical stimulation for extra contour-lifting and muscle-tautening.

What It's Like

The facial workout is divided into a 'warm-up', which is a nice firm massage, followed by a 'cardio' section where the therapist thrums her fingers across my jawline and up my cheeks at such speed and in such a continuous flow that all tension is forced out of my face.

Then there's even 'strength training' to pep up flagging face muscles. For the finale, my face is worked over with the FaceGym Pro device, which looks like some futuristic insect and whose metallic antennae deliver mild electrical charges to the face, to make my dozy face muscles contract and tighten. It tingles, but it's not unpleasant.

Comfort Level

Good. The massage is strong and fabulous, and the electrical aspect of it isn't too challenging.

Verdict

It all feels fantastic, much more relaxing than I had expected from such a strong, hands-on treatment. Afterwards, my face looks both relaxed and more awake than before – my cheeks sit a bit higher, and my eyes seem more open. It's everything that a great facial massage should deliver, and I could see the benefits of a more consistent skin colour (from improved blood flow and lymph drainage) and of relaxed face muscles for several days.

Cost and Location

Signature Electrical Workout, £85, www.facegym.com.

TREATMENT REVIEW: RADIOFREQUENCY SKIN TIGHTENING: THE VENUS FREEZE FACIAL

Venus Freeze is not so much a facial as a high-tech treatment which delivers a combination of radiofrequency energy and magnetic pulses into the skin for 20 minutes, to tighten the skin and refine its contours.

What It Is

Radiofrequency (RF) is a type of energy derived from radio waves. As a tweakment, it heats up the lower levels of the skin, where the collagen lies, to the extent that the collagen contracts. This has a small but instant shrink-wrapping effect on the face and also stimulates the skin to produce more of its own collagen. Used at high intensity, radiofrequency treatments are great for serious skin tightening (see page 257 onward for more on this), but even adding a quick session of radiofrequency into a facial can give skin a noticeable boost.

What It's Like

With my face covered in a delicious-smelling gel that will help the treatment head to slither around on my skin, this starts off feeling like an indulgent facial, rather than a medical treatment. The beauty therapist starts scooting a device with a smooth, flat head around my face in swift, overlapping circular movements. I can feel it is warming my skin as it goes, but it's perfectly comfortable. I relax.

The therapist tells me that the radiofrequency energy waves are causing damage deep down in the skin, to stimulate my skin's own healing mechanisms. I don't like the sound of 'damage', but I'm told it is a carefully controlled dose of heat – enough to kick-start my skin into producing new collagen and elastin, which together give skin its firmness, plumpness, and springiness. The radio-frequency waves also have the knock-on effect of shrinking the existing collagen within my skin, which is what gives the instant contouring effect. The magnetic pulses, apparently, have the ability to liquefy fat into fatty acids. I don't like the sound of that, either – my face doesn't need to lose any more of its padding – but she reassures me that for use on the face, the magnetic pulses are turned down very low. (The Venus machine can also be used for non-surgical body-contouring, and that's when its fat-busting magnetic pulses are more useful.)

Ten minutes in, my face is starting to feel quite hot, and the therapist explains the treatment has to heat the skin to 40C or more in order to make the collagen shrink, to get the tightening-contouring effect. She keeps whizzing the little heat-blaster around my cheeks, my forehead, and under my jaw. And it's getting really quite hot; if she pauses for even a fraction of a second, it's scorching, rather more challenging than the 'wonderful warming massage' promised by the promotional literature.

Comfort Level

Very comfortable – as long as that heated treatment head is kept moving

Verdict

I'm not expecting much of a result, although my face feels taut all over, as if I'd been out in the sun for too long. So it's a nice surprise to see that my forehead is smoother and my eyebrows have risen up a fraction. The skin on my browbone and beneath my eyebrows is tighter, making my eyes look more awake, and I would swear that my cheeks and jawline definitely have more definition, as well as a lovely glow to the skin. Very impressive.

I'm still baffled as to why the treatment is called Venus Freeze, when it is all about heat. I'm told it is because it's 'freezing' the ageing process, by boosting collagen production, which I suppose makes a sort of sense.

Cost and Location

Venus Freeze costs £120 at www.nevillehairandbeauty.net and nationwide (for locations, see www.venustreatments.com).

Microneedling Facials

Microneedling is – or can be – a much more serious sort of skin treatment than should be included in this chapter, but because many facialists are including a quick session of light microneedling in their treatments, I'm going to discuss it here and then return to it later in the book.

Microneedling involves using either a small roller covered in tiny sharp spikes, or a pen type device tipped with a grid of tiny sharp needles, to punch thousands of very small holes in the skin. That might sound like a terrible idea, but there are a couple of compelling reasons for doing it.

One reason is that making holes though the tough protective outer cells of the epidermis means that any skincare product that you slap on immediately afterwards can get direct access into the skin – so if that's a high-tech serum with skin-repairing benefits, it will be more effective.

The other reason is that, if the needling is done with long enough needles, it can stimulate a wound-healing response in the skin which floods the skin with growth factors and prompts the skin to create new, firming collagen.

These two reasons tend to get run together and conflate in people's minds into seeing microneedling as something really scary that will leave their faces smeared with pinpricks of their own blood (I looked up a Kim Kardashian post, which didn't help).

But when microneedling is on offer as part of a facial, it will be done with short needles – say, 0.5mm long, which really don't hurt as they don't sink far enough into the skin to hit the nerves or to cause bleeding. By contrast, collagen-stimulating needling requires needles that are more like 3mm long – and yes, they will cause pinpoint bleeding, and you will need anaesthetic cream beforehand.

TREATMENT REVIEW: MARIE REYNOLDS: THE MASTERLIFT

Marie Reynolds is a leading UK facialist with a rare gift for improving complexions.

What It Is

Marie's latest facial involves a good deal of microneedling with a neat device called a Dermapen, followed with light therapy to calm the skin down.

The Dermapen is an automated device with a grid of tiny needles that punch in and out of the skin 110 times a second. Its needles can be adjusted from an eye-watering 3mm to a barely-there 0.5mm; for the Masterlift, Marie uses it on the lightest setting. 'There is no need for it to be painful,' she says. The needling is used to drive a special rejuvenating serum into the skin, after which the skin is massaged with copper wands before the full-face LED light mask is balanced over your face.

What It's Like

After a quick cleanse, Marie covers my face with a special rejuvenating serum and gets out the Dermapen. I'm apprehensive about the needling, but Marie points out that she is only using 0.5mm needles, so it will barely hurt – and she's right. She moves the device smoothly and swiftly round my face, and most of the time, I hardly feel it, even when she works over my lips (when I do, it's mildly uncomfortable, rather than painful). Then she puts on a soft biocellulose mask full of hydrating serum, then tops this with the shield-shaped light mask. What does this feel like? Lovely, as alternating doses of red (healing), blue (antibacterial), and purple (skin-energy-boosting light work their magic.

Comfort Level

Only mildly uncomfortable, unless you are having a sensitive day (see the 'What Makes Tweakments Hurt More' sidebar on page 32 for details on what makes skin more sensitive).

Verdict

Very good. My skin was a little pink afterwards from all the needles, but my face looks instantly improved – before and after snaps that Marie took show how the needling and special serums that she used have plumped out fine lines around my crow's feet wrinkles and lips. Marie tells you to use no makeup until the following day, as all those tiny pinprick holes take a few hours to heal up, and you don't want to smush makeup into them during that time.

By the next day, my skin was glowing with health and felt a bit tighter, too. Great result.

Cost and Location

From £222 at Fortnum & Mason's beauty room. To book, go to www.mariereynoldslondon.com.

TREATMENT REVIEW: CRYSTAL CLEAR COMCIT ELITE

Comcit stands for Cryo Oxygen Microchannelling Collagen Induction Therapy – how high tech is that? – but don't let that put you off. Facialists refer to it as 'the popcorn facial' because of the way that pressurized oxygen and rejuvenating serums instantly plump the skin.

What It Is

Before you get to the pressurized oxygen part, there's a light microdermabrasion to shift dead skin cells from the surface of the skin, and a session of microneedling to stimulate the skin to make more collagen. Stimulating collagen production is the aim of the treatment, though I'd take issue with this based on what I said above about the length of the needles needed for collagen stimulation.

What It's Like

More 'treatment' than pampering. There is lovely, soothing cleansing first, then the microdermabrasion, which I find mildly uncomfortable, and ditto the needling, which means having the 'microchannelling' roller, with its many sharp spikes, raced around my face, over and over.

A special serum containing skin-repairing ingredients including vitamin C, plant stem-cell extract, and moisturizing hyaluronic acid is applied to my face before the rollering, and creating all those tiny holes – the 'micro channels' – allows the serum easy access to the skin. But even if it's done with a light hand, 20 minutes of this is plenty.

The next step is the puncture-jet oxygen machine, which blasts out oxygen at such pressure that it squeaks as it is moved across my face – the 'popcorn' bit. The therapist does one side of my face first, then sits me up and gives me a hand mirror so I can see there is a real difference between the two sides. Somehow, the machine has smoothed and plumped up my skin cells at the same time.

Comfort Level

Mild-to-moderate discomfort from the roller – it's prickly, rather than actually painful.

Verdict

Definitely a stimulating treatment for the skin, so not one to have done just before a big occasion. Much to my amazement (after all that microdermabrasion and the roller), my skin was only a little bit red, and that went in the next hour or two. It also felt really plumped up, though it felt rough for the next couple of days as the skin repaired itself after the microneedling. After that, it looked really good, clear and smooth, for the rest of the week.

Cost and Location

From £90, nationwide; see www.crystalclear.co.uk for your nearest salon. Crystal Clear recommends doing a course of treatments, a month apart.

The Skin-Peeling Facials

Skin peels might sound horrific, but done lightly, as part of a facial, they work brilliantly as skin-smoothers and glow-boosters.

TREATMENT REVIEW: iS CLINICAL FIRE & ICE FACIAL

A not-too-hard-hitting medical-grade facial, the iS Clinical Fire & Ice Treatment bridges the gap between a mild salon treatment and a high-tech medical-clinic procedure.

What It Is

The Fire & Ice Treatment aims to make dull skin look smoother, brighter, and more radiant. What it takes to do this is two professional-strength masks. The 'fire' mask is 18% glycolic acid with retinol, to exfoliate the skin; the 'ice' mask is soothing and moisturising, with aloe vera, antioxidants, and hydrating hyaluronic acid.

Both the treatment masks and the other products used alongside them come from the well-accredited and hard-working cosmeceutical skincare line iS Clinical.

What It's Like

Less fearsome than it sounds. After thorough cleansing, the 'fire' mask is painted on to my face with a brush, and I lie there waiting for the tingling to start as the glycolic acid dissolves the bonds that are holding old, dead skin cells onto the skin's surface. It doesn't take long. I'm torn between staying calm and letting the mask stay on as long as possible (five minutes is the absolute maximum) and shouting 'enough already' just in order to get the itchy stinging to stop. I last about two minutes, and the relief when the acid is neutralized is immense.

You could go straight on to the soothing, cooling 'ice mask' from here, and some clinics do, in order to wrap up the treatment within half an hour. But Dr Preema Vig's clinic likes to take a bit longer and add a little more TLC into the treatment before the second mask, extracting gunk softened by the glycolic peel from congested pores, and, after the second, soothing mask, massaging all the surplus hydrating serum from the mask into my skin.

Comfort Level

Moderately uncomfortable – but only the glycolic mask bit. The rest of it is very agreeable.

Verdict

Fabulous. My skin has shed its drab and slightly dry urban façade and looks brighter and bouncier, with a youthful glow to it. If there was a red-carpet event going on, I'd be ready for it. Celebs like Halle Berry and Gwyneth Paltrow love this facial for a quick boost. I can see why, as my skin looked terrific for days afterwards.

Cost and Location

From £120, Dr Preema Vig, drpreema.com. To find a practitioner in your area, go to www.thetweakmentsguide.com.

Light-Therapy Facials

When you are sitting or lying under a canopy of LED lights – small bright bulbs not unlike the ones you'd find in fairy lights, but with a rather higher wattage – it may feel as if nothing is happening, but this is one of the most helpful, gentle, and utterly painless types of skin treatment. LED light has been known to improve the skin for decades, but it is only recently that this sort of treatment has become widely available both in cosmetic doctors' clinics and in beauty salons. Here's why it's such good news.

TREATMENT REVIEW: THE LIGHT SALON: NEAR INFRA-RED LIGHT THERAPY

Light treatments are quick, utterly non-invasive, and anti-inflammatory, so they are good for even the most sensitive skin. Depending on the colour of the light, they can help to neutralise the bacteria that cause acne (blue light), or boost the production of collagen, elastin, and hyaluronic acid in the skin (red light and near infra-red light).

What It Is

Before having this treatment, I was well aware of the benefits of blue light and red light; what I didn't know was that a one-minute dose of yellow light, which is what the Light Salon treatment starts with, has been shown to improve cellular communication in the skin. Nor did I know that near infra-red light, which makes up the main 11 minutes of this treatment, not only has the skin-boosting effects of red light but travels 15cm deep into the body and strengthens bones against degeneration, too. In addition, near infra-red light also lowers levels of the stress hormone cortisol and also has a positive effect on the body's feelgood hormones.

What It's Like

The Light Salon is in a small, attractive room on the ground floor at Harvey Nichols, where canopies of LED lights hover over the comfy easy chairs. My face is given a quick cleanse before the treatment began – though if you are wearing make-up and would prefer not to take it off, you don't have to, as the light will get through it. I sink into the cocooning chair under the lamp, noticing behind my closed eyelids the way the light appears to slide from side to side of the canopy (it's just the yellow tinted panel that is moving to reassure customers that something is happening), relax, … and then find I've slipped into a slight trance, a bit like in meditation. When the time is up, I feel incredibly calm and relaxed; this goes on for the rest of the day. Two minutes of facial massage finish off the treatment.

Comfort Level

Very comfortable. If you are good at napping, it's the ideal opportunity to sneak in a quick one.

Verdict

Because I hadn't known about the de-stressing effects of near infra-red light, I am taken by surprise to find myself feeling so very serene at the end of the session. My skin looks clear and smooth and fresh, too. Even though you need multiple treatments to gain the most effects in the skin, this is just lovely. Next time I'll put my hands on my shoulders, so their backs get the benefits of the rejuvenating light, too.

Cost and Location

Express LED Rejuvenation, from £35, The Light Salon at Harvey Nichols, London, www.thelight-salon.com.

To find a practitioner offering LED light therapy in your area, go to www.thetweakmentsguide.com.

TREATMENT REVIEW: THE TT FACIAL

Teresa Tarmey is one of London's best facialists, with a keen following of celebs, socialites, and beauty editors. Her clinic has an impressive line-up of lasers and a light canopy for treating the skin.

What It Is

Teresa's signature TT facial is bespoke, adapted for each client's needs, but generally involves thorough cleansing, a quick exfoliating glycolic peel, extractions if you need them, wonderful face-sculpting massage, and 10 minutes under a canopy of tiny glowing red LED lights which calm any inflammation in the skin and stimulate collagen production.

What It's Like

Teresa's premises in west London are in an elegant private house with a large sitting/waiting room that looks out over the gardens behind. The facial is a real treat – Teresa's hands are superb and massage out tension from my face even while she's doing the initial cleansing. She gives me a quick acid peel to slough off dead skin cells and brighten my skin, then settles down for some necessary extractions. I don't have any thread veins worth lasering – something that she will do as and when necessary – but I get to enjoy 15 minutes' relaxation under her canopy of LED lights and am amazed to find that she has done all this in just over an hour.

Comfort Level

No discomfort at all. Apart from the extractions, which are very minor discomfort.

Verdict

Terrific. My skin is as fresh, clear, and glowing as if she has turned the clock back and sent me on a detox holiday. It's the sort of thing that makes you want to take no-make-up selfies, even at my age.

Cost and Location

TT facial, from £220 with Teresa, £120 with a senior facialist, www.teresatarmey.com. To find a practitioner in your area who offers laser facials, go to www.thetweakmentsguide.com.

Laser and Intense Pulsed Light Facials

If you're wondering whether lasers sound a bit too much like serious and possibly painful bits of equipment to be deployed in something like a facial, well, you're not wrong. The lasers you'll find in skin clinics are powerful devices capable of burning the skin – but it depends what intensity, or what power setting, they are used at.

There's more on lasers in later chapters, as they're good for clearing pigmentation, resurfacing, and tightening the skin; but if used on lower settings, they make a useful addition to a facial. Clearly, if you have a light sweep of a laser at the end of a facial in a beauty salon, you won't see the same sort of results as you would with a full laser treatment in a clinic, but if you repeat that laser-facial experience often enough, you will get a cumulative improvement in your skin.

TREATMENT REVIEW: SKIN LAUNDRY LASER AND IPL FACIAL

This super-quick treatment (you're in and out in 15 minutes) uses two high-tech machines on low settings to brighten the face. First, a light dose of laser vaporizes dirt, grime, and bacteria that are clogging your pores, then a quick blast of intense pulsed light (IPL) helps give a more even skin tone. Have these regularly, and you'll see pigment-busting and collagen-boosting effects, too.

What It Is

Skin Laundry is a laser salon in Liberty, the London department store, and its aim is to be a quick fix for the skin in the way that blow-dry bars are to hair. This treatment uses an Nd:YAG laser and an intense pulsed light (IPL) machine on a low setting, so no skin numbing is needed and you are left looking fresh rather than reddened. In case you're wondering, Nd:YAG is short for Neodymium Yttrium Aluminium Garnet – the laser shines its light through a yttrium aluminium garnet crystal 'doped' (coated) with neodymium.

The laser beam is used to vaporise dirt, oil, and bacteria on the skin's surface and in your pores to deep-clean the skin, while IPL adds an extra element of brightening. I had been sceptical of these 'vaporising' claims – how could a low-level laser 'vaporise' anything? – but a quick bit of phoning round skin-and-laser experts put me straight. This sort of low-power application of an Nd:YAG laser is what is used to clean years of grime and pollution off old stone buildings; the British Museum even keeps a laser like this for cleaning ancient artefacts such as papyrus scrolls. If it's gentle enough for that, my face ought to be ok!

What It's Like

First, a pen-like laser device which blasts out low-level laser light is wafted over my face. It feels as if tiny drops of hot fat are being spattered across my skin, but they are so small and so light that the sensation is just a sort of exciting prickling, rather than actual pain. I'm more disconcerted by the fact that there's a sort of frying smell, which I reckon is my blackheads being dissolved and sautéed by the laser. That takes about five minutes, and after that I have a conductive gel applied to my face before the IPL light device is fired across my face, section by section. I can't even feel it. Afterwards, my skin is patted with a moisturising sunscreen, and I'm done.

Comfort Level

Comfortable, with only very slight discomfort.

Verdict

Because of the gentle power settings, you need repeated treatments to get results on age spots. But what I see instantly is how much fresher and brighter my skin looks after its laser deep-cleaning.

Only 12 minutes have passed, but it looks airbrushed – fresh and smooth, as if my pores have shrunk. My scepticism is gone. I can see why people get hooked on this treatment.

Cost and Location

First treatment free, subsequent treatments, £60. Liberty, London W1, skinlaundry.com.

TREATMENT REVIEW: SKIN MATTERS FACIAL WITH IPL OR LASER

Although this Skin Matters treatment is very much a facial, a lovely long one that lasts up to two hours with a good deal of indulgent pampering along the way, it is much more than that. Joanne Evans, the super-facialist who leads Skin Matters, describes this treatment as more of a skin health check. Every step of the process is customized for your skin and Joanne is constantly alert to what your skin needs more (or less) of.

What It Is

The treatment has eight stages: a three-step cleanse; a light peel to loosen up dead cells on the skin's surface; steaming to soften the skin and open pores; extractions of debris done the old fashioned way, by hand; something called a hydra-quenching derma jet, which deluges your clean, fresh skin with moisture and vitamins; a fabulous face mask; a reflexology foot massage; and finally, a dose of either laser or intense pulsed light (IPL).

What It's Like

Heavenly, apart from the extractions – but then in a perverse way I rather enjoy those, because they get rid of my blackheads. I've had enough facials over the years to know when I'm in good hands, and Joanne's are excellent. Her face massage is superb, and I drift through stages one to eight in a happy daze – while the infusion mask is on my face, she gives my feet a blissful reflexology massage. I get off lightly in terms of the technology, with just a bit of intense pulsed light (like being flicked lightly with elastic bands) to get rid of some thread veins.

Comfort Level

Blissfully comfortable, apart from the extractions.

Verdict

My skin looks clear and fabulous. The massage has taken away the tension from my face and that, together with the hydrating serums, has made my fine lines vanish. No wonder Joanne's regulars book straight in month after month.

Cost and Location

From £380, skin-matters.co.uk.

DEBBIE THOMAS LASER FACIAL

Debbie Thomas is the laser-facial queen, and her treatments are customised for each client. Most facialists with a laser at their disposal have only one, but Debbie has several and finds that 'layering' a number of different laser procedures within one treatment session gives enhanced results.

I've written up her 'DNA laser facial' later in the book, because it's a serious laser treatment rather than a facial (in the chapter on treating sagging skin; see page 276), but I'm mentioning it here because if you see Debbie for a bespoke facial, she can include as much or as little lasering as you want or need. Her Illuminate facials use what she calls 'baby laser' – ie a very light dose – which will give a nice brightening result and can help persuade laser-phobics of how easily a quick once-over can leave the skin looking plumper and more glowy. These treatments reduce redness and rosacea, too.

Illuminate facials from £130. Debbie Thomas, 25 Walton Street, SW3, www.dthomas.com.

CHAPTER 5

Home-Use Devices

Perhaps you like the idea of tweakments but can't really afford them or live too far away from the top aesthetic practices. Or maybe you would simply like to step up your home skincare routine, or to see what improvements you can bring about in your face before visiting the tweakment maestros.

There is a huge selection of home-use beauty devices offering watered-down versions of the sort of tweakment technology that you find in clinics. Here's my selection of the best.

DEEP-CLEANSING BRUSHES

The aim of these brushes is to add extra oomph to your cleansing routine.

If you're wondering what place a cleansing brush has in a chapter about devices set to improve the face... that's a fair question, but I do think good skincare is fundamental to how good your face looks, certainly to the quality of the skin. And if you are using skincare products with active ingredients such as vitamin C, retinol, or other retinoids, or alpha hydroxy acids, they will all work that much better if they can actually get into your skin. A lot depends on the formulation of the products, but it also helps if their path is not impeded by the sort of everyday accumulation of dead cells that sit on the surface of our skin, cluttering up the complexion.

You don't have to exfoliate like a maniac to get rid of these dead cells, just do a slightly deeper cleanse than usual, and a powered brush can be helpful for that. The best-known cleansing brush is the Clarisonic (from £89, www.clarisonic.co.uk), which is brilliant, though I find it is a bit harsh on the face for everyday use. So if you do go for this, keep its use down to once or twice a week.

I prefer the vibrating Foreo brush (from £119, www.foreo.co.uk), which has soft silicone 'bristles' that don't harbour bacteria and never wear out. It buzzes its way through a 'sonic' cleaning routine which removes make-up, dirt, oil, and dead skin cells very effectively and with absolutely minimal irritation. Each recharge of the device seems to last for weeks, too.

FACIAL TONING DEVICES

With one of these high-tech devices, you can turn your home face-care routine into more of a salon experience. They all promise visible results if used diligently.

HOME-USE DEVICE REVIEW: CLARISONIC MIA SMART PLUS MASSAGE HEAD

Can you really improve lines and wrinkles with mechanical massage? It's a concept called 'mechanobiology' and is the premise behind the massage attachment that can be used with the this device.

What It Is and What It Does

Clarisonic is famous for its cleansing brushes and the latest one, the Mia Smart, can be used with a number of different click-to-fit treatment heads. One of these is a face-massaging attachment with three rubbery bumps on it, which Clarisonic claims that it will tighten and lift the skin at the same time as softening wrinkles.

The rubbery bumps vibrate and deliver 'micro-massage motions' into your skin, 27,000 of them per minute, and these in turn stimulate collagen production in the skin. You can use the device with any skincare serum, cream, or oil that you like (it helps products sink deeper into the skin, too), for three minutes at a time, morning and evening. Results from trials look encouraging – users report tighter, smoother skin and less visible pores.

What It's Like to Use

Very easy: you clip on the attachment, apply a product to your face to give it some 'slip', and off you go. The device glides easily over my face, and although three minutes seems a long time to spend pushing this around my face and up the sides of my neck, it is curiously addictive. I find it works well with cleansing oil and that I spend as much time burrowing it into the tight knots of muscle in my cheeks, jaw, and neck as smoothing it along my forehead.

Verdict

Needs commitment, but surprisingly nice to use.

Where to Buy It

Clarisonic Mia Smart, £185; Clarisonic Firming Massage Head, £22.95, currentbody.com.

HOME-USE DEVICE REVIEW: THE MICROCURRENT MACHINE: NUFACE TRINITY FACIAL TRAINER KIT

Running low-level microcurrents through the face improves the circulation, helps reduce fine lines and, by tweaking and toning the face muscles, helps give the face a lifted appearance.

What It Is and What It Does

This nifty device is hugely popular in the USA and is the only one of its kind to have FDA approval (which means it does what it claims, including improving the contours of the face if you use it regularly). Because it works by toning the muscles, you would think it was an antidote to Botox, but it works well as an adjunct to Botox treatment. This is because it plumps up the muscle fibres and keeps them in good shape even if, thanks to Botox, those muscles are temporarily inactivated.

What It's Like to Use

Very easy: you just switch it on and – having applied conductive gel to the skin first – slide the smooth bobbles of the device slowly upwards and outwards across the cheeks, nine times on each side, then slowly upwards from the eyebrows, again nine times on each side, which takes less than five minutes. Having watched a demonstration where a middle-aged model's eyebrow was hoisted by at least a centimetre in just five minutes, I have been experimenting at home and can just about do this, which is thrilling. It tingles a bit, but it's not remotely painful. Some people use it while watching TV. That's only possible if you're watching alone as the beep the device gives to tell you to move to a different spot soon becomes really annoying for anyone else in the room.

Verdict

Terrific, portable and slightly addictive. I love the way that, when I have worked over my forehead and tweaked up my eyebrows, I feel much more awake, simply because my forehead is lifted and so my eyes are that little bit more open. Strange but true. What I haven't managed to do is use it consistently enough to get lasting results, but I know it is proven to give results if you keep at it.

Where to Buy It

£300 (mini version, £199), currentbody.com.

HOME-USE DEVICE REVIEW: THE LIP PLUMPER: PMD KISS

Any non-surgical method of making your lips look bigger – even temporarily – is worth a closer look.

What It Is and What It Does

A compact device which uses a pulsating vacuum to apply a suction force to your lips, which makes them swell. It's like a kinder, electronic version of the shot-glass trick. (This trick – you can look it up online, though I wouldn't recommend trying it – involves pushing your lips into an empty shot glass, then sucking out the air, creating a vacuum whose pressure causes your poor lips to swell in protest.) And if you apply the serum that comes with the device, it is meant to help hydrate the lips and boost their volume a bit, too, for two or three hours.

I can see this being popular with young women looking to achieve fuller-looking lips without injections of filler, as well as with older women whose lips are starting to shrink. Daily use is meant to boost collagen production, to create plumped-up lips for as long as six weeks.

What It's Like to Use

Easy enough. It vacuums up a chunk of your lip at a time, and you move it around your lips until each bit of them has been treated. It doesn't hurt, and it takes about three minutes to do.

Verdict

It certainly boosts your lip volume and colour (due to the increased blood flow) for an hour or two, but I found that going too near the lip edge could leave a red ring around the outside of the mouth, which looks really odd and which you can't hide with lipstick. Call me old-fashioned, but this is something I can't really be bothered with. Why have I included it in here if I wouldn't use it myself? Because it does give a result, and you might feel differently about it.

Where to Buy

£125, currentbody.com.

HOME-USE DEVICE REVIEW: GLOPRO MICROSTIMULATION FACIAL TOOL

Microneedling is increasingly popular as an at-home treatment to stimulate collagen production in ageing skin

What It Is and What It Does

A sophisticated home-use microneedling device designed to stimulate the skin's natural healing response. It also vibrates and beams soothing, collagen-boosting red LED light at the skin as it is used. The roller is covered in tiny 0.3mm stainless steel spikes. Rolling the device across the face creates thousands of tiny holes in the skin. These allow any skincare products you apply to get right into the skin so they will be more effective, and, the theory goes, as the skin races to repair the damage caused by the needles, it produces growth factors and collagen that help strengthen the skin.

What It's Like to Use

Very easy and only lightly prickly on the skin, rather than painful. When I tried it out, I rolled it enthusiastically around my face for the recommended minute, then carried on a bit until I could see my poor face was going a bit pink – but no harm done, that just means the needles are doing their job. Then I slapped on my retinol-based night cream and retired for the night.

Verdict

Fabulous. It's sophisticated, clinically well-proven, and I love it. I have found myself using this with dedication and also experimenting with the larger body-roller head with its 0.5mm spikes, which is meant to be brilliant for stretch marks and cellulite – though I appreciate you could get all the same benefits of the microneedling, minus the LED light and vibration, with a £10 dermaroller off the internet. So is it worth it? Depends on your budget.

Where to Buy

£199, currentbody.com.

> Since trying this device and writing this up, I have had a bit of a re-think on home needling, because I have been speaking to a few dermatologists who are not keen on it. They say that it causes unnecessary trauma to the skin and that few of the products that people apply after needling are designed to go as deep into the skin as they will through the needled holes (if a product has fragrance in it, for instance, that is very likely to cause irritation). So I have included this review because this is a lovely product and a very popular one. But I'm not totally convinced that it is good for your skin. So bear that in mind.

SKIN-TIGHTENING DEVICES

Radiofrequency and laser treatments are popular in clinics as ways to tighten and firm the skin. Here are two home-use devices that are well worth trying.

HOME-USE DEVICE REVIEW: THE FACIAL SHRINK-WRAPPER: THE TRIPOLLAR STOP

Radiofrequency energy is a popular in-clinic choice for tightening the skin and reducing wrinkles, and this device offers a home-use version of the same technology.

What It Is and What It Does

Like a clinic-based radiofrequency treatment, the Tripollar Stop works by creating heat within the skin, which has two results. Initially, it has a quick tightening effect as the heat makes the collagen in the skin contract; and longer term, the heat will prompt the skin to make more of its own, new collagen. The device can be used on the hands and the neck, as well as the face.

What It's Like to Use

I apply a thin layer of conductive gel all over my (clean, dry) face, switch on, and get going. The head of the Tripollar device has four rounded metal pegs on it, and these all need to be in contact with the skin in order for it to work. As instructed, I work on a small area of face, sliding those four pegs around in a slow circle. It feels very warm, and just as it is becoming alarmingly hot, the green indicator light on the device turns orange, which tells me that that patch of skin is cooked – or at least, hot enough to stimulate new collagen formation. Phew. Then I move onto the next patch. It takes just over 20 minutes to go over my whole face, which is left a bit red – but this redness goes within half an hour.

Verdict

As with all home-use devices, you need patience and commitment to get the best results out of this. And because it takes 20 minutes, you need to set that time aside two or three times a week for a special spot of self-care. Having tried it, I have found that if I earmark half an hour on a quiet evening for this, it's quite possible. What I'm really interested in seeing is what difference it can make to my neck, which is in more need of attention than my face, so I'm more motivated to keep going with it. I'm pretty sure it will work if I do.

Where to Buy

£249, currentbody.com.

HOME-USE DEVICE REVIEW: THE SKIN-TIGHTENING LASER: TRIA

This laser deploys a lighter version of the same fractional, non-ablative laser technology that you find in professional salon treatments, and it is FDA-cleared, too.

What It Is and What It Does

Tria uses targeted laser light to reduce discolouration, improve skin texture, smooth wrinkles, and rebuild collagen. The 'fractional' technology drives tiny pinprick beams of laser light into the skin, and as these micro-channels of damage heal, you begin to see the benefits.

And if you are worrying that a laser sounds like a dangerous thing to have around at home – this one has a number of built in safety features. You don't need to wear goggles when using it, and each zap of laser won't fire until the treatment head is properly in flat contact with the skin.

What It's Like to Use
By Karen Heath

It's very user-friendly, and the little zaps of laser light it delivers feel no worse than gentle pinpricks, even after I have skipped past levels 1 (introductory) and 2 (normal) and cranked it up to level 3, the maximum dose. One major attraction is that you use it on clean, dry skin and don't need any gloopy expensive conduction gel that so many home devices require.

The whole treatment takes 15 minutes – that's five minutes on each side of your face and five on the forehead. Initially I was a little pink for about an hour afterwards, but now my skin is used to it, there is only slight pinkness for about 10 minutes.

When I was new to the Tria, I had to watch what I was doing in the mirror but now I relax on the sofa, watch TV or even lie in bed while gliding it over my face. It's recommended to use the device for five days a week for 12 weeks and then to do another 12-week treatment when needed. I can never manage that, but I do use it a couple of times a week.

Verdict

I love a home beauty gadget and have found I use this regularly –
just because it is so easy to use. I love the way it brightens up my
skin when it's a bit dull and smooths out the surface. I'm hoping
it's keeping some lines and wrinkles at bay, too.

Where to Buy

From £450, www.triabeauty.co.uk.

LIGHT-THERAPY DEVICES

Using LED light therapy is increasingly popular as a clinic
treatment, either to promote collagen production with red light or
to quell acne bacteria with blue light. Its only drawback is that you
need frequent treatments, several times a week, to see best results.
Here are the devices that bring the treatment into your home.

HOME-USE DEVICE REVIEW: THE COLLAGEN-BOOSTING LED LIGHT
DEVICE: THE PHOTIZIO BLUSH

LED light has genuine skin-boosting properties, and this device can
help smooth and soften the skin by boosting collagen production,
reducing inflammation, and improving lymphatic drainage within
the skin.

What It Is and What It Does

The Blush began life as a vetinary device – or rather, it is a toned-
down version of a Photozio device which is used on animals; and,
as the company told me, you don't need as heavy a dose of light to
stimulate repair in human skin as you do to encourage healing in
the dense muscle of a horse's hindquarters. The device looks like
a slimline shower-head, and dispenses red and near infra-red light
together.

What It's Like to Use

Blissfully easy. You press the button, and the head of the device
lights up. You place it in your chosen spot on your face. After 16
seconds, it beeps and turns off. You move it to a new spot, press

the button again, and so on. That's it. It is safe to use all around the eyes and even on the eyelids, and also on the lips.

Verdict

I really like this device, because it is so simple to use, and because the light it delivers will definitely do your skin good if, as with all these other devices, you can just commit to using it enough. Because the vetinary model is designed for easing animal arthritis, I'm experimenting with this on a finger joint which is showing early signs of swelling and stiffening, and have been advised to give it six cycles of light every day. At the time of going to press, it seems to be helping.

Where to Buy

£299 at www.danetrehealthproducts.com.

HOME-USE DEVICE REVIEW: THE LIGHT MASK FOR CROW'S FEET WRINKLES: DR DENNIS GROSS SPECTRALITE MASK

The ideal beauty device would be something so very quick and simple to use that you wouldn't hesitate to pop it on every day – backed up by technology capable of delivering genuine results. Something like this odd but fabulous little light mask.

What It Is and What It Does

72 little LED light bulbs are tucked inside this curvy little eye-mask, clustered at either side, to aim directly at your crow's feet, and in the centre, to target frown lines. These bulbs give out gentle rays of red, deep-red, near infra-red, and amber light, at wavelengths that have been clinically proven to stimulate collagen production. Wear it for three minutes every day, and you should see results after two weeks, and these should go on improving for 10 weeks.

What It's Like to Use

So easy. It clings gently to the contours of your face (you can secure it around the back of your head with the strap provided, but I didn't always bother), switch it on, then relax for three minutes. The rubbery inside of the mask makes it very comfy. And although it is very bright at the sides of my vision, I can still see out and use my hands – so I can, say, still answer the door while wearing it (and yes, truly scare the poor postman).

Verdict

Brilliant. The technology is proven, all you have to do is use it enough and you ought to get results. It's really easy to use and also – a useful plus for the careless among us – it charges with a common-or-garden USB-to–micro USB cable.

Where to Buy

£168, spacenk.com.

HOME-USE DEVICE REVIEW: THE SPOT-BUSTER: NEUTROGENA VISIBLY CLEAR LIGHT THERAPY ACNE MASK

Using blue LED light to denature acne bacteria is a well-proven strategy for improving spotty skin. This device means you can treat yourself.

What It Is and What It Does

The mask is a solid plastic face-shaped shield, with a slot at eye level so you can still see out. On the inside, there are LED lights which emit blue and red light. The blue light destroys the bacteria that cause acne on the skin, while the red light helps stimulate collagen formation. To make it work, you press 'start' on the 'Activator', the lights flick on and the countdown starts on your 10-minute light therapy session.

What It's Like to Use

Surprisingly comfortable, and you can see enough not to feel shut off from the world. But read the instructions several times before you start. I didn't, and inadvertently set off the mask. When I stopped it, I found I'd used up one of the 30 sessions you get from the Activator – when those run out, you need to buy a new Activator for £14.99.

Verdict

Very helpful if you use it regularly and consistently. (If you went to a clinic, you would need 20 minutes of blue light twice a week.) In

Neutrogena's tests, 98 per cent of acne sufferers saw improvements after using the mask every day for 12 weeks.

Where to Buy

£59.99 at Boots, Tesco, and Superdrug.

HOME-USE DEVICE REVIEW: THE FULL-FACE LIGHT MASK: MZ SKIN GOLDEN FACIAL LED MASK

Gold-coloured and offering several varieties of LED light, this device offers glamour as well as high-spec lights.

What It Is and What It Does

This solid shield of a mask has gaps over the eyes, nose, and mouth, so you can still see out (and breathe). On the inside, there are LED lights which emit red (collagen-boosting, anti-inflammatory), or blue (acne-busting), or clear near infra-red (regenerating and calming), or green light (to reduce pigmentation) or even red and blue light together. The countdown timer offers a 20-minute session as a default, but you can change this as you like.

What It's Like to Use

The mask is quite heavy, so even though it will stay on if, say, I sit upright and meditate with it on, it is easier to use it lying down. Also, whichever way I wear it, I get swimming-goggle-style indent marks below my eyes which take an hour or two to soften. The eye holes are large enough to see out without being blinded by the light, so it is possible to watch TV while wearing it, as long as you are close enough to be able to plug the device into an electrical socket. Apart from these quibbles, it is fab.

Verdict

A terrific product. Anyone with any skin type can use this and will see benefits if they use it regularly enough.

Where to Buy

£385, currentbody.com.

PART 2: THE TWEAKMENTS

NAILING YOUR CONCERNS, AND PICKING YOUR TWEAKMENTS

Over the next few chapters, I've put together the main skin and face concerns, along with the tweakments that can be used to improve them and, where it's relevant, where skincare can help. The roll-call goes something like this:

- Dynamic lines and wrinkles on the forehead (the ones that get worse when you move your face) – wrinkle-relaxing toxin injections
- Dynamic lines and wrinkles around the eyes – wrinkle-relaxing toxin injections
- Skin texture issues, including: fine lines all over the face; dry, rough, or dull skin – LED light, skin peels, PRP, medical needling, dermaplaning, laser skin resurfacing, radiofrequency skin resurfacing, injectable moisturiser, mesotherapy
- Pigmentation problems such as brown age spots and melasma – intense pulsed light (IPL), laser, skin peels
- Thread veins, rosacea, redness, large pores and acne – IPL, laser, microneedling, LED light
- Loss of volume which leads to flatter cheeks, looking hollow in the cheeks, hollow eyes and puffy eye bags, nose-to-mouth lines and 'marionette' lines (at the sides of the mouth) – facial filler injections, fat transfer injections, stem cell injections
- A pouchy or saggy jawline – facial filler injections
- Thin or asymmetric lips, loss of lip volume, 'barcode' lines above the lips – lip filler injections, injectable moisturiser
- A nose that isn't straight, a weak chin – facial filler injections
- Hooded eyes – skin tightening with Tixel, radiofrequency, and Plexr
- Loose, sagging skin on the cheeks – skin tightening with radiofrequency, focussed ultrasound, and laser, thread lifts

- Double chins and fatty jowls – fat freezing, fat-dissolving injections
- Stringy or wrinkly neck – wrinkle-relaxing toxin injections, focussed ultrasound
- Crepey décolletage – skin tightening with radiofrequency and focussed ultrasound, injectable moisturiser

That's a big old list, and put all together like that, it sounds more than a bit negative, even if these are all perfectly normal things to find on a face. If you're younger, there may be aspects of your face you want to change or enhance. If you're older, there may be things which have niggled for years and which are gradually becoming more of an issue. Whatever it is, and to take a more positive line, all these concerns can be worked on and improved, and the following pages should give you an idea of how to begin to tackle the bits that bother you most.

For each tweakment, I've explained what it is and how it can help, and for many of them I have included a first-person account of what it is like to have the treatment done. That way, you can get an idea of what to expect from each procedure – how long it takes, whether it hurts, whether there is any downtime afterwards, and what sort of results you might expect. I've also mentioned the clinic or salon where the treatment was done, and what the treatment costs. Costs tend to vary according to location, the expertise of the practitioner, and how difficult it is to force yourself into his or her schedule.

I realise that a disproportionate number of the clinics in this book are in London and the surrounding area. It's not that there aren't many brilliant doctors and nurses outside London, it's just that when I'm visiting clinics for work to try out new procedures, I usually go to the closest ones. For a wider range of practitioners, go to my website, www.thetweakmentsguide.com, which has search tools for both finding suitable tweakments and for locating practitioners who offer particular tweakments.

As I mentioned, most of the treatment reviews are by me; where they're not, I've put in the name of the person who tried it. In case you are wondering what on earth my face looks like after such an onslaught of treatment, I haven't scampered through all these in the past six months; they are things I have tried out over the course of several years.

HOW TO USE THIS INFORMATION TO COME UP WITH A TREATMENT PLAN

It's hard for me to advise on this, because it completely depends on you – on what your face is like now, what you want to achieve, and how much time and money you have to dedicate to this.

If the world of tweakments is completely new to you, be sensible. You don't have to jump in at the deep end.

- Start by developing a more consistent skincare routine.
- Consider adding in skin-boosting supplements and home-use beauty devices.
- Try one of the 'facials plus' type treatments, to see how they can help
- When you are ready to try a tweakment, do your homework, find a good practitioner, and book in for a proper consultation about your concerns. Listen to their suggestions, and go away and think about what they have said before deciding what to do.
- Have a play with the interactive tools on my website, www.thetweakmentsguide.com, which can help you identify tweakments and the practitioners who offer them, as well as skincare, supplements, home-use beauty devices and 'facials plus'.

Good luck – and let me know how you get on. You can contact me through the website, www.thetweakmentsguide.com and find me on Instagram at @alicehartdavis.

CHAPTER 6

Managing Lines and Wrinkles on the Forehead

The lines and wrinkles that crop up on our foreheads are usually the first indication we get that we're not as young as we used to be.

In this chapter, I first explain why we get lines and wrinkles, suggest the right time to start dealing with them, and tell you how to improve matters with suitable skincare. I then devote the bulk of the chapter to tweakments for lines and wrinkles on the forehead, starting with the gold-standard tweakment – Botox – and moving on to other tweakments, including skin peels, laser skin smoothing, radiofrequency skin tightening, and microneedling. Finally, I cover what you can do about crow's feet wrinkles around your eyes, either by treating them yourself or by having tweakments.

WHY WE GET WRINKLES

There are two reasons those lines arrive. The first is the most obvious one – that when you frown or raise your eyebrows, the muscle movements involved ('dynamic' movements, as they're called in the trade) scrunch up the skin of the forehead into wrinkles. Foreheads are expressive, which is great for communicating emotion, but if you carry on making these expressions for long enough, these wrinkles start to become set in. They're most noticeable if you have a habit of pulling your eyebrows together when you frown, creating the '11' vertical lines between your brows ('glabellar lines', as doctors call them) or if you raise your eyebrows higher than average when you're curious or surprised.

Why these lines become entrenched also has to do with the way that skin becomes less firm and springy as it ages. That's the second reason, and this happens because the levels of collagen (the protein that keeps the skin firm) and elastin (another protein, one that keeps the skin springy) drop the older we get. That makes skin less resilient, so when it is continually squashed into a crease, it loses the ability to spring back. When you're young, and you relax your brow, the wrinkles go away. When you are a tad older, those forehead wrinkles tend to hang around, even when your face is relaxed.

WHEN SHOULD YOU DO SOMETHING ABOUT IT?

When it starts to annoy you, continually. People often ask me at what age they should start having Botox, but it's impossible to give a one-size-fits-all answer. Cosmetic doctors will usually say: 'When your face is relaxed and you still see lines on your forehead,' but it also depends how you feel about those lines. (Plus there's no 'should' about having Botox. It's not the law.) But if those lines are making you look cross or sad when you're not, it's very irritating. It was when my mother told me not to look so anxious about something trivial – when I wasn't remotely anxious, I was just… thinking – that I realised it might be time to do something about my own forehead.

START WITH SKINCARE – AND SUNSCREEN

Skincare can genuinely help improve the appearance of wrinkles. The first and most useful skincare product you can own is a moisturising sunscreen, which you must wear every day – because what really hastens ageing in the skin is daily exposure to ultraviolet light. All the details on why I feel so strongly about sunscreen are in the chapter on pigmentation, from page 157 onward, so for now I'll just say: before all else, sunscreen.

So, assuming you've got sunscreen, here's what else you might want to know. Dry skin wrinkles more swiftly that well-hydrated skin, so if your skin is on the dry side, and you are not already using a moisturising serum containing hyaluronic acid (HA), add one of these into your skincare routine as a first step.

Add Hyaluronic Acid for Hydration

I so wish this ingredient wasn't termed 'acid', just because that word alone makes people suspicious of it. It's the gentlest thing in the skincare ingredient-book, a naturally occurring substance that has a near-miraculous ability to hold onto water – each hyaluronic acid molecule can hold up to 1,000 times its own weight in water. We have hyaluronic acid in our connective tissue, in our nerve tissue, and in our eyes; and it's a major component of the skin. So the skin knows it and likes it.

Over the past 10 years, hyaluronic acid has become hugely popular as an ingredient in skincare, because it sinks into the upper layers of the skin (it is quite a large molecule, so even if it is broken up into fragments, it doesn't go that far into the skin), hangs on to moisture, and plumps the skin up so it feels more comfortable and looks better. I like to use a few drops of hyaluronic acid serum – a lightweight, runny concoction of the product – on my skin after cleansing if it is feeling particularly dry. This serum vanishes into the skin, so you wonder where it's gone, but it will be sitting there in the upper layers, preventing that tight, dry feeling, and drawing water into the skin from the atmosphere. A quick word of warning: if you are somewhere where the air is very dry, hyaluronic acid will start to draw water from the deeper layers of your skin, which isn't ideal.

You can use hyaluronic acid under moisturiser, sunscreen, makeup, or whatever you are putting on your face (it works best when sealed into place with a product on top of it). If you're the sort of person who reads ingredient labels, hyaluronic acid may be listed as Sodium Hyaluronate, which is the salt form of hyaluronic acid.

HYALURONIC ACID SERUMS TO TRY

Here is a short list of some of my favourite hyaluronic acid serums.

- **La Roche Posay Hyalu-B5 Serum**, £37, www.boots.com.
- **Vichy Mineral 89 Hyaluronic Acid Booster**, £16.50, vichy.co.uk.
- **Garden of Wisdom Hyaluronic Acid Serum**, £9, victoriahealth.com.

- **Novexpert Instant Lifting Serum**, £34, www.novexpert-lab.fr/en/catalogue/our-products-shop.1.html.
- **The Hero Project Hyasoft Gel**, £19, www.heroproject.com.

For an intensive course, try Fillerina Dermo Cosmetic Filler Treatment Grade 3 (£79, www.cultbeauty.co.uk). This is a kit naughtily designed to look as if it is for self-administered injection: the gel comes in a vial with a syringe-type applicator. But in fact there is nothing injectable about it. Using this applicator, you put the stuff onto your worst wrinkles for 10 minutes before bedtime, then wipe off the excess before you go to sleep. I thought this was all a bit of a performance and unlikely to work until I trialled it for a newspaper a couple of years ago and found it made a measurable improvement in my skin's hydration levels – so yes, it really works.

HOW TO USE HYALURONIC ACID IN YOUR SKINCARE ROUTINE

If you are using a vitamin C serum, apply this after cleansing in the morning, then once it has been absorbed into your skin, apply your hyaluronic acid serum. If you're not using vitamin C, just apply the hyaluronic acid to clean dry skin, and spread it around your face. Wait for this to be absorbed, then judge how your skin feels. Because my skin is on the oily side, I just apply a lightweight, moisturising sunscreen after my serums. If your skin is drier, you might want to use a separate moisturiser next, before finishing off with sunscreen.

Add a Vitamin A Cream for Regeneration

The next step is to start using a cream containing some form of vitamin A, such as retinol. This ingredient is part of the retinoid family and is chemically related to vitamin A. It can be transformative for the skin because it kick-starts collagen production and at the same time reduces the rate of collagen breakdown in the skin, so your existing collagen lasts longer, and new collagen is made faster.

Retinol also speeds up the rate at which ageing skin cells renew themselves, which has an exfoliating effect on the skin; reduces oiliness, so it helps to unclog blocked pores; and quietens down the production of excess pigment in the skin. Put together, all these effects make the skin look clearer and less wrinkled, so products containing retinol are a great addition to any skincare regime from aged 35 onwards, and are also very helpful for younger skin suffering from acne. See the nearby sidebar 'Retinol, Retinoids: Which Is Which?' for information on what the various types of retinoids are and how to use them.

The idea that retinol 'speeds up' skin cell turnover may sound like a bad idea – after all, isn't too much cell-proliferation associated with cancer? But what retinol and other retinoids do, more accurately, is normalise skin cell turnover. So in older skin, where skin cell turnover has slowed down, retinol will speed up turnover. But in skin that's producing skin cells too fast (hyperkeratosis), retinol can slow this down.

WHICH TYPE OF RETINOID IS BEST FOR YOU?

Before you decide that what you need is the strong stuff (the retinoic acid), the other thing to know about retinoids is that there is a direct link between how well they work and how much they irritate the skin. Side effects of using retinoids include redness, dryness, itchiness, and skin peeling – not things that any of us would voluntarily step up for. That's why there is such a large market for over-the-counter retinol products.

But having said all that, cosmetic technology is advancing fast, and there are now ways of tweaking retinoid molecules in the lab to give them cosmetic super-powers. Let me explain the science: the experts are creating cunning new forms of retinoids, like retinyl retinoate, which is gentler on the skin than retinol, yet produces results that are eight times as good as retinol. Another development is Hydroxypinacolone Retinoate (HPR for short), which is described as 'a non-prescription ester of all-trans direct retinoic acid'. HPR is said to offer 'a multifold better effect against signs of ageing than retinol, retinyl palmitate, and nearly all other forms of non-prescription retinoid'.

RETINOL, RETINOIDS: WHICH IS WHICH?

There are few topics on which skin experts agree – but the fact that retinoids help make the skin look fresher and smoother is one of them.

'Retinoids' is the group name for a bunch of ingredients which are all derived from vitamin A.

The strongest and most effective of these is retinoic acid (also known as tretinoin), which has a marked effect on skin. It is also only available on prescription, because it is so potent and its use needs to be supervised by a doctor or dermatologist. Our skin cells have receptors for retinoic acid and know exactly what to do with it.

Then there is retinol, which is widely used in skincare products that are available in shops and online. Once it's on the skin, the retinol has to be converted into retinoic acid in order to work its magic, so it works in the same way as retinoic acid, but a bit more slowly and gently.

Or there's retinyl palmitate, which needs to go through one conversion process in the skin to become retinol, then another to become retinoic acid. These conversion processes make retinyl palmitate a gentler and weaker option than retinol. Retinyl palmitate is also not proven to have the same rejuvenating effect as retinol unless it has been tweaked in the lab and put together with, say, some high-strength peptides.

I hope you're still with me, but essentially what you need to know is that you can find Hydroxypinacolone Retinoate in The Ordinary's Granactive Retinoid 2% Emulsion (£8, theordinary.com), and retinyl retinoate in Medik8's R-Retinoate (£135, medik8.com). But the net result of all this is that new types of active retinoids are continually being launched that are really effective at improving the skin than their older cousins, and, oh joy, much less irritating, too.

HOW TO USE RETINOIDS

The standard advice for when you are starting to use any sort of retinoid is to use it twice a week for the first week *and no more*. It's active stuff: your skin needs a while to become accustomed to it, and you need to work out what sort of dose your skin can tolerate. The twice-a-week start is also vital because if your skin is going to find your chosen retinoid irritating (and it may well do), it will take 72 hours for this irritation to show up in your skin. So if you just wait 48 hours, think it's all fine, then apply another dose, all may be well until that third day, when suddenly your skin goes haywire, you think 'Oh no!', and the reaction carries on for longer than you expect, because you have already given yourself a second dose of it.

But start gradually, and you'll soon find out how your skin feels about retinoids. If you're fine with using it twice a week without your skin looking dry, red, scaly, or irritated, then step up to three times a week. Everyone's skin is different. I find I don't tolerate straightforward retinol very well. If I stick with a product containing 0.5% retinol, then I'm ok for every second night, but if I wanted to progress towards using 1% retinol, then I'd need to creep up on that target slowly and gradually. But since discovering the 'adapted' types of retinoids like Hydroxypinacolone Retinoate and retinyl retinoate, which are so much easier to tolerate, I haven't bothered much with straightforward retinol.

CHOOSING A RETINOID: IT'S NOT JUST ABOUT NUMBERS

When choosing a product, keep in mind that the percentage of retinol that it contains is key to the sort of result that you are going to get. Except the choice is more complicated than that. How well that active ingredient can get at the skin also depends on the formulation of the product. So it is not necessarily the case that a higher percentage will mean a better or more effective product.

If you are finding a retinoid drying, then pop a moisturiser over the top of it. As well as being moisturising, this may have the effect of 'buffering' the retinoid and softening its effects. Or just stop using the product for a few days. You're playing a long game when it comes to skincare, so there is no need to push your skin too fast.

WHEN TO USE RETINOLS AND RETINOIDS

Most retinols and retinoids should be used at night. One reason is because most retinoids are sensitive to daylight, which makes them break down, so they lose their effectiveness. Another is that night time is repair time as far as the skin's internal biology is concerned. But having said that, just to confuse things, there are a handful of great new products containing retinoids that are designed to be used during the day, and which are fine to be used by day because the retinoids in them have been engineered – tweaked in the lab – so as not to be vulnerable to daylight. I'm thinking of products like DCL's brilliant Profoundly Effective A Cream SPF30 (£59, spacenk.com) which contains a non-irritating vitamin-A 'polypeptide derivative', so it repairs and protects the skin at the same time.

Whichever product you choose, follow the instructions, which probably will tell you to apply the product to a cleansed, dry face in the evening and to use it sparingly. I'd suggest also using the product on your neck and the backs of your hands, since these areas usually need even more help than the face.

If you're not already in the habit of wearing a sunscreen during the day – and I do hope you are – you need to raise your skincare game and do this, because using a retinoid may make your skin more reactive to daylight. You'll also want to protect the fresher, new skin that the retinoids are helping to give you.

RETINOL PRODUCTS TO TRY

Here is a short list of some of my favourite retinol products.

- **Skinceuticals 0.3% Retinol** (£55, skinceuticals.co.uk). A well formulated, time-release retinol.
- **Murad Resurgence Retinol Youth Renewal Serum** (£70, murad.co.uk). Nice-to-use and easy-to-tolerate product from Hollywood dermatologist Dr Howard Murad. There's a cream version if this serum isn't moisturising enough.
- **Sunday Riley Luna Sleeping Night Oil** (£45, www.cultbeauty.co.uk). Gorgeous blue oil with cold-pressed avocado oil and chia seed oil alongside retinol.

- **Medik8 r-retinoate** (£135, medik8.com). With a key ingredient engineered in a Korean super-lab, this is gentler on the skin than retinol yet with eight times the results, so you can use it both morning and evening without skin irritation. If this is too pricey, start with one of Medik8's straightforward time-release retinoids (start with the one called 3TR), from £29.
- **The Ordinary Granactive Retinoid 2% Emulsion** (£8, theordinary.com). This is the product with Hydroxypina-colone Retinoate, mentioned above, which is also gentle on the skin but which gives good results.
- **Image Skincare Total Overnight Retinol Mask** (£80, www.imageskincare.com). This product is nice to use – it has a special hydrating technology within it to keep the skin moisturised while the retinol is doing its work. It's an interesting concept, to stick retinol in an occasional-use mask rather than a regular-use cream, but the net effect will end up being much the same.

DON'T BOTHER WITH 'BOTOX GELS'

I really wouldn't waste money on the creams and serums that offer a 'Botox-like effect'; the ones I have tried in the past, such as Biotulin (which is heavily marketed as a favourite product of famous women from Oprah and the Duchess of Cambridge to Madonna and Michelle Obama) have proved totally ineffective.

If you do want to try this sort of product, the key ingredient to look for is Argireline, which technically is able to inhibit the communication of superficial nerves in the skin and thus have a relaxing effect on the wrinkles. As so often, The Ordinary has a bargain version, a 10% Argireline solution (price £5.50).

TWEAKMENTS FOR LINES AND WRINKLES ON THE FOREHEAD

I think you know what's coming. The main way to quieten lines on the forehead is with injections of wrinkle-relaxing toxins, and the best-known and most widely used of these is Botox.

The Gold-Standard Tweakment: Botox

Botox is considered by cosmetic doctors and dermatologists and cosmetic surgeons to be the gold-standard treatment for softening lines and wrinkles on the forehead and elsewhere. It is quick and very effective, and the effects last for several months. It's also a treatment that makes many people shudder. 'But it's poison!' they say. 'How could you ever consider it?'

Botox, even though it is one of the best-known drug names in the world, is a brand name, and it is utterly dominant in its market. There are several other wrinkle-relaxing botulinum toxins available, such as Azzalure, BoCouture, and Dysport, which do the same job, but you won't find them so frequently. So although technically I should be referring to this injectable drug treatment for wrinkles as 'Botulinum toxin type A', I'm going to call it Botox, just because that's how most of us think of it, and Botox is the brand of botulinum toxin A that most practitioners use.

Why Botox Alarms People

I know why people shudder. Yes, Botulinum Toxin Type A, to give it its proper name, is derived from a nerve poison. And yes, there are lots of badly Botoxed faces around, particularly in the beauty industry. Bad Botox is very easy to spot, and it gives the whole business of aesthetics a bad name.

Even though most people have a fairly good idea of what Botox does, they usually think it 'freezes' the face, removing all expression and making that face look distinctively bizarre, with a blank forehead, and eyebrows that are either springing upwards in permanent surprise, or flying up at the outer corners, or pressing down heavily on the eyes. People think this because, well, we've all seen pictures of famous faces that look like this, and they look terrible. So when people think of Botox, they think of this 'bad Botox' look, and fear that if they went for treatment, that's how they would look.

But It Can Be Great – Honest!

But honestly, hand on heart, it doesn't have to be like that. All of the best cosmetic practitioners, who spend more time treating patients with Botox than doing any other procedures at their clinics, are appalled by that sort of look. They would hate for anyone to be able to spot that their regulars even have Botox. That's because their work is cautious and subtle, and every treatment is personalized to suit a patient's face and their style. That way, they can make a face look rested, with eyebrows that sit a fraction higher and eyes that look a little more open and less tired than they did before. Most of us have faces that are asymmetrical to some extent, or where the muscles that make expressions pull harder on one side than the other. A spot more Botox on the side that is working harder will even things up.

Personalised Treatment Can Give the Result You Want

Some people want to get rid of the obvious lines altogether, which needs heavier treatment. But most people who go for Botox just want their face to look a little softer and fresher, but still to be able to move. That's certainly what I want from a Botox treatment.

I don't get those 'eleven' tramlines between my eyebrows, but I do get a very obvious sort of thick pleat of skin there which makes me look more cross and anxious than I feel. So I like to have that softened, but I mind far less about the horizontal wrinkle lines across my forehead. I still want to be able to lift my eyebrows, so I have a minimal dose of Botox across the centre of my forehead; just enough to take the movement down a few notches. I don't want my forehead immobilized, not least because it confuses my poor dog. He has learned to read my face as well as most humans, and he is baffled if I try to tell him off with a stern voice and a perfectly serene face.

How to Avoid Bad Botox

In short – choose an experienced practitioner who has a reputation for giving people a natural-looking result. All practitioners say they do this these days and will tell you that the fashion for overtreating went out in the Noughties, but some of them still have quite a heavy hand.

Also, always book in for a review two weeks after treatment, by which time the full effects of the treatment will be showing. That way, if you end up with, say, one eyebrow arching higher than the other, your practitioner can make a small adjustment to even things out.

What Should I Ask For the First Time?

If you are nervous about what the results may be like – and the first time you try the treatment, or the first time you try it with a new practitioner, it is hard not to be – ask them to keep it light. You will have had a consultation with your practitioner before he or she prescribes Botox and then sets about your face with a needle, and during that conversation he or she will have been observing your face and how it moves when you talk. You can always ask for 'mobile Botox' or 'baby Botox', just a very light dose, to give you an idea of how the treatment works.

Potential Problems with Botox

As with any injections, there can be bruising or bleeding at the injection site, but the main issues with Botox stem from over-treatment. Aesthetically, too much of it results in a frozen-looking face that can't express emotion. If muscles are poleaxed with Botox for too long or too often and don't get a chance to regain their full range of motion, they may begin to waste away through lack of use. Inexpert injecting can lead to drooping (ptosis) of the eyelid or brow, which will last until the effects of the toxin start to wear off – another good reason for starting with a low dose.

The product can drift a little from the injection site, but usually not by much, and only within the first hour after injection. This is why practitioners used to advise not lying down for four hours after treatment, though this is now thought to be unnecessary and overly cautious. Still, I wouldn't advise rubbing at the treated area, or having a facial massage, for a day or two, just in case.

Softening frown lines with Botox is the most popular and the most common tweakments of all.

What It Is

Botulinum Toxin Type A, to give the drug its proper name, is a dilute form of nerve toxin. When it is injected into the facial muscles that help pull our faces into expressions, it interferes with the nerve signals that tell the muscles to contract. These effects last until the drug is dispersed by the body and the muscles recover their function – which, amazingly, they do, time after time. It doesn't take much Botox to have a cosmetically-pleasing effect of damping down the muscles, which leads to a subtle relaxation of frown lines and a fresher-looking face.

What It's Like

I've had enough Botox with different doctors over the past 15 years to know good injectors when I find them, and Dr Tapan Patel, who spends a lot of time teaching Botox masterclasses to other practitioners, is one of the very best. He takes pictures of my face – at rest, smiling, frowning, and gurning – to see which of my face muscles are overactive. He then injects tiny amounts of toxin into the muscles that produce that annoying pleat of skin between my eyebrows, and even less into the ones that lift my brows up and down. He does it so calmly and carefully that I barely feel the needle – and that's without anaesthetic. It takes all of 10 minutes.

Comfort Level

Comfortable – only the slightest pinpricks from the injections.

Verdict

The Botox begins to kick in after four days. It feels as if my forehead is becoming sluggish when I try to move it. But that's what I want. After two weeks, when I return to be assessed, my face looks terrific. The frown-pleat is smoothed away, but I can still show interest by lifting my eyebrows, just not as much as before. And he's done it without giving me the dreaded 'Joker' eyebrows, which shoot up too sharply at the corners. Magic. Over the next two months, the lines on my forehead almost vanish, because the skin isn't constantly being squeezed up into furrows, and it is four months until I need to go back for more.

Cost and Location

Botox at www.phiclinic.com, from £250; with Dr Tapan Patel, from £495. To find a practitioner in your area who offers Botox, go to www.thetweakmentsguide.com.

Would It Work for You

Yes. Botox treatment is straightforward and very effective. The main question is whether you would like the results. To end up with a result you're happy with, you need to find a sympathetic practitioner who will listen to what you want in terms of treatment (rather than simply doing what they always do or what they think would be best for you) and discuss it all thoroughly before moving on to treatment.

Potential Problems

See the section 'Potential Problems with Botox' on page 96 for what can go wrong with Botox.

Other Ways of Treating Fine Lines on the Forehead

What Botox does is relax the muscles beneath the skin. It isn't actually treating the skin itself. So another approach to forehead-smoothing is to choose one of the many treatments that work directly on the skin to help soften and smooth the forehead and plump up the skin itself, all of which helps soften frown lines and expression lines.

SKIN PEELS

Skin peels sound drastic, but they are now a much gentler kind of treatment than they used to be. A skin peel or chemical peel is a deep exfoliation which is done using ingredients such as glycolic acid or lactic acid (rather than, say, a physical scrub type of exfoliator). How it works is that the peel solution is painted on to the face, where it helps to loosen the chemical bonds that are holding old dead skin cells onto the skin's surface, so those old cells can be swept away, revealing fresher skin beneath. You could try:

- A glycolic peel (see the section 'iS Clinical Fire & Ice Facial' on page 62) will also help the skin to hydrate itself better – and anything that hydrates the skin makes the epidermis swell a little, which means it looks fuller and less dry and wrinkly.

- The Neostrata Retinol Peel (see page 129), which stimulates the skin to produce new, firming collagen as well as exfoliating it.

- The PRX-T33 'no peeling' peel (see page 130), which manages to stimulate the skin to regenerate itself at a deep-down level with almost no visible peeling on the surface afterwards.

LASER SKIN SMOOTHING

Again, lasers sound like a heavy-duty approach, but they can be very effective for smoothing and tightening the skin. I've covered specific laser treatments in the chapters on skin texture (see page 140) and skin tightening (see page 275). Many facialists are adding a light dose of laser into their treatments because of its skin-smoothing effects.

RADIOFREQUENCY SKIN TIGHTENING

Also known as a way of 'shrink-wrapping' the skin, radiofrequency treatment uses an alternating electrical current to create an electromagnetic field of radio waves. It heats up the skin – bearably – to the point where the collagen within the skin tissue contracts and tightens, so you get an instant tightening effect, and it also makes the skin cells think they have been damaged (well, they have...) which kicks them into wound-repairing mode. That means the creation of more new collagen to keep the skin firm. Again, there is more on radiofrequency in the 'Tightening Sagging Skin' chapter; see page 257.

MICRONEEDLING

If a cosmetic doctor says to you, 'So I'm going to work over your face with this device tipped with sharp spikes which will create thousands of tiny perforations in your skin...', that may be as far as the conversation gets. But if you can get your mind round the concept, it's a great way of stimulating the skin into renewing itself and creating a fresher, smoother, firmer surface. Again, there are many facials that include a light needling treatment (see Chapter 4, page 49, for examples); for a treatment review of microneedling, see page 59.

STAY SERENE

I know staying serene is easier said than done, but don't laugh – it works. In the mirror, frown at yourself, then relax your forehead and your eyebrows, and observe the difference. Breathe in, breathe out, and stay relaxed. You may think you can't learn to do this in real life, but with a bit of practice, you can.

One way to reinforce the learning is to use stick-on face patches such as Frownies (www.frownies.co.uk), which you stick onto your face when it is relaxed. (You can even use sticky tape, though that isn't so kind to your skin when you take it off.) Then, as soon as you start to scrunch up your face or frown, and the patch tugs at your skin, you become very aware of your facial movements.

No, staying serene or using these patches won't get rid of your wrinkles, but it's a good way of trying to get yourself out of the habit of frowning or of scrunching your face up when looking at a screen. Also, in the way that forcing a smile, even when you're not happy, can lift your mood, relaxing your face, even when you are stressed, can make you feel a bit calmer.

DEALING WITH CROW'S FEET WRINKLES AROUND THE EYES

You might, if you were feeling kind, view them as laughter lines. But the fine lines that radiate out from the outer edges of the eye are more commonly known as crow's feet. They're some of the first lines to set in on the face, because the skin in this area is finer and dryer than elsewhere on the face, and fine, dry skin is quick to wrinkle.

Start with Skincare

Appropriate skincare is really helpful for the eye area. Because the skin here is delicate, you don't want to overload it with rich, oily creams (those can lead to clogged white spots known as milia), nor do you want to traumatise it with ingredients that are too hardcore. Having said that, it's well worth trying hyaluronic acid serums (see page 87), and specialised hydrating eye-mask patches – the sort of tear-shaped ones that you stick onto the skin below the eye – which give a quick hydrating boost.

HYDRATING EYE PATCHES

Here are three of my favourite hydrating eye patches that you could try:

- **Bioeffect EGF Eye Mask Treatment** (£75, bioeffect.co.uk)
- **Sanctuary Spa Awakening Cucumber Hydrogel Under Eye Masks** (£5, sanctuary.com)
- **Estee Lauder Advanced Night Repair Concentrated Recovery Eye Masks** (£38, esteelauder.co.uk)

SPECIALISED EYE CREAM

I'm not a huge fan of eye creams – I feel most of them aren't worth the bother – but here are two which I like for their proven ability to improve the skin.

- **Alpha H Liquid Gold Firming Eye Cream** (£52, www.cultbeauty.co.uk) has peptides to firm up the skin, AHAs (exfoliating alpha hydroxy acids) to smooth the skin surface, and ingredients to relax expression lines, reduce puffiness, and brighten dark circles. All this while smoothing and hydrating the skin, too. Worth a try.
- **Olay Pro-Retinol Eye Cream** (£29.99, www.boots.com). Olay's latest eye cream contains retinyl propionate, which is gentler than retinol but nonetheless strong enough to show proven results on entrenched wrinkles within four weeks.

SUNSCREEN

Don't forget to wear a sunscreen around your eyes – especially since the eye area is so vulnerable to ageing. I just use the same one that I use on the rest of my face. If your eyes are sensitive, make sure your sunscreen is fragrance free (most eye products should be fragrance free, but some aren't, and they can be irritating). These two are good even on sensitive eyes:

- **Clinique Superdefense Age Defense Eye Cream SPF20** (£31.50, clinique.co.uk)
- **SkinCeuticals Mineral Eye UV Defense SPF 30** (£28, skinceuticals.co.uk)

Next Steps for Crow's Feet Wrinkles

If you are up for a more proactive approach to softening crow's feet lines, these innovative patches can help.

SPIKY EYE PATCHES

Spiky eye patches might sound like something from the torture chamber, but they are a novel way of getting active ingredients deeper into the skin around the eye and helping it to rejuvenate itself, and they're an at-home treatment. They're like the eye-mask patches, above, except that they have a prickly side covered in tiny spikes which you smooth against the skin.

RADARA EYE PATCHES

These shield-shaped stick-on patches are designed to fit around the outside edges of your eyes, exactly over your crow's feet wrinkles. Each patch is flexible and has 2,000 tiny spines on it, each less than half a millimetre long, which create 'micro-channels' into your skin – a gentler form of microneedling, if you like. They feel more bristly than prickly when you press them onto the skin. There's a slight 'scrunch' as they go on, but they don't feel painful.

The regime is to press the patches onto the skin to create those micro-channels, then peel them off and apply a few drops of the pure hyaluronic acid serum that is supplied with the patches, then press the patches back on over the serum, and leave them in place for five minutes. They seem to have a good grip on the skin, so you don't have to sit still or lie down to do this. Although the prickly bristles aren't long enough directly to stimulate the growth of new collagen and elastin in the skin, the tiny channels they create in the skin allow that hydrating serum right into the epidermis, the outer layers of the skin. After five minutes, you peel off and discard the patches, and massage in any serum that hasn't been absorbed.

There is a month's supply of patches in each box, and you should start to see improvements after two weeks. Radara's clinical studies have shown that the average reduction in wrinkles is 35 per cent (35 per cent!) if they're used every day for a month. I find my wrinkles are definitely softer when I use them, but I haven't had before-and-after measurements done to offer any statistics.

The eye patches cost £200. See www.radara.co.uk for where to buy them, because you need to get them from a clinic.

NATURA BISSE INHIBIT CORRECTIVE PATCHES FOR WRINKLE LINES

Even more high-tech than Radara (described in the previous section), these small, stick-on anti-wrinkle patches also look like the wrinkle-smoothing mini masks that fit around the outer curve of the eye and also have a mass of tiny pointed 'needles', built into each patch, but – get this – each 'needle' is composed of dried, compressed anti-ageing ingredients.

When the patches are smoothed onto the face – one beside each eye, one along each nose-to-mouth line, and one onto the wrinkly bit between your eyebrows – the 'needles' prick through the outer layers of the skin, and those concentrated, compressed skincare ingredients dissolve into the skin over the next two hours. The wrinkle-relaxing ingredient they contain, Conotoxin, is said to work in a comparable way to Botox to reduce muscle contractions, and – of course – there's hyaluronic acid, too, to plump out wrinkles from the inside.

Like the Radara patches, these patches are lightly prickly when you smooth them on. They're thinner, made from clear material, and so are less obvious than Radara. I find that once they're on, I can hardly feel them and am only reminded that I am wearing them for the next two hours when I squeeze up my eyes. Nobody notices them as I go about my business nosing around shops in central London. There are no marks when I peel the plastic off, and all the ingredients that made up the 'needles' have melted into my skin. There's no immediate change in my crow's feet, but the brand's clinical trials promise impressive results if I were to repeat this process twice a week for a month.

This is a whole new leap forward in skin-rejuvenating technology, which helps explain the high price point – and which makes it a tempting and more natural alternative to Botox injections.

The Natura Bisse patches cost £350, www.naturabisse.com.

Radara and Natura Bisse were the first into the area of spiky eye patches – but the trend is spreading. Beauty members club Beauty Pie has Hyaluronic Acid Microneedle patches (10 sachets for £150, or £24.56 for members, see www.beautypie.com) while on the high street, Vichy LiftActiv Micro Hyalu Eye Patches (£20, at major chemists).

TREATMENT REVIEW: BOTOX TO SOFTEN CROW'S FEET LINES AROUND THE EYES

The first place you'd think of using Botox is the forehead – as explained in the section 'Botox in the Forehead' on page 97, for frown lines – but it is also really effective at softening crow's feet lines.

What It Is

The toxin needs to be injected into the muscles around the edge of my eyes, to deactivate the lively muscles that are so good at crumpling my skin up into creases. The fact that the treatment lasts for several months means that, during this time, it will discourage new lines from forming, as well as making existing lines less obvious.

What It's Like

You can have numbing cream if you're a real needle-phobic, but I have never found Botox injections to be particularly painful, so I always skip it. Dr Tracy Mountford cleans the area around my eyes, then asks me to give a mega-watt smile so she can see precisely where lines are forming. Once she has pinpointed where the toxin needs to go, she places four injections on each side of my face, where my crow's feet radiate outwards towards my temples and down onto my cheek and under my eye. This takes a few minutes and scarcely hurts at all, just a tiny pinprick of a sting with each injection.

Comfort Level

Only very mild and momentary discomfort.

Verdict

Over the next week nothing startling happens, but the over-active muscles around my eyes gradually lose their strength, so although I can still smile as usual, and the skin around my eyes still creases up a bit when I do, the lines are definitely softer. The thing is, I have so many crow's feet lines, and they are so obvious, that I really need this sort of treatment just to tone them down every few months (I have this done about three times a year).

Cost and Location

From £300, at The Cosmetic Skin Clinic, cosmeticskinclinic.com. To find a practitioner in your area who offers Botox, go to www.thetweakmentsguide.com.

Would It Work for You?

Yes, especially if, like me, you have an eye area that scrunches up into a mass of tiny wrinkles when you smile. It is effective, and it's a nice treatment because it gives a subtle result. A few small injections of Botox at key points into the relevant muscles means the whole area crinkles up 50 per cent less. It doesn't mean that you can't smile, or that your smile doesn't reach your eyes.

Potential Problems

As with any injections, there is a possible risk of bruising. If your practitioner overtreated you around the eyes, you might find it hard to give a genuine smile. For other potential concerns with Botox, see the section 'Potential Problems with Botox' on page 96.

ALSO WORTH TRYING FOR CROW'S FEET WRINKLES

The next tweakment is a relatively hardcore option, in that it is not comfortable and also requires a few days of downtime, but it is certainly effective.

TREATMENT REVIEW: TIXEL SKIN TIGHTENING AND RESURFACING

Tixel uses heat energy to deliver smoother, firmer and tighter skin.

What It Is

Compared to some of the sophisticated sorts of technology on the market, which work off radiofrequency energy, or use focused ultrasound, or miniature lightning bolts of 'plasma' energy, Tixel is very straightforward. All of these skin-rejuvenating technologies work by creating a trauma in the skin, which stimulates the skin's own wound-healing process. That means your skin begins to produce not just more collagen and elastin, the proteins that keep skin strong and flexible, but also the growth factors that assist the formation of new skin tissue, to give you fresher, tighter, smoother skin in the treatment area.

But all Tixel uses to do this is heat. Nothing fancier than that. The treatment head of the device is 1cm square, and packed into that space are 81 titanium rods with gently pointed ends. These are heated up to 400 degrees C, then lightly touched onto the skin to create the necessary trauma.

You may be wondering, 'Did she really mean 400 degrees C?' Yes, I did. That's incredibly hot, searingly hot, so that 'touch' on your skin has to be very light in order to create tiny pinpoint burns (rather than, say, permanent branding) on your skin. The point about there being 81 rods is that each hot rod tip creates a channel of damage into the skin, but the fractions of skin between the rod-tips are left intact, which helps the treated skin to heal swiftly.

What It's Like

I hadn't quite appreciated how serious a treatment this was until the anaesthetic cream is applied. Not just your average clinical numbing cream with 4 per cent lidocaine (local anaesthetic), but the clinic's own special super-strength numbing cream, with 23%

lidocaine. Within 20 minutes, the goggle-shaped area of skin around my eyes, neatly marked out for the treatment with a white pencil, is nicely numb, which is reassuring.

As Dr Patel begins treating the area, I can feel each touch of the device clearly enough, but it feels hot, rather than painful. On the skin just below the eyes, I feel it more acutely but not enough to make me shout for him to stop. And then he dials down the intensity to treat the skin on my eyelid – I can't think of any other treatment that can be carried out on the eyelid, but for Tixel, it's part of the treatment protocol – and that, strangely enough, is perfectly comfortable.

By the end, I look as if I am wearing a pink eye mask. My skin feels fiery-hot for the rest of the day and I wish I hadn't arranged to go out for supper because I look pink and puffy, enough to catch curious glances in the restaurant (there's no way you can wear makeup for 24 hours, until your skin has started to heal up). It isn't painful overnight, and by the next morning my skin is almost its normal colour, though the treated area is a bit swollen, but nothing that a large pair of sunglasses won't cover.

Over the next week, the skin feels a bit rough, and if I look really closely in a magnifying mirror, I can see the grid-mark of pinpricks etched on my skin as they heal up, and after that it is fine. When I go back for reassessment four weeks later, I am amazed at the difference in the before-and-after photos. Crow's feet are softer, the skin below my eyes is more taut, and the skin above the eyelid is tighter, too.

Comfort Level

Mostly, very tolerable. Some patches uncomfortable.

Verdict

A remarkable improvement, much more that I would have expected from a single treatment (a course of three treatments is recommended).

Cost and Location

From £495, at the PHI Clinic in Harley Street (www.phiclinic.com) and also at Belgravia Dermatology (belgraviadermatology.co.uk), which has clinics in London, Birmingham, and Cardiff. To find a practitioner in your area, go to www.thetweakmentsguide.com.

Would It Work for You?

Yes. Heat treatment is straightforward and effective and relatively inexpensive. But be prepared for the swelling afterwards.

Potential Problems

This treatment needs to be done with great care, by an experienced practitioner. Too much heat could result in a deeper burn.

CHAPTER 7

Smoothing the Texture of Dry, Rough Skin

There is a whole bunch of things to do with ageing skin that don't fall into the standard boxes of 'wrinkles' or 'looking a bit hollow in the face' or even 'age spots' – see the next chapters for those last two – but which none the less make a big difference to the way skin looks. These things usually get lumped together under the heading of 'skin texture problems'.

We all know what we'd like our skin texture to be – smooth, firm, pliable, and not dry, with nice small, nearly-invisible pores – but most of us have a few issues with how our skin actually is. I'm going to start this chapter by looking at the various factors that affect skin texture, then walk you through what can be done to help and how to go about it.

WHAT CAUSES SKIN TEXTURE PROBLEMS?

The surface of your skin has a tendency to become drier, rougher and more crepey with the years, in a way that none of us wants. (When I say 'crepey', I mean thin, dry, and softly wrinkled, like crepe paper.) In this section, I dig into the various factors that affect the texture of your skin.

Dehydration

The first factor is dehydration, where, yes, the skin is just generally drier than it used to be. Dehydration occurs when the skin barrier isn't doing its job of holding moisture in the skin as well as it used to, because it isn't making enough of the natural moisturising factors (NMFs) that it needs to do this. That leaves little gaps in the skin through which moisture can escape (a process known as Trans Epidermal Water Loss, TEWL, if you want to get technical), and the skin cells, being less plumped up with moisture, deflate a bit.

Once the skin cells deflate, the skin begins to look less lively than it ought, and wrinkles up more easily into fine lines, which just makes the situation worse. It's an unfortunate double-whammy, and one that has been proven by scientific studies, that dry skin wrinkles faster than oily or well-moisturised skin.

Losing Collagen and Elastin

The next factor is the loss of collagen, the supportive protein that gives skin its structure and also keeps it firm. Our skin keeps on producing collagen, but in decreasing amounts as the years roll by. For women, collagen production declines gently from the age of 25 until the menopause, at which point it plummets to almost nothing as oestrogen levels tail off. Cue loss of skin firmness, which means more of those fine, creasy lines. In men's skin, collagen production also drops off from the mid-twenties, but it's a steady process, without any sudden acceleration.

Much the same thing is happening with the elastin in the skin. That's the protein that gives skin its bounce. You know you're losing it when you pinch the skin on the back of your hand and, instead of springing back to where it was immediately, the skin stays momentarily in that startled pinched shape.

Feeling Rough

Skin roughness is another part of this picture. Roughness is partly due to dehydration and to over-exposure over the years to ultraviolet light. It's also because of not producing enough natural moisturising factors from below and not being cosseted from above with soothing moisturisers.

Shrinking Fat Pads

Another factor is the way that skin slackens as the loss of collagen and elastin is compounded by the shrinking from within the face of the fat pads that give youthful faces their lovely smooth convex surfaces. These pads – at the temples, around the eyes, in the midface – not only wither away, but can redistribute themselves unhelpfully in bags under the eyes, or around the jaw or under it.

Shrinking Bones

At the same time as these other changes occur, the facial skeleton changes too; the eye sockets get a bit larger with the years, and the bones around the mouth shrink a bit, and the face loses a bit of its height. Put together, that means there's more, looser skin and less structure beneath it, which is what leads to sagging of the skin – which in turn affects the texture and the way the skin feels.

I've lumped all these elements together because they all affect the texture of the skin, and there are plenty of treatments that address most of them at the same time. I'll get on to replacing lost volume in the face, with injectable fillers, in the next chapter.

WHERE TO START IMPROVING SKIN TEXTURE

Skincare can be a big help in improving skin texture. Softening any roughness in the skin obviously makes the skin smoother. Hydrating the skin cells with moisture plumps them out and helps disguise fine lines. Encouraging the skin cells to turn over faster and boost the production of collagen and elastin strengthens the skin and makes it look fresher and smoother, too.

The key ingredients you need to help make this happen are

- Hyaluronic acid
- Vitamin C
- Glycolic acid
- Retinol
- Ceramides and cholesterol

I feel you sigh and flinch; this sounds hardcore – it sounds like a science lesson. But I will keep it brief, and honestly, it's worth knowing this stuff. If you have some idea what these ingredients do, then you'll know why you want them in your skincare, and why it makes sense to use certain products. So give it a whirl. Maybe come back to it later. After a bit, it will all start to make sense.

Hyaluronic Acid

Hyaluronic acid (HA) is good for hydration, which helps to make skin smoother; and giving the skin more moisture helps it to function better, so it's an all-round win. See the section 'Hyaluronic Acid Serums to Try' on page 87 for more on hyaluronic acid and a list of products to try.

Vitamin C

Vitamin C is a brilliant anti-ageing ingredient for the skin, because it brightens dull and discoloured skin, fades age spots, helps to strengthen the skin against the damage that UV light inflicts, and also boosts the production of collagen and elastin in the skin. Vitamin C is an antioxidant, so it tackles free radicals, the unstable molecules that accelerate ageing in the skin, and it has been well proven, clinically, to work wonders in the skin – *if* it is well formulated and used at a high enough concentration.

That 'if' is crucial. Vitamin C is a tricksy ingredient, as it oxidises easily when it sees UV light, so it needs to be carefully formulated and then contained in dark or airtight packaging. Vitamin C products often have a low pH of around 3.5, which keeps the ingredient stable, but it does mean they're acidic and may sting a bit when you apply them; any stinging doesn't usually last long.

To get the most benefit from a vitamin C product, look for a serum with 10–20% vitamin C in it; 20% concentration is about as much as the skin can absorb, and the higher the concentration, the more likely it is that the product will irritate your skin). And because of the complexity of formulating them, effective vitamin C products are usually on the pricier side. This is not always the case; as ever, The Ordinary has a fantastically good-value strong Vitamin C product, *but* it feels very sharp on the skin, and if you have sensitive skin, you should use it with great caution.

Vitamin C comes in various forms on the ingredients label – there's retinyl ascorbate, L-ascorbic acid (which may ring a bell from long-ago chemistry lessons), sodium ascorbyl phosphate, and ascorbyl palmitate. All have a good deal of scientific research behind them, though what you really want to look for is a product that has been put through clinical trials to show that it, the product, produces good results in the skin.

How well a vitamin C product performs isn't only about the pH and the percentage of vitamin C it contains: it also depends on what that vitamin C is combined with. One of the best-known products sold in skincare clinics is Skinceuticals' CE Ferulic, which adds ferulic acid into the mix to create a product that works even better than the sum of its parts would suggest.

Here are some of my favourite Vitamin C products:

- **Skinceuticals CE Ferulic**, which I just mentioned – though, because I've got slightly oily skin, I prefer Skinceuticals' Phloretin, which is a vitamin C serum with a lighter texture to the formulation. £108, www.skinceuticals.co.uk.
- **Clinique Fresh Pressed Daily Booster** with vitamin C 10%, £58 for a month's supply, www.clinique.co.uk.
- **DCL C-scape High Potency Night Booster 30**, £108, spacenk.com. This is strong stuff. It's brilliant, but even my skin, which has been toughened up over the years, so to speak, by regular use of active ingredients, found it a bit of a surprise. It feels slightly gritty when it goes on, and it tingles – which is fine – but the tingling is quite pronounced and goes on for quite a while. I've now learned to put it on a good half-hour before bedtime, otherwise I find I'm lying there trying to get to sleep and being distracted by the slight itchiness it brings.
- **The Hero Project Vit-C 30 Ultra Brightening Serum**, £39, www.heroproject.com. Brilliant high-strength, time-release, very effective serum at a bargain price. It's in a clear bottle, but its clever formulation protects the vitamin C within it from deteriorating in the light.
- **Medik8 C-Tetra**, £35, www.medik8.com. A very light-weight formula, so it's easy to wear, and great for oilier skins.
- **The Ordinary's Vitamin C Suspension 23% + HA Spheres**, £4.90, theordinary.com. This is another product to use at night. This also feels quite gritty and tingly as it goes on, but it settles down after a while.
- **bea Skin Care Vitamin C 20% and HA serum**, £49, www.bea-skincare.com. A small dark bottle of goodness with essential fatty acids and hyaluronic acid alongside a hefty dose of vitamin C (an ascorbic acid complex).

HOW TO USE VITAMIN C IN YOUR SKINCARE ROUTINE.

The simplest way to introduce vitamin C into your skincare routine is to apply a vitamin C serum to clean, dry skin after cleansing in the morning. Follow it with hyaluronic acid serum if your skin feels it needs it, then with a moisturising sunscreen. There's no reason you can't use vitamin C serums at night as well – and two of the products above are best used at night. If you want to use a vitamin C product at night and also want to use a retinoid product at night, use them on different nights.

Glycolic Acid and Other Alpha Hydroxy Acids

Glycolic is more of an 'acid-y' acid; it's not as gentle as hyaluronic acid, but it's an excellent addition to your skincare cabinet, because it both exfoliates the skin and makes skin better at hydrating itself.

Glycolic is from a family of acids called alpha-hydroxy acids (AHAs); other acids in the same ballpark are lactic acid, which is gentler; mandelic acid, which has bigger molecules and so doesn't penetrate as far into the skin; and malic acid. Because glycolic acid has the smallest molecules, it is the most direct and effective.

If you've heard of the trend for 'acid toners', these are usually based on alpha-hydroxy acids.

When glycolic acid is wiped onto the skin, it gradually dissolves the bonds – the inter-cellular glue, if you like – that are keeping the outermost layer of dead skin cells stuck to the surface of your skin. Dissolving the top layer of skin with an acid sounds drastic, but it is a much gentler means of exfoliation than physically scrubbing off those cells with an abrasive face scrub. So using a product containing glycolic acid or a toner containing AHAs can help keep skin clear and glowing.

If you're worried that exfoliating with acid is going to 'thin the skin', don't be. All it is doing is encouraging the shedding of skin cells that die as they reach the surface of the skin (don't worry, they are continually being renewed from below). And at the same time, the glycolic acid helps to trigger skin regeneration and boosts collagen production, which makes the skin firmer and thicker. So it is very slightly thinning the epidermis by removing the dead cells on the surface, but improving the health and structure of the dermis, the lower layers.

Here are some of my favourite glycolic acid products:

- **Alpha-H Liquid Gold**, £33.50, www.marksandspencer.com. A leave-on liquid to be used twice a week, at night. I always have this on my bathroom shelf; it gives immediate (well, overnight), noticeable results.

- **Pixi Glow Tonic**, £10, pixibeauty.co.uk. With 5% glycolic acid, this hugely popular 'acid toner' is a good one to start with.

- **Superdrug Naturally Radiant 5% Glycolic Toner**, £5.99, www.superdrug.com. Also a great product for an introduction to glycolic acid, and a complete bargain.

- **Neostrata Foaming Glycolic Wash**, £32.96, www.skincity.co.uk. The idea of a cleanser that is both foaming and acid based sounds all kinds of awful, but this is one of my all-time favourite cleansers. The glycolic acid gives a freshening edge to cleansing, and it doesn't leave skin dry.

- **Dr Philip Levy Switzerland 3 Deep Cell Renewal Micro-Resurfacing Cleanser**, £39, www.cultbeauty.co.uk. Expensive, but it can also be used as a glycolic treatment mask, and lasts for ages.

If your skin is sensitive, and glycolic acid sounds like it might be too much, lactic acid is a gentler take on the same idea. You could try this product:

- **Ren Ready Steady Glow Daily AHA Tonic**, £25, www.renskincare.com. This tonic uses lactic acid rather than glycolic acid for gentle exfoliation.

Retinol

Retinol is the best-known, most studied, and best-proven anti-ageing ingredient of all and will help improve skin texture. See the section 'Add a Vitamin A Cream for Regeneration' on page 88 for information about retinol and products containing it.

HOW TO ADD GLYCOLIC ACID TO YOUR SKINCARE ROUTINE

As with any type of exfoliation, you want to keep it gentle. The easiest way to start is to use it in the evening, twice a week at first. After cleansing, give your skin a wipe-down with your chosen AHA lotion or tonic and leave it on. That's it. It will tingle, but this shouldn't go on for long. If you feel it is too tingly, put a moisturiser on top of it, as that will soften the effect of the AHA.

This is what I do – using a glycolic lotion twice a week, on nights I am not using retinol – and I find that it is enough. You could use a glycolic tonic in the morning before your other serums and sun-screen. Or you could use it in the evening before using retinol; if your skin is used to both ingredients, this is fine. But don't over-use it. If you find your skin is becoming red and irritable, do the sensible thing and stop using the AHA product until your skin is back to normal. Glycolic acid and other AHAs make your skin more sensi-tive to ultraviolet light, another reason for not using them too often, and for always using sunscreen.

Ceramides and Cholesterol

Ceramides and cholesterol are types of lipids, or fats. They're vital for skin texture because, along with essential fatty acids, they make up the skin's 'lipid layer' – the fatty 'mortar' that surrounds the 'bricks' of skin cells in the outer layers of the epidermis – which makes our skin such a good waterproof barrier against the outside world.

'Healthy skin starts with a healthy skin barrier, and the healthiest skin is made up of the correct balance of three key lipids: cholesterol, ceramides, and free fatty acids,' says cosmetic derma-tologist Dr Mervyn Patterson of Woodford Medical. 'They are skin's natural protection and, ideally, they exist in a ratio of 1:1:1.'

If your skin's self-defence mechanisms aren't working as well as they ought, tiny gaps appear in the skin barrier, and your skin can't hold onto moisture so well. So keeping the skin barrier in good shape is crucial.

Cholesterol has become something of a dirty word, so obsessed is modern medicine with bringing its levels down in our bodies. But leaving that argument aside, one thing that is less disputed is that cholesterol is very good for your skin. In fact our skin needs cholesterol so much that it makes its own supply, regardless of the levels of cholesterol in the blood; it is cholesterol which enables our skin to create vitamin D when it is exposed to the sun.

You might find you need lipid-repair products more in winter: our skin often becomes dry in winter, thanks to the everyday challenges of both the cold and wind outside, and central heating indoors, which all help to strip moisture from the skin. But for some people, dry skin and the rough texture that goes with it are a year-round problem.

Rather than putting a really rich cream on, research has found that it is more useful, particularly for older skin, to use a product that includes cholesterol in its formulation. Scientists from skincare company Skinceuticals found that, while dry skin in younger people is mostly short of ceramides, cholesterol is what is really lacking in ageing skin.

And no, putting cholesterol onto your skin doesn't in any way affect your blood cholesterol levels. Cholesterol found in the skin is distinct from cholesterol found in blood, and there is no scientific link between using skincare formulations containing cholesterol and blood serum cholesterol levels. Nor do levels of cholesterol in the blood have an effect on skin cholesterol levels – and in case you're wondering, taking statins doesn't affect the cholesterol levels in your skin.

Here are some of my favourite products with barrier-repairing lipids:

- **Vis Viva Retinyl + Frankincense Restorative Oil Serum** (£39, visvivaskincare.com). A light-feeling 'oil serum' with added cholesterol for improving barrier function.
- **Skinceuticals Triple Lipid Restore** (£130, www.skinceuticals.co.uk). A non-oily cream which is great for older skin, as it contains double the ratio of cholesterol to ceramides and fatty acids. Studies show that it can improve skin texture by 40 per cent within minutes and boost skin hydration by up to 39 per cent within 24 hours.

- **Paula's Choice Resist Anti-Aging Omega Serum** (£32, www.paulaschoice.co.uk). A light lotion that's packed with all the lipids you need: omega fatty acids, ceramides, and cholesterol. Really good for dry, rough skin.
- **Elizabeth Arden Advanced Ceramide Capsules Daily Youth Restoring Serum with Cholesterol** (£66 for 60 capsules, www.elizabetharden.co.uk). Elizabeth Arden has always been big on ceramides; these, with added cholesterol, fatty acids, and skin regenerating retinyl palmitate, are great for older skin. In clinical tests, Elizabeth Arden's scientists showed that using the product for 12 weeks could take 10 years off the appearance of ageing skin.

HOW TO USE CERAMIDES AND CHOLESTEROL IN YOUR SKINCARE ROUTINE

Use ceramides and cholesterol as and when you need them. In the morning, you could layer this between your serums and your sunscreen. At night, you could use them on their own, or after a glycolic toner, or after a retinoid. I find a cream packed with ceramides and cholesterol makes a much more satisfying and nourishing skin treat than a traditional night cream.

EAT YOUR SKIN SMOOTHER

Stepping back from the skincare and tweakments for a minute, there's a good case to be made for the 'beauty from the inside out' argument. What you eat certainly affects the way your skin looks. I'm sure you don't need me to labour the point about a healthy diet, but in general, eating more vegetables, lean protein, and healthy fats, and cutting back on sugar, refined carbohydrates, and alcohol will benefit your skin no end.

Beyond those general guidelines, here are some specific supplements which I have found helpful.

With EFAs (Essential Fatty Acids)

Another helpful thing to do which will contribute to better skin texture is to cram your diet full of omega-3 essential fatty acids. Although their reputation for improving heart health has been called into question, omega-3s are vital for the health and good functioning of the skin, because they're a crucial part of the lipid (fatty) membrane that surrounds every cell in the body. When the skin-cell membranes are in good shape, they hold onto moisture more effectively, and so keep the skin softer. Can you make your skin softer and better hydrated simply by loading up on essential fatty acids? You probably can.

The quickest way to pack in the omega-3s is to eat oily fish (salmon, mackerel, sardines, fresh tuna) but without overdoing it, because although this fish is really good for us, it tends to contain low levels of pollutants like mercury, which can then build up in the body (unless you're buying wild Alaskan salmon, but that is super-expensive). Two portions a week is the usual amount suggested as the maximum by health experts, though I tend to think that, being well past child-bearing age, and less bothered about heavy-metal accumulation, I may as well scoff as much oily fish as I can, because of the benefits.

What oily fish gives you is two particular omega-3 fatty acids called docosahexaenoic acid (DHA) and eicosapentaenoic acid (EPA). There is a third, plant-based omega-3 fatty acid called alpha-linolenic acid (ALA), which is found in foods like walnuts, flaxseed oil, and chia seeds; such foods are worth adding into your diet for omega-3 backup, as it were, but fish is a better source (unless you're vegan). That's because once you've eaten ALA, your body has to convert it to DHA and EPA, so it ends up being only about 10% as effective as the marine-based omega-3s. This is why nutritionists are always going on about eating oily fish.

With Vitamin C Supplements

We have all grown up with the idea that vitamin C is good for our body and, by extension, for the skin – and that we need to get vitamin C from our diet because, along with monkeys and guinea pigs, humans are the only mammals whose bodies can't make their own supplies of vitamin C.

Lots of us take vitamin C supplements, particularly if we are feeling under the weather, with a view to boosting our immune systems and warding off coughs, colds, and viruses. And I can't be the only person to be disappointed often to read in the papers about new studies showing that vitamin C has no special powers in this area, and that because it is a water-soluble vitamin and our bodies cannot store it, if we ingest large amounts of it, we will simply excrete it, thus creating expensive urine but no great benefit to our bodies.

I had given up on Vitamin C as a supplement until recently, when I heard that a special sort of vitamin C, called Altrient C, had just completed clinical trials – proper double-blind, placebo-controlled, medical-grade clinical trials. These trials showed that if you took enough of their product – three 1,000mg doses a day – for three months, it could achieve impressive improvements in skin elasticity and hydration, as well as boosting collagen levels in the skin.

Would I like to be the first writer to try it out? the company asked. You bet. So I stopped all the 'active' skincare that I usually use (the retinoids, the glycolic acid, and the vitamin C serums), stopped having any of the tweakments that I have to keep my skin in good shape, and stopped taking collagen supplements which I also take for the same reason (yes, they work, too; see below). Then I had detailed measurements taken of my skin elasticity, hydration levels, and collagen density with the most sophisticated machines available in London, and started taking the vitamins.

What's different about Altrient C is that the active part of it, sodium ascorbate, is encapsulated in tiny fatty particles called liposomes which make a great delivery system (if liposomes sound familiar – yes, they are the same things used to transport active ingredients into the skin in face creams). In this supplement, the liposomes enable the vitamin C to get through the stomach, without being broken up by the stomach acids, into the gut, where it is absorbed into the blood stream. The advantage of this is that your body gets the benefit of around 98% of each dose of vitamin C, whereas from normal high-street supplements of the stuff, you can absorb as little as 10-15 per cent – and if you have ever tried taking more than 2,000mg of those a day, you will know how much normal vitamin C upsets the stomach and irritates the gut.

Altrient doesn't taste great, but it's not revolting. Each individual dose comes in a sachet that you squeeze out into a small amount of water, swill around, and gulp down. Really not too difficult, even if it has the consistency of orange snot.

I really didn't think Altrient would make a difference to my skin. I thought my skin would get a lot worse before it showed any improvement – if there was any. But guess what? It worked. My hydration levels were picking up before the end of the first month, and after three months I had notched up 22.8 per cent more collagen, a 30 per cent rise in hydration, and a whopping 64.3 per cent improvement in elasticity.

Altrient C isn't cheap, at around £1 a sachet, but I've started buying it in bulk, I'm so impressed by these results. (Now I've finished the trial, I'm on two sachets a day, for maintenance.) And of course it improves the skin all over your body, not just on your face, and gives your immune system a helping hand, too.

With Collagen Supplements

I used to be hugely sceptical about collagen supplements too, but became a convert a few years ago. Collagen drinks and collagen powders are one of those newish arrivals on the beauty scene that look like so much snake oil (Drink this potion! Look more lovely!). But the brands which contain enough of the right sort of collagen can make a measurable difference to your skin, and several brands have conducted clinical trials which demonstrate the improvements that their products can make.

The new collagen drinks contain 'hydrolysed' collagen – that is, collagen that has been broken up into tiny fragments. What I couldn't understand at first was why consuming collagen supplements would do you more good than eating lots of lean protein, which would be broken down into protein/collagen fragments in your stomach. But then I learned that providing the body with a ready supply of hydrolysed collagen has two effects. First, it encourages the body to use this collagen for repair where repair is needed. And second, by some curious internal alchemy, when our bodies detect a lot of these hydrolysed collagen fragments in the blood, it presumes there has been some trauma to the skin that is needing repair, so it starts to make more collagen of its own.

The hydrolysed collagen in these supplements is usually marine collagen, from, say, the skin of freshwater fish; sometimes it is bovine collagen, from cow hides.

In order to make a difference, trials have found that you need to consume somewhere between 3,000mg and 10,000mg a day of this hydrolysed collagen.

Lots of supplements offer this – including Absolute Collagen, Pure Gold Collagen, Pink Cloud Beauty, Rejuvenated Collagen Shots, LQ Liquid Health Hair, Skinade, Skin and Nails and Totally Derma. The other consideration, to get technical for a sec, is the molecular size of the hydrolysed collagen – because the smaller its molecules are, the better they will be absorbed by the body. Molecular size (or, more accurately, molecular weight) is measured in units called *daltons*, with larger molecules being measured in kilodaltons (kDa) – thousands of daltons.

Several of the supplements mentioned above have a molecular size of 2 or 3 kilodaltons, and some brands boast clinical studies showing how well their products work.

If you are familiar with the world of beauty supplements, you might be wondering whether Imedeen should be on this list. It's not, just because its key ingredient is a patented 'marine complex' that contains fish extract including collagen, but it isn't totally collagen-focussed like these other supplements. But it also improves the skin measurably; the company has a good deal of data on its website detailing all the studies they have conducted to prove this. Imedeen also had 'Advanced Beauty Shots' which offer 2,500mg of hydrolysed porcine collagen – ie not as much collagen as the other supplements, though it should be enough to show some skin smoothing over time; and it is derived from pigs, which won't suit everyone.

I will happily consume any of the above. They're not cheap and, depending on which you choose, will add up to £100 a month to your skincare bill. If that's within your budget, they are worth considering, in order to firm up your beauty-from-the-inside-out strategy.

Don't go over the top and take more than the recommended dose of collagen supplements. While doses of up to 10,000mg a day have been shown to be effective, it is thought that taking too much collagen could have a negative effect on collagen building, though the chaps who are working on the studies for this can't yet say how much is too much. Just so you know.

SKIN SMOOTHING AND TIGHTENING TREATMENTS

If you want to pick a treatment that will improve skin texture and help soften lines, there is a huge range to choose from, everything from the super-gentle – such as lying down under a canopy of warm red lights, which feels too easy to be effective (but it's not, read on!) – to the more challenging, like microneedling.

All these treatments mentioned in this section will improve the texture – the surface smoothness – of your skin, but most of them will do a good deal more as well. But they seemed to fit well into this chapter, which is why they're here rather than elsewhere.

Red Light Therapy

Treatment with red light involves nothing more taxing than relaxing for around 20 minutes in the gentle glow from a large canopy studded with small LED bulbs, or wearing a phantom-of-the-opera–style face-shaped mask which has LED bulbs on the inside.

It feels like nothing is happening. It might even be a touch boring. The first time I tried it, years ago, I thought I was having my leg pulled. Seriously, how could this be good for my skin? But that was before I learned about the remarkable body of research that has piled up in favour of 'photobiomodulation', as light therapy is more properly called. What can it do? Well, it helps to heal wounds, calm inflammation in the skin (the sort you get with acne, for example), and encourage cell renewal, for a start. Then there is the way that it smooths the skin, grows new collagen, and helps skin glow. It's also the only treatment I can think of that defies the usual maxim of 'no pain, no gain' which applies to most tweakments.

The light needs to be used at an appropriate intensity and for long enough – the standard treatment time is 20 minutes – and to be repeated regularly. But the fact that it works isn't in doubt. Most cosmetic clinics will have one of these canopies and will use it as an add-on to other treatments as well as on its own.

One cosmetic doctor I know even went as far as to say that it made much more sense to spend your money on red light therapy than on an anti-ageing moisturiser. A session costs around £50 and, if you have it once a month, he said, the treatment is far more productive and efficient than a cream; it would soften fine lines and make skin more radiant as well as smoother and stronger. Back that up with a decent, inexpensive moisturising sunscreen by day and a serum or night cream overnight, and you would definitely get results.

Dr Ravi Jain, who runs the Riverbanks clinic in Harpenden, has been using Omnilux, the original and now leading brand of LED light therapy, on patients for 12 years. 'The standard treatment is to have this twice a week for eight sessions,' he says. 'That on its own is a remarkable treatment, but people are impatient, they want quicker fixes, maybe something like a more advanced peel. Also, because all LED treatment involves is lying under the lamps, people lose confidence that it's actually doing anything. But all the scientific evidence is not just good, it's amazing. Once you've finished a course of this, it will go on working for another 8–12 weeks, because when you are asking skin to grow, you don't just grow skin cells overnight – skin has to go through the whole natural process of developing cells.'

WHAT RED LIGHT THERAPY DOES FOR THE SKIN

'What red light therapy does is trick the body into thinking that there has been a wound in the skin,' says Dr Jain. 'Then the skin releases growth factors and stimulates collagen growth, which is what the body does when it needs to repair the skin, so you get younger-looking skin.'

'What makes it so good for improving skin texture is that, when you have newer, healthier skin cells being produced, they can do their job more efficiently. They absorb fluid and hold onto it better than old, damaged cells, so they are fuller, which plumps up the skin, makes it feel smoother and reflect light better. That's why periorbital rhytids [aka crow's feet wrinkles around the eye] improve dramatically with red light therapy.'

As Dr Jain points out, red light therapy is also a useful treatment to offer patients who want to have something done to their face but don't want to go as far as injections. Given that red light therapy works best if you are having a course of sessions twice a week for a month, it's easiest if you live close to a clinic that offers the treatment, and you have plenty of time to spare.

Top London facialist Teresa Tarmey, who looks after the complexions of beauties including Rosie Huntington-Whiteley, is a big fan of red light therapy, too. "LED light therapy is one of my favourite treatments simply because it suits everyone,' she says. 'I've seen it transform so many of my clients' skin, we use it at the end of every treatment whether it be to calm the skin, heal, or treat acne. It's so good for brightening the skin too. It's a very under-rated treatment."

It's worth pointing out that red light therapy is doing a good deal more than just improving skin texture, but your skin texture will certainly benefit from it.

Where Can You Find Red Light Therapy?

Most cosmetic clinics and many beauty salons now offer light treatments. The most common is red light treatment, and they will usually offer separate sessions of this, as well as tacking it onto the end of other treatments where it is helpful for calming down any inflammation in the skin generated by previous parts of the treatment, and for stimulating skin renewal.

Are There Any Potential Problems with Red Light Therapy?

Red light therapy has no potential problems that I've been able to unearth. This is a very gentle and healing type of treatment.

LED LIGHT AND SKIN REJUVENATION

The LED light energy that you get in skin-rejuvenating treatments is the same type that you find powering electronic clock displays and fairy lights – but used at a greater power and intensity, and at a variety of wavelengths and in different colours, for different treatment effects.

Red Light

The most popular and most commonly available is red LED light, which has been well proven to help stimulate the production of collagen, elastin, and hyaluronic acid in the skin. Red light reaches several millimetres into the skin and also has an anti-inflammatory effect, so it soothes the skin by calming inflammation within it. This makes red light a popular add-on to everything from beauty treatments to non-surgical procedures.

Blue Light

Blue light helps denature *P. acnes*, the bacteria that causes acne. It won't stop spots from forming in the skin, but it will reduce the redness and inflammation by knocking out the bacteria on the surface of the skin that are provoking spots.

Because blue light only works at a surface level, it doesn't kill bacteria deep in pores in the skin. As with red light, you can get treatment at a clinic or salon, in which case you will need to visit once or twice a week, or you can try using a home-use device. These are less powerful than the light sources you'll find in clinics but can be helpful if you are diligent about using them. See the section 'The Spot-Buster: Neutrogena Visibly Clear Light Therapy Acne Mask' on page 80 for a treatment review of one such device.

Yellow Light

Amber or yellow light has a shorter wavelength, so it can't reach the dermis in order to stimulate collagen production, but it is useful to improve the communication between skin cells. What it can do is enhance the absorption of near infra-red light into the dermal cells, which is why it is part of the LED rejuvenation treatment, below.

(continued)

LED LIGHT AND SKIN REJUVENATION (continued)

Near Infra-Red Light

Near infra-red light is invisible, is more powerful than red light, and travels much deeper into the body – up to 15cm. As well as kick-starting collagen production and improving levels of elastin and hyaluronic acid, it is able to stimulate bone tissue development. That's a real incentive for those of us who are realising how much difference the normal process of bone resorption makes to the face. It's something that happens with age and there's not much you can do about it – but I reckon near infra-red treatment is worth a try, which is one of the reasons I like the Express LED Rejuvenation treatment at the Light Salon (**www.thelight-salon.com**; see the review on page 63).

Near infra-red light also lowers levels of cortisol, the stress hormone, and boosts levels of serotonin, the feelgood hormone. Near infra-red light can have these effects even within a swift 10-minute session.

SKIN PEELS

Chemical peels used to be one of the standard procedures offered by dermatologists in the 1990s, but they have had something of an image problem since the 2002 episode of *Sex and the City* where Samantha turns up at Carrie's book launch with a face like a skinned tomato after having 'a little something' done.

It's true that old-fashioned peels were hardcore; rather than just freshening up the surface of the skin, the acids that were used made most of the top layer of your face peel off and meant you needed to spend a week or so in hiding while new, fresh skin frantically grew itself fast enough to repair the damage. Why were they popular? Because this new, fresh skin grew through without the wrinkles and pigmentation spots that had besmirched the old skin, and with a lovely softer, smoother texture.

But what goes around comes around, and the past five years have seen a huge resurgence in peels on offer in cosmetic clinics. Today, peels are back in a new format – as super-swift treatments that pack a proper rejuvenating punch but without the pain and the downtime of their predecessors. Rather than being done in one big old dose, they are often offered as a course of gentle peelings, which will give great results that will improve skin texture no end – and which at the same time will brighten the skin, soften pigmentation and wrinkles, and improve hydration, but without the need to take time off and hide from the world.

Will Peels Thin My Skin?

Many people flinch from the idea of peeling as something that will 'thin the skin' and therefore be harmful. Do peels thin the skin? Yes. A little, and just on the very surface. But here's why it's not a bad thing. What a chemical peel will do is dissolve the cellular 'glue' that keeps old dead skin cells stuck to the surface of your face. That's a very small thinning of the stratum corneum, the outermost layers of the epidermis. Peels reveal a fresher surface beneath, and that's good, because that fresher surface is smoother, reflects light better, and absorbs skin products better.

People feel that 'thinner' skin will mean skin that is more fragile and worse protected, but because the ingredients used in chemical peels – whether glycolic acid, or retinol, or new complex mixtures – also stimulate skin repair in the lower levels of the skin, they actually thicken the dermis (the lower layer of the skin) and improve its health, so overall, your skin will be left in better shape.

Potential Problems with Peels

If peels are relatively light and superficial, they are unlikely to cause problems beyond a bit of stinging at the time they are done, though it's always a good idea to be extra vigilant with sunscreen after a peel, to protect your newer skin and reduce any chance of developing hyperpigmentation.

What's not a good idea is to do too many of the old-style, doctor's-office aggressive peels, or you end up with a strange, unhealthy, translucent look to your skin. But moderate use of the sort of peels mentioned here will do your skin good rather than harm.

The NeoStrata Retinol peel is a quick and painless smoothing and brightening peel with hardly any down-time.

What It Is

Unlike most light peels (which use glycolic acid, which stings a bit and gives a gentle exfoliation), this peel deploys retinol, one of the genuine wonder-ingredients in skincare. Retinol speeds up the turnover of skin cells to improve texture and minimise fine lines and dark spots. It also makes skin more even in tone... but it has a reputation for irritating the skin, especially if used in a concentrated form.

This peel involves 3% retinol – that's quite strong: if you were using a retinol serum at night, it would at most be 1% – plus a 'retinol-boosting complex'. It also has an ingredient called 'Aminofil', derived from amino acids which help 'enhance collagen and hyaluronic acid', so it's extra helpful for improving skin texture.

What It's Like

After a consultation to make sure I understand what I am letting myself in for and how to look after my skin afterwards (be gentle; use lots of sunscreen), Kristin, the 'medical aesthetician' (aka highly trained skin specialist), cleans my face, solemnly cracks open the tiny 3ml treatment vial of Neostrata peeling potion, pours it into a small tray, and carefully paints it onto my face with a feathery fan brush. And that's it. There's no tingling, no stinging, no redness, and it takes all of two minutes.

But even if it feels as gentle as a moisturiser, it is strong stuff. The protocol is to leave it on for eight hours while it goes to work – or, if you're gung-ho and want to get the maximum result, you can leave it on overnight, so I do.

For 72 hours my face looks and feels normal; then, quite suddenly, it begins peeling. Not a dramatic, sloughing-off-of-snakeskin sort of peeling, but a network of fine cracks appears all over my face and soft, fine scuffs of skin begin to lift away. It isn't that obvious as long as I pat it down with moisturiser, but it takes a superhuman effort not to pick at the edges to help things along.

Which is fine, except that on day seven, I have to give a talk to beauty-industry colleagues and really don't fancy doing it with my face free from make-up and adorned only with wisps of shedding skin. I nearly cry with relief when, on the morning of day seven, I wipe my cleanser off carefully with a clean flannel and find all shreds of dead skin are gone and my skin looks fantastic – clearer, fresher, and with a healthy sheen to it.

Comfort Level

Completely comfortable. No stinging or tingling either at the time or application, or later.

Verdict

This was so quick and easy and, after the shedding, my face definitely looked smoother, brighter, tighter, and more glowy. Would I go back for more? Absolutely – on a Tuesday, so that I can schedule a very quiet long weekend for the peeling.

Cost and Location

£275 per treatment (for best results, you should have three or four, a month apart) at Eudelo, www.eudelo.com. To find a practitioner in your area, go to www.thetweakmentsguide.com.

Would It Work for You?

Yes – but allow yourself plenty of time to complete the peeling phase and don't be tempted to pick at the peeling bits.

Potential Problems

See page 128 for information on possible issues with peels.

PRX-T33 – The Gentle 'Non-Peeling Peel'

Back in the day, a TCA peel was a fearsome thing. TCA stands for trichloroacetic acid, one of the more savage deep-peeling ingredients. TCA could achieve a substantial peeling effect, but at the cost of several days where you wouldn't want to show your face to the world.

Now, though, the TCA peel has reappeared in a much-modified form called PRX-T33. It's not a catchy name, but it's a great treatment which gives all the surface-smoothing, skin-freshening, and strengthening benefits of a deeper peel, with minimal discomfort – just a bit of stinging and redness as it is massaged in. There is also – get this – almost no actual peeling, apart from perhaps a bit of dry flakiness around the nose and chin, and no interruption to your social life.

PRX-T33 does this by combining TCA with low-dose hydrogen peroxide, which protects the skin while the TCA slips past the skin barrier without damaging it and kick-starts the skin-remodelling process in the skin's deeper layers. It's more than a peel, really, as this skin-remodelling effect makes the treatment more of a biostimulator, which is why it is so good for skin texture.

Aesthetic nurse Lee Garrett, whose practice in Harley Street is popular with celebs, is a big fan. 'Because of the way PRX-T33 is engineered, you don't get any of the side effects,' he says. 'The hydrogen peroxide causes growth factors to release from the fibroblasts in your skin.'

The peel solution has to be massaged onto the skin for a few minutes, during which time it can feel hot and prickly, but the instant glow and firmness that patients feel after treatment makes it worth it and more inclined to come back; the treatment protocol is to have one treatment a week for three weeks, after which the effects should last for 18 months. 'Everyone is adding this into their treatment regimes,' Lee says. 'It works well with fillers and Botox, and because it doesn't make the skin more sensitive to sunlight, it can be done at any time of year.'

PRX-T33 costs £850 for a course of three treatments at freedomhealth.co.uk.

Will PRX-T33 work for you? Yes, it seems to work well and to be a good add-on to other treatments.

PRP – Platelet Rich Plasma – to Improve Skin Texture

Another increasingly popular way of improving skin texture is with injections of Platelet Rich Plasma (PRP), plasma derived from your own blood.

If the letters PRP are ringing a slight warning bell – this may be because you've heard this treatment referred to as the Dracula Facial or the Vampire Face Lift. That's more because it makes use of your blood than because it leaves your face looking like it has been attacked by a vampire.

What It Is

First, you have a small amount of blood – about 15ml – taken from your arm. Vials containing this blood are placed in a centrifuge, which looks like a small medical version of a spin-dryer, and spun for five minutes until the red blood cells in the blood separate from the clear plasma. This plasma is packed with platelets, which are able to generate growth factors, which in turn can spot any damage within the skin and set about repairing it. That means the PRP is providing a home-grown tonic to regenerate the skin, once it is reinjected.

PRP is good for improving skin texture because, along with that regeneration, comes a nice fresher, smoother top layer to the skin. For anyone with an aversion to having foreign substances such as fillers injected, this is a viable alternative. It won't give you the volume boost that dermal fillers provide, but it should smooth the skin and give it a glow, soften wrinkles, and plump up the skin's surface.

What It's Like

Disconcerting. It is bizarre yet rather exciting to think that my own body is able to provide a rejuvenating cocktail for my face. Some doctors inject PRP all over the face using a needle (the neck and décolletage can also be treated), but Dr Olivier Amar, who is doing my treatment, prefers to reintroduce the PRP into the face via a cannula rather than a needle.

A cannula is like a blunt needle, which sounds like a bad idea, but once it is under the skin, it can be steered gently around just under the skin, without stabbing through any fibrous bands or blood vessels in its path, which a needle might do. Using the cannula, Dr Amar distributes the PRP evenly around my cheeks and that troublesome saggy bit at the side of the mouth by the chin, on both sides of my face. The big advantage of using a cannula for this treatment is that you don't end up with a face covered in pin-prick injection marks.

Comfort Level

Good, as long as you are ok with needles. Having the blood taken from my arm is no more painful than having a blood test, and having the cannula burrowing under my skin as Dr Amar puts the PRP in place is, surprisingly, perfectly comfortable. (There's a video of this on my YouTube channel. You can see I'm not even flinching.)

Verdict

Impressive. A month later, the treated area of skin looks softer, clearer, and smoother. You are meant to do two or three sessions, six weeks apart, for best results (I only did one).

Cost and Location

£875 with Dr Olivier Amar at www.cadoganclinic.com. To find a practitioner in your area, go to www.thetweakmentsguide.com.

Would It Work for You?

Yes, as long as you're not needle-phobic.

Potential Problems

Few, apart from possible bruising and swelling at the injection site or sites. One of its big selling points is that you can't possibly be allergic to a substance that comes from your own body.

Microneedling (Medical Needling)

Microneedling – also known as *medical needling* – is a simple enough premise. A small, spiky roller tipped with slender 3mm stainless steel spikes is rolled gently but firmly around the face in order deliberately to create thousands of tiny puncture wounds. Why on earth? Because the healing process that takes place as the skin scrambles to mend itself after this sort of assault releases growth factors and creates new collagen and elastin, all of which makes the skin fresher and firmer than before.

'Medical needling is a wonderful, completely natural anti-ageing treatment that helps the skin to help itself,' says specialist dermatologist and medical director of the Eudelo clinic Dr Stefanie Williams, who is a big fan of the process. Another benefit of making all these holes in the face is that it is a bit like aerating the lawn with spiked shoes. Whatever you apply on the surface afterwards will sink in much further, much more quickly. More on that later.

The other sort of microneedling which is very popular at the moment is done not using a roller, but a motorized needling device. The best-known brands are the Dermapen and the Innopen, which are pen-shaped devices with a grid of tiny needles at their tip.

One key attraction of these pen-type devices is that their needles move straight up and down into the skin, as opposed to the rolling movement of a spiky roller, which creates a very slight rip in the skin with each movement because of the way the needle spikes into the skin, then moves forward a fraction with the movement of the roller, before being pulled out of the skin. Some doctors like this rolling movement because it creates a little more of a wound, some don't.

Also, the needle-pad at the tip of the device oscillates at such speed (120 times a second) that it can be kept moving smoothly around the face, stabbing away as it goes. I'm not really making this sound hugely appealing, am I? But it's a good treatment and will help greatly to improve skin texture as well as softening wrinkles.

The other advantage of these motorised devices is that you can adjust the length of the needles from a barely-there 0.5mm to an eye-watering 3mm. 0.5mm will just create holes in the stratum corneum, the very outer, dead, protective layers of skin tissue; whereas 3mm will drive down to the dermal-epidermal junction in even the thickest areas of skin and cause the pinprick bleeding that stimulates the wound-healing response that produces more collagen and elastin and tightens up the skin.

This might sound like too much information, but bear with me, because it's important. Microneedling has become more widespread and more popular over the past five years. Cosmetic clinics and beauty salons have started adding microneedling into their more advanced facials, and people have cottoned on to the fact that you can needle your own skin at home with a roller bought off the internet. And somewhere along the line, it has become accepted skincare wisdom that all microneedling, including the DIY version with super-short 0.2mm needles, will help stimulate collagen production. It sounds great. But unfortunately, it's not true.

Tracy Tamaris, who is education director at the International Institute for Anti Ageing (IIAA) has been explaining this distinction for more years than she cares to remember. The cornerstone brand of the IIAA is Environ, a line of skincare built by the South African plastic surgeon Dr Des Fernandes, who also pioneered the use of medical needling for reviving ageing, sun-damaged skin.

'We need to be clear,' says Tracy. 'There's needling that you do at home to enhance the penetration of active ingredients, and for that you only need to penetrate the stratum corneum, which is 0.02mm thick. So a 0.1mm roller is plenty for that. But to stimulate collagen production, you need to bleed. If medical needling is not creating pinprick bleeding, then you are not producing the growth factors and platelets which are in the blood and which stimulate collagen production.'

As you might imagine, the IIAA has stacked up a good deal of research on medical needling over the years. 'Just from medical needling, you can gain a 205% increase in the thickness of the dermis,' says Tracy. That's very much what ageing skin needs. This research was done independently by Professor Mattius Aust at Hanover University. He also showed that when you add Vitamin A to the mix you increase the collagen production by a whopping 658%.

'There is no limit to the number of needling treatments you can have,' says Tracy, 'because medical needling, or collagen induction therapy, as it is sometimes called, is the only treatment that causes proper regeneration in the skin. That's because it stimulates production of a growth factor called TGFb3 [transforming growth factor beta 3, if you want its full name] which in turn encourages the production of collagen I – and collagen I is the sort of lattice-frameworked collagen that you find in really young skin, as opposed to collagen II or collagen III, which is laid down in parallel lines and which is more akin to scar tissue.'

AND WHAT ABOUT HOME MICRONEEDLING?

As for home micro-needling, which anyone can do with a roller bought off the internet for not much more than a tenner... I have been a fan of home micro-needling for a few years, but have had a bit of a rethink on that recently.

First, as explained in the main text, using a short-needled roller won't help stimulate collagen growth. All it will do is create holes in the outermost layers of the skin so that your active skincare ingredients can penetrate that bit deeper. That sounds like a great idea, but it rather depends on the products you are using.

Yes, it will be getting the active ingredients in the products more directly into your skin – but what about all the other ingredients in the product? The product will have been designed to be applied to the surface of the skin and may well contain ingredients, such as fragrance, which will irritate the skin if delivered more deeply.

Then I met with Dr Eric Shulte, the creator of the QMS! range of skincare. His expertise is as a trauma and cosmetic surgeon with a special interest in wound-healing, and his is one of the beauty industry voices who feels that as a concept, home microneedling is 'going in the wrong direction' for our skin. He is happy for needling to be done by an expert under clinical conditions, but feels that 'aggressive procedures like this don't belong in the hands of laymen at home.'

'It seems that we want to destroy the skin with needles, creating artificial wounds,' he says, 'which in the long term will not be good for the skin. What you want for the skin is lifelong stimulation, but you don't want irritation or a weakened skin barrier which is prone to dehydration.'

Since hearing that, I've been a bit more cautious about needling my face. In fact, I've stopped for now.

The only drawback to this miraculous-sounding procedure is, as you may have already guessed by now, it's hardcore. For treating normal ageing, Tracy suggests 1mm needles and topical anaesthetic. For heavy scarring from burns or acne, she would recommend 3mm needles and stronger anaesthetic. That will leave your face looking rather red and sore. The redness will take a couple of days to go down, and you'll need to treat your skin with scrupulous care as it heals.

TREATMENT REVIEW: DERMAROLLER

Because of the way that medical needling encourages the release of growth factors and the remodelling of the skin, it is a terrific treatment for improving skin texture – as well as generating fresher-looking, firmer skin.

What It Is

Passing a roller covered in 3mm stainless steel spikes repeatedly over the face creates multiple punctures in the skin. If these punctures are deep enough to create pinprick bleeding, then this will kick-start the skin's wound-healing response. As part of this wound-healing response, growth factors are released that stimulate the growth of new collagen and elastin and improve skin hydration, all of which will make the skin softer and smoother.

What It's Like

Challenging, to be honest. My face is anaesthetized with numbing cream 20 minutes before we start, and while some parts of the treatment – over the better-padded parts of my cheeks – feel fine, it feels very spiky over the bonier bits of my jawline and my forehead. I had my treatment done by Dr Stefanie Williams, who is a big fan of microneedling with a roller and who has no truck with my whingeing. 'Nearly done,' she says briskly, moving the roller smartly back and forth, and continues until she is satisfied every bit is properly spiked. I had this treatment along with sessions of Restylane Skinboosters (see page 153), so, yes, that was an awful lot of needling.

Comfort Level

Uncomfortable. Not impossibly painful, but I can't claim it was a breeze.

Verdict

Immediately afterwards, my skin is really quite red, even though the pinprick bleeding has stopped; but by the following morning, my face has calmed down and is only a bit pink. After three sessions, each six weeks apart, my skin is certainly firmer, clearer, and smoother – so a really good result.

Cost and Location

Gel needling with Skinboosters and Medical Needling in one session, £995 at eudelo.com. To find a practitioner in your area, go to www.thetweakmentsguide.com.

Would It Work for You?

Yes. It's a bit brutal as treatments go, but very effective. Needling is well-proven to stimulate the growth of new collagen in the skin, which will give you a smoother skin surface. Adding the hyaluronic acid gel skin-boosters is another well-proven texture-booster, so the two together work a treat.

Potential Problems

Your skin may well be red and sore for a couple of days after this – some practitioners needle more heavily than others – but the wounds are being created deliberately, with a purpose in mind, so this shouldn't be a problem, just a means to an end.

TREATMENT REVIEW: DERMAPLANING

Dermaplaning is a close shave with a scalpel for super-smooth skin.

What It Is

The idea of having your skin shaved, free-hand, with a scalpel may not sound like fun, but this is a gentle if rather advanced form of facial exfoliation, carried out by a well-trained skin specialist using an ultra-fine scalpel. It's a swift way to improve skin texture on the surface, because careful shaving not only removes the top layer of dead, polluted skin cells that make the face look dull, but also all the 'peach fuzz' vellus hair on the face, so your newly-denuded skin feels extra smooth. It will also be that bit more receptive to skincare ingredients and that bit more sensitive to UV light, so stock up on sunscreen.

What It's Like

Signing the form saying I understand that the therapist will be using a scalpel on my skin gives me pause for thought. But once Beata, the therapist, starts work on my face, my anxiety subsides. The scalpel is used so lightly I hardly feel it, and the soft scuffing movements are so hypnotically soothing that, as the treatment carries on (it takes the best part of an hour), I am nearly lulled to sleep. When she has finished my whole face, Beata treats my skin to some hydrating and plumping skin serums, which sink in very easily.

Comfort Level

Extremely comfortable. As exfoliating techniques go, this is much gentler than either microdermabrasion (intense exfoliation with a special tool to even out skin tone) or a chemical peel.

Verdict

With all its tiny hairs shaved off, my skin feels as smooth as porcelain and looks miles younger, because it reflects the light so evenly. Make-up glides on, too. I can see why the clinic is besieged with requests for this treatment before the spring awards ceremonies, the Cannes film festival, and Christmas, as it gives skin a preternatural smoothness that looks great in photographs.

Cost and Location

£160, HB Health Clinic, hbhealth.com. To find a practitioner in your area, go to www.thetweakmentsguide.com.

Would It Work for You?

Yes. I don't know anyone who hasn't been delighted by this treatment, once they have got over the very reasonable anxiety about having a scalpel working over their face, and once they have been reassured that the hairs will not grow back stubbly (I don't know why, but they just don't).

Potential Problems

Apart from the fact that someone is wielding a brand-new scalpel blade around your face? Not many.

Laser Skin Resurfacing

You can also try laser treatment to make your skin smoother. A laser uses a precisely focused beam of light, which is a powerful tool. What a laser can do depends on where it is focussed – and the power at which it is used.

Older-style 'ablative' lasers that scorch away the surface layers of the skin (CO_2 lasers – carbon dioxide lasers – such as the Fraxel Re:pair) have become less popular over the past couple of decades. They're effective but require a lot of recovery time. Then there are non-ablative lasers which heat up the lower layers of the skin without charring the surface.

LASER is an acronym that stands for Light Amplification by the Stimulated Emission of Radiation. Always a good one to know for a pub quiz.

Many of the most popular lasers are 'fractional', which means that the laser beam is fired at the skin through a grid of tiny holes. Using the grid means that in between each channel of damage that is burned into the skin, there is a scrap of intact skin, which reduces the damage on the skin's surface and speeds up the healing process.

Laser skin resurfacing is a confusing area – for instance, the best known brand of fractional laser, Fraxel, has both an ablative version (the Re:pair) and a non-ablative version (the Re:store). But the general message is that there are many types of laser that can work on the skin in a variety of ways. So ask the clinic that you are thinking of visiting about which brand of laser they use, and get them to explain what it can achieve and why it would help you get the results you are looking for.

One of the newest developments in laser is the arrival of the 'pico' lasers, such as the Picosure from Cynosure or the PicoWay from Syneron Candela. A pico laser fires its beam so quickly – in a picosecond, a trillionth of a second – that it manages to bypass the surface of the skin altogether and gets straight to stimulating healing in the lower layers with pressure waves. A pico laser is brilliant for breaking up the pigment in tattoos, which it shatters by acoustic vibration, and can also be used for skin rejuvenation.

POTENTIAL PROBLEMS WITH LASER SKIN SMOOTHING

Most of the potential problems with lasers stem from their potential for heating and damaging the skin. So make sure that whoever is doing your treatment knows exactly what they are doing with the laser they are using, has plenty of experience of using it for treatment, and uses it with care and caution.

You may find your skin is red after treatment, and this may persist for a day or two, depending on the intensity of the treatment; that is normal, as the skin heals and recovers from treatment. Over-treatment can lead to problems with pigmentation within the skin – either hypopigmentation, where the skin shows pale patches that have become depigmented, or hyperpigmentation, where the melanocytes (the cells that make pigment in the skin) have gone into overdrive after treatment, leaving darker patches. These problems are much more common with old-style ablative lasers and when darker skin tones are treated with laser without sufficient care.

TREATMENT REVIEW: LASER GENESIS

This treatment uses a non-ablative Genesis Nd:YAG laser to generate renewal within the skin.

What It Is

By gently heating the upper dermis with a laser beam, the Genesis triggers the skin's own regeneration mechanisms. This stimulates collagen production, plumping fine lines and improving pore size and texture. It also helps improve the look of the skin by reducing redness, which it does by clearing away broken blood vessels.

What It's Like

Much more gentle than I had expected. My skin is given a light acid peel first (a mixture of lactic, mandelic, and malic acids) – which tingles, but not enough to sting – to sweep away dead cells and provide a clean surface for the laser to tackle. After that my skin looks a bit pinked-up in patches. Then on go the laser goggles, and the aesthetic therapist starts with the laser, first on my forehead, then the upper cheeks, then the lower cheeks.

The machine chirps and chirrups as she moves the laser beam continually around the chosen section of my face, heating up the lower layers of the skin to 42 degrees. Oddly, it is not creating more redness in the skin, but rather taking it away – because this wavelength of laser (1064nm) has the effect of shrinking the capillaries.

Comfort Level

Very tolerable. It feels hot, but not so hot that it stings.

Verdict

This gave a really nice instant brightening result just from one treatment. The surface of my skin looks fresher, and my pores seem invisibly small. To be honest, I didn't see much of a resurfacing effect because, as so often, I failed to go back for the further treatments that the clinic suggests – they recommend a course of five, each three weeks apart, for longer-term results. But I am confident that I would have seen this deeper regeneration if I'd persevered.

Cost and Location

From £95 per session, www.medicetics.com. To find a practitioner in your area, go to www.thetweakmentsguide.com.

Would It Work for You?

Yes. Everyone I know who has tried this, from people with acne to people with older skin like mine who are mainly looking for smoothing and brightening, has seen a really good result.

Potential Problems

Few; this treatment offers a lightweight dose of laser so it will give gentle but definite benefits without the risk of provoking hyperpigmentation or hypopigmentation.

> The Fraxel fractional laser is, as mentioned above, a great treatment for improving the skin texture. There's a review of non-ablative Fraxel treatment in the next chapter (see page 173), because it is also good at reducing pigmentation in sun-damaged skin.

TREATMENT REVIEW: LASER SKIN REJUVENATION WITH THE PICOWAY RESOLVE

This skin-rejuvenation treatment uses a PicoWay Resolve laser, which has a photoacoustic effect (which means sound waves are created as the laser light is absorbed into the skin) rather than a photothermal effect (where the laser light creates heat), so it does not heat up the surface of the skin.

What It Is

Each pulse from this laser lasts only a picosecond, which is a mere trillionth of a second. That's so fast that the laser manages bypass the surface of the skin without damaging it, but creates a 'photoacoustic' vibration within the skin. This vibration generates a wound-healing response. It is also meant to be pain free, with no need for the numbing cream that most other laser procedures require.

What It's Like
By Karen Heath

I was lured into trying the treatment by the 'no pain' promise, but every time the laser fires, I find I am wincing. The pain isn't dramatic, but it's like having a rubber-band snapped against my skin. Thank goodness it only goes on for 15 minutes.

My skin is red afterwards, and by the evening, it feels as if my face is on fire with sunburn and it itches horribly, too. I keep applying aloe vera gel every time I wake up in the night, which soothes it a bit, but it is just as painful the next day, and my face has developed a rash of small spots all over. After three days it all starts getting back to normal, though my skin feels very dry.

Verdict

After a month, as the new skin grows through from beneath, there is certainly an improvement in my crow's feet wrinkles, and my skin is firmer and brighter. But I haven't found the strength to go back for follow-up sessions (three are needed for best results).

Cost and Location

From £300. For clinics offering the treatment nationwide, see www.syneron-candela.com).

Would It Work for You?

Yes. Laser is a reliably effective treatment. If you found Karen's description off-putting, it's worth noting that she was one of the first people in the UK to try this treatment a couple of years ago, and the protocol is now to treat at a lower, more tolerable intensity.

Potential Problems

Lasers can damage the skin, particularly if they are used at too high an intensity, or by an inexperienced practitioner. With any laser treatment, make sure your practitioner explains to you beforehand very clearly what treatment will involve, what it will feel like and whether there will be downtime afterwards.

RADIOFREQUENCY SKIN RESURFACING

Yet another way of convincing the skin that it has been injured enough to kick-start the process of repair is with radiofrequency energy. Unlike laser, which mainly works on the surface of the skin, radiofrequency energy travels a short distance into the skin.

As with other treatment technologies, radiofrequency energy can be used in different ways, and that's the case with this next treatment, which is done with an EndyMed radiofrequency machine on the 'FSR' setting (this stands for Fractional Skin Resurfacing). Within the FSR handpiece are 112 tiny electrodes which deliver a concentrated shot of focused radiofrequency energy to the skin. This creates 112 tiny channels of damage into the skin which, as they heal up, will generate new, tighter, stronger skin. So this machine can not only heat up the lower layers of the skin, to shrink-wrap the collagen and kick-start the creation of new collagen from beneath, but can resurface and repair the skin at the same time, which makes it a powerful tool.

HOW RADIOFREQUENCY WORKS

Radiofrequency (RF) devices use a brilliant type of technology for tightening up the skin. Radiofrequency is commonly referred to as a tweakment that can have a 'shrink-wrapping' effect. It does this by heating up the lower layers of the skin (the dermis) to 42 degrees C, at which point the existing collagen contracts (I don't like the analogy, but think of flash-frying a steak, and how it shrinks in the pan). The radiofrequency energy also makes the skin think it is injured so that it starts throwing out growth factors and new collagen to heal the perceived wounds. In due course, this collagen will show up on the surface of the skin as smoother, firmer, tighter skin.

There are two main ways of getting RF energy into the skin to heat it up. The gentle way is with the smooth end of a pen-like device, which is moved around the skin in little circles and kept in constant motion, heating up the skin as it goes. There's a thermometer on the device, too, so it can monitor the temperature in the skin as it works. The intensive, medical-clinic way is to use a more powerful machine which delivers a precise dose of RF energy via a handpiece, which has to be worked, zap by zap, very precisely across the treatment area. Other RF devices use needles to deliver the heat more deeply into the skin.

TREATMENT REVIEW: RADIOFREQUENCY SKIN RESURFACING WITH ENDYMED FSR AND ENDYMED INTENSIF

Radiofrequency treatments are usually used to tighten the skin – you can read a treatment review of Thermage, which does this, on page 265 – but the following treatment is a way of using radio-frequency to resurface the skin to make it smoother.

MONOPOLAR, BIPOLAR, AND TRIPOLAR RADIOFREQUENCY – WHAT'S THE DIFFERENCE?

RF energy is an alternating electrical current which creates an electromagnetic field that sends out radio waves, and RF devices are either monopolar or bipolar. Monopolar machines, such as Thermage, have a treatment head that delivers the RF energy, while a metal pad attached to the machine is placed under your shoulder. This RF energy can be fine-tuned to hit precise depths within the skin, up to 2cm deep.

Bipolar RF machines, on the other hand, have two electrodes on the treatment head, and the current passes between them, which means it can't go far into the skin at all (like, only 2mm), unless it is helped to go deeper by being passed through needles (yes, ow) that have sunk a small way into the skin.

You'll find RF machines called 'tripolar' or 'multipolar', but given that electrical polarity is a plus-to-minus sort of thing rather than a plus-to-minus-to something-else-in-the-middle sort of thing, these other machines just use variants on bipolar technology. Practitioners who like using RF treatments usually prefer monopolar machines, because they offer a more flexible way to treat patients.

What It Is

The treatment head of the EndyMed machine delivers micro-blasts of radiofrequency energy which create small channels of damage within the skin. As these heal up, the new skin that is created, and the growth factors and new collagen that is released as part of the process, both tighten the skin up and leave it a good deal smoother.

The FSR treatment head works more on the skin surface, tightening and brightening; the Intensif head sends the radio-frequency deeper into the skin through a set of fine microneedles, so it is better for skin texture improvement and reducing the appearance of pores.

POTENTIAL PROBLEMS WITH RADIOFREQUENCY TREATMENT

The most common side-effects of treatment are redness and swelling, because the radiofrequency is generating heat within the deeper layers of the dermis. It's also possible that the treatment could burn, if the practitioner is not careful. Also, monopolar RF treatments can reach deep enough into the body to hit the fat beneath the skin, and the radiofrequency can kill the fat cells it reaches. Great in a bottom-shrinking treatment; less great in a face which is already losing its fat pads, though I'm told this rarely happens these days now that practitioners are so much better at aiming the energy precisely where it is needed.

What It's Like

My face is covered with a thick layer of anaesthetic cream for 20 minutes before treatment, and I'm glad of it. Those blasts of RF energy may be micronized, but they're still powerful. But it's not intolerable, and within 45 minutes, my whole face and neck has been treated.

I do look a bit scorched, as if I'd been sunburned, and it takes a day or two for this to calm down, days during which my skin feels rough to the touch. It's not itchy, thank goodness, so I cover it with moisturiser and sunscreen and concentrate on not touching it as it heals up. It feels normal again after a week, but looks a little speckled as the damaged skin works its way to the surface.

Comfort Level

Moderate to challenging.

Verdict

After four rounds of treatment, each a month apart, my skin is markedly smoother. A very good result.

Cost and Location

EndyMed FSR (the fractional skin resurfacing), from £300 for a single session. EndyMed Intensif (needling with radiofrequency), which works deeper than FSR and has more focus on texture, from £400 per session. The whole 'EndyMed Workout' of two sessions of each of these over four months for both face and neck that I tried costs £2,150, including all the supporting skincare. Go to www.waterhouseyoung.com for all the details. To find a practitioner in your area, go to www.thetweakmentsguide.com.

Would It Work for You?

Yes, as long as you are committed to doing enough treatments to achieve the promised results, and prepared for the discomfort of treatment and a couple of days of post-treatment redness each time.

Potential Problems

See the sidebar titled 'Potential Problems with Radiofrequency Treatment' on page 147.

Under-the-Skin Moisturisers That Give the Face a Complete Reboot

And now, something you might not have thought of, but which is brilliant for improving skin texture all over your face (and your neck, and décolletage, should you want to go there).

You'll be familiar, if you've read this far, with the idea of injecting fillers into the face in order to give back volume to, say, gaunt cheeks. These fillers are made from hyaluronic acid gel, which is great at holding onto water within the skin. And now there is a whole new category of extra-runny hyaluronic acid gels which are designed not to give volume and structure to the skin, but to provide extra hydration just beneath the surface.

You need to be comfortable with the idea of needles if you are going to try these moisturisers, as they need to be injected in order to place them beneath the skin, but once they are in place, that extra hydration will improve your skin texture and make it smoother and more supple, give your complexion the lit-from-within glow that it tends to lose in the approach to middle age, and last for 6–9 months. There are several different brands of these moisturisers, all of which work in slightly different ways, though they are all in effect doing much the same thing.

WHAT YOU NEED TO KNOW ABOUT CROSSLINKED
HYALURONIC ACID

Hyaluronic acid is a naturally-occurring molecule often found in moisturising serums. The kind used in most products quickly breaks down, which is why you have to reapply it morning and evening, but the hyaluronic acid in these injectable moisturising-from-within tweakments is lightly 'crosslinked' – an industry term meaning the bonds between the hyaluronic acid molecules have been intensified though a chemical process – so that it stays in the skin, holding onto moisture for months before it is broken down by the body.

Would these under-the-skin moisturisers work for you? Yes. They're expensive but give terrific results. Everyone I know who has tried these has been really delighted with the way these make older, drier skin feel fresher, softer, and more springy.

POTENTIAL PROBLEMS WITH INJECTABLE MOISTURE
TREATMENTS

Are there any potential problems with injectable moisture treatments? Not really – apart from short-lived redness following the injections, and possible bruising, which is always a possibility for a treatment delivered by needles, I've yet to hear of any issues with these treatments.

TREATMENT REVIEW: INJECTABLE MOISTURE – PROFHILO

How exciting is Profhilo? Well, it's not unusual for cosmetic doctors to rave about new products and treatments, but it's quite rare for so many of them to be quite so keen on a product all at once.

Every clinic I know that has taken on Profhilo in the past couple of years is hugely enthusiastic about it and finds it gives reliably impressive results. Why? It's the most innovative of the new 'injectable moisture' treatments, and it has been shown in clinical tests to not just improve hydration in the skin but to boost the skin's elasticity and collagen levels too, so it is now classed as a 'biostimulator', something that kickstarts significant renewal within the skin. Will we be seeing more of these biostimulators in the future? You bet. Other companies are already working on them.

Another selling point for Profhilo is that it contains no BDDE (butanediol diglycidyl ether), an ingredient used to 'crosslink' the hyaluronic acid molecules in more durable forms of hyaluronic acid gel, to stop it being broken down so quickly by the body. Is that an advantage? Possibly, in the eyes of people who like a 'free from' tag, though BDDE has been shown in plenty of tests to be completely safe and not problematic. (And before you ask – yes, the hyaluronic acid in Profhilo is crosslinked, but only lightly and via heat treatment.)

What It Is

Profhilo is such a runny substance that it only need to be injected at five key points on each side of the face. From these injection sites, it will spread, finding its way underneath the surface of the skin, to treat the whole face. Once in place, the Profhilo solution boosts skin hydration by enabling the skin to hold more moisture. It also stimulates production of elastin and collagen, which is what, in two months' time, will make the skin firmer and bouncier.

What It's Like

Very quick and easy. I visit Dr Saira Vasdev at the Waterhouse Young clinic just off Harley Street in central London to try it out, and the injections take less than five minutes on each side of the face. I don't ask for anaesthetic cream, as I'm used to having injections in my face, and these injections are neither deep nor painful. Dr Vasdev injects the Profhilo on the outer point of my cheekbones, on the corner of my jaw, and in three places across my cheek (on each side of my face), and we're done. That's it.

The injections look a little like alien wasp-stings, all swollen up with liquid, but she assures me that these will vanish as the liquid disperses within my skin over the next 12 hours, and so they do. There's no downtime as such, but given that I have five of these swellings on each side of my face, it wouldn't be a good look to take to a meeting, say, or out to supper with friends.

Comfort Level

Minor discomfort, just 10 pinprick injections in total.

Verdict

Definitely one of the quickest and most effective cosmetic fixes that I have ever tried. You are told not to expect results for two months, but I could see and feel a change after a month, when I went back for the second round of injections. Also, I only needed half as much moisturiser as usual. This happy state of affairs lasted for at least six months.

Cost and Location

Profhilo costs £975 for two treatments, one month apart, www.waterhouseyoung.com. To find a practitioner in your area, go to www.thetweakmentsguide.com.

Potential Problems

Few; see the sidebar 'Potential Problems with Injectable Moisture Treatments' on page 149.

TREATMENT REVIEW: INJECTABLE MOISTURE – JUVEDERM VOLITE

Another runny form of injectable hyaluronic acid gel, Volite is from Juvederm, the well-known and highly reputable brand of facial fillers, and is owned by Allergan, so it has a great pedigree. Again, it doesn't just hydrate the skin; it is being marketed as a skin-conditioning treatment.

If you're trying to choose between these treatments, one of the big attractions of Volite is that it's a one-off treatment. One appointment, and you're good for nine months of smoother, well-hydrated skin. That said, it does require hundreds of tiny pinprick injections in order to place the product neatly beneath the skin (into the mid-layers of the dermis, to be precise) all over your face. After that, you may well look as if you've run into a swarm of bees, so you'll want to do it at the end of the day and/or drive to your chosen clinic so you can just go straight home afterwards and wait for your face to calm down.

What It Is

Volite is a very liquid form of hyaluronic acid gel which is injected all over the face (around 200 injections in all). Once the gel is beneath the surface of the skin, it is able to hold onto moisture, and over the next two months, it will both soften and plump up the skin and improve its texture and elasticity.

What It's Like
By Sharon Walker

I have anaesthetic cream on for 20 minutes beforehand, which numbs me up a bit. The injections aren't that painful, but there are a lot of them, and I appreciate the way that Dr Vicky Dondos, who does my injections, changes the needle every now and then so that it is always very sharp. It takes the best part of an hour, and feels like quite a serious treatment, even though these are superficial injections (ie they are only just into the dermis) to introduce the droplets of Volite under the skin. Dr Dondos takes the injections all around my lips and into the 'barcode' lines on my upper lips, too. That is quite challenging.

I'm not too red afterwards, but there are an awful lot of tiny puncture marks on my face, so I wouldn't want to go out and see people. There's no puffiness from the fluid that was injected, just the tiny red dots from the injections, so yes, I do feel a bit like a pincushion, but I only have one or two tiny bruises, even after all those injections.

Comfort Level

Moderately uncomfortable, but I wasn't screaming with pain, either.

Verdict

I start to see the results after about a month. The fine lines on my upper lip have really softened significantly, and so have my crow's feet, which go on improving during the second month. I know it is working when I run out of moisturiser – and realise I don't really need any. What's really interesting is that the whole quality of my skin feels better. It's softer, and there's more radiance to it. Would I go back? Yes, definitely.

Cost and Location

Juvederm Volite, from £400 per session, depending on the extent of the area covered, www.medicetics.com. To find a practitioner in your area, go to www.thetweakmentsguide.com.

Potential Problems

Few; see the sidebar 'Potential Problems with Injectable Moisture Treatments' on page 149.

TREATMENT REVIEW: INJECTABLE MOISTURE – RESTYLANE SKINBOOSTERS

Another brand, another similar treatment. Restylane is a well-known and highly reputable brand of hyaluronic acid gels, and Skinboosters is their ultra-liquid, under-the-skin injectable-moisturiser option. The results of this will last six months, but it takes three rounds of treatment to build up the full effect; that means three rounds of 200 pinprick injections, each a month apart.

What It Is

Injecting a dose of moisturising hyaluronic acid gel into the top layers of the skin gives long-lasting smoothing and plumping effect so, again, it's great for improving skin texture and giving older, drier skin back its glow and vitality.

What It's Like

Getting the product into the skin involves hundreds of tiny injections, which are done freehand with a very fine, sharp needle. Thanks to the numbing cream and the aesthetician's delicate injection technique, the whole process is much less uncomfortable than I was expecting, but it does take a good 40 minutes to get them all done. Best to put your mind somewhere else while this is going on, rather than counting the injections.

Comfort Level

Mostly not too uncomfortable – though the injections in my forehead aren't much fun.

Verdict

I don't look my best after all this – my skin is red and inflamed from the injections – but after a couple of days this has calmed down. The effect is subtle: my skin is definitely smoother and feels well hydrated, and appears just that little bit plumper, rather than puffy; and unlike most beauty treatments, it lasts for months. For best results, you should do a course of three treatments three or four weeks apart.

Cost and Location

£950 for a course of three treatments at clinics nationwide (www.restylane.co.uk).

Potential Problems

Few; see the sidebar 'Potential Problems with Injectable Moisture Treatments' on page 149.

TREATMENT REVIEW: MESOTHERAPY

Injecting a cocktail of vitamins and moisturising ingredients into the middle layer of the skin – the 'mesoderm' – is a treatment that has been popular in France for 50 years. In the face, it is used to smooth and rejuvenate the skin, and on the body, to improve the appearance of cellulite – but exactly what is injected and how tends to vary from practitioner to practitioner, and it is not an area where there has been much scientific research conducted on how well it works.

Despite that, many aesthetic clinics offer mesotherapy as an entry-level tweakment which will give the skin a bit of a boost, providing hydration, smoothing the surface, and helping skin to regenerate itself from within.

What It Is

In Britain, the idea of injectable skincare is often met with a shudder. But at Medicetics, mesotherapy is hugely popular, and Dr Vicky Dondos uses it as an interim step to ease cautious patients onwards from just having facials towards trying injectable products.

The 'meso' cocktail is injected using the U225 injection gun – which is slightly terrifying because it is quite large and automated and has a 3mm needle which chugs back and forth, slowly, into the skin to deliver the goods to where they're needed. Once in the skin, that liquid mixture of vitamins and hyaluronic acid is intended to help revive the skin by providing the right nutrients to encourage regeneration of collagen and elastin. Also, each of the little wounds created as the needle of the meso-gun stabs into the skin should stimulate the production of collagen and elastin in the skin as said wound heals.

What It's Like

I'm braced for a painful impact as the aesthetic nurse doing my treatment hefts the meso gun, which starts knocking a 3mm needle repeatedly into my skin, but to my great surprise (and relief) I can feel only minute pinpricks as it does its work. Phew. She works steadily around my face injecting the serum cocktail, then turns up the speed of the needles to create more miniature wounds in the skin. But even that doesn't hurt. For the final 20 minutes, I lie peacefully under a canopy of soothing red LED lights to calm down the redness and inflammation in my traumatised skin.

Comfort Level

Not half as painful as you might think. Honestly. Really quite comfortable.

Verdict

I was warned that I would look as if I had been stung all over, but I only look a bit freckly and sunburned after the treatment, and even that redness has subsided by the end of the day. What I do notice, particularly the next day, is how amazingly plumped up my skin is – which isn't really surprising as there is a whole 5ml teaspoonful of the magic meso cocktail now trapped between the upper and lower layers of my skin. On the third day, it looks particularly good. I can see why this glowy smoothness is addictive, and why it is so popular before big events. The glow and the plumpness dwindles over the next week; if you do more sessions, the results are meant to last for longer.

Cost and Location

From £150, at www.medicetics.com. Three sessions are recommended, two weeks apart. To find a practitioner in your area, go to www.thetweakmentsguide.com.

Would It Work for You?

Yes. It won't give as long-term or as noticeably rejuvenating result as the three injectable-moisture treatments above, but it is much cheaper, and when you see the boost it can give to the skin, it might inspire you to try one of the other treatments.

Potential Problems

Few; see the sidebar 'Potential Problems with Injectable Moisture Treatments' on page 149.

CHAPTER 8

Softening Pigmentation

Pigmentation always sounds like a dull topic. But skin discoloration – whether it's from age spots; the redness of rosacea or thread veins; obvious, grubby-looking pores; or spots – has an even bigger impact on how fresh the skin looks than wrinkles. It is also an area where the right tweakments can help a great deal.

UNEVEN SKIN TONE

If we stop to think about what makes an older face look its age, the things that spring to mind are obvious ones like lines and wrinkles, hollowness, and sagging skin and pouchy jawlines. But it's not just those things that indicate age. In fact, uneven skin tone with brown marks or redness is an even bigger giveaway of skin age than lines or wrinkles.

This sounds unlikely at first, but if you think about it, young skin is a lovely consistent colour, and as soon as you have weathered cheeks, patchy pigmentation marks, a sprinkling of age spots or a red nose, it makes a face look much older – and the human eye is very good at assessing this. If you'd like more detail, look up the studies done by evolutionary psychologist Bernhard Fink, along with Karl Grammer and Paul Matts, which show that the way colour is distributed in the skin is a very clear indicator of how old and how attractive we perceive a face to be; the attractiveness element comes in because, as these studies argue, we are hard-wired by evolution to see clear, smooth skin as highly attractive in a potential mate. And just think how much time and money we spend smoothing on foundation and concealer to give ourselves that fresh-faced look.

PIGMENT, MELANIN, AND SKIN TONE

What makes skin tone even or uneven is the way melanin, the black or brown pigment that gives our skin its base colour, is distributed through our skin.

We all have melanin in our skin, and it is there for a reason: to protect our skin cells from the sun. Generally, the closer your ancestors lived to the equator, the more melanin your skin will contain by way of defence. When ultraviolet light hits the skin, it prompts the melanocytes – the cells that produce melanin – to make more melanin to help the skin protect itself. That's the response that results in a tan – but it is also a sign of damage in the skin. (If you're a redhead, you have a reddish kind of melanin which results more in freckles than a tan).

Yes, I just said that a tan is a sign of damage to the skin. Almost a century after Coco Chanel first popularised the concept of the sun tan as a chic hallmark of health and wealth – previously, tans had belonged to the rural poor who worked in the fields – we still persist in seeing tans as healthy and desirable, even if your skin cells would beg to differ.

AGE SPOTS, PATCHY PIGMENTATION, AND HYPERPIGMENTATION

But back to melanin. We don't even notice a nice, even distribution of melanin – it just looks good – and we tend to be blissfully unaware of pigmentation as a potential problem for the skin. Pigmentation builds up so gradually that it is hard to notice it happening, because whatever stage you are at just tends to become your new 'normal'. But as soon as the melanin begins to cluster and show up as patches or brown age spots, it is more obvious and not such a good look. The technical term is 'hyperpigmentation', and if it is something that bothers you, take heart, because there is a good deal you can do about it.

- The most common type of hyperpigmentation is the result of overexposure to daylight. (I say 'daylight' rather than 'sunlight' because what does the damage is ultraviolet light, which is present in daylight all year round, whether it is sunny or not.) This hyperpigmentation shows up as ragged brown patches or as small dark age spots that build up over the years.
- Then there's melasma, a condition where the pigmentation seems to be forming more of a 'mask' of colour across the face, and which is brought on by hormonal fluctuation. See page 177 for more information on melasma.
- The third type is called post-inflammatory hyperpigmentation (PiH), where the brown spots that show up are the result of acne scarring, or eczema, or overenthusiastic pigmentation treatment with, say, lasers.

WHAT CAUSES PIGMENTATION PROBLEMS?

Before we get on to how to treat pigmentation problems, I'm going to back-track and talk about the skin and what UV light does to it over a lifetime.

UV Light, Sunshine, Sunscreen, Broad Spectrum Protection, and What It All Means for the Skin

Time for a statistic – it's much used, but it's still a cracker: up to 90 per cent of what we think of as the 'signs of ageing' – all the wrinkles, the age spots, the rough texture – are all due to exposure to UV light.

If you're wondering whether 'exposure to UV light' means 'being outside in the sun', the answer is yes – being outside in the sun is the most direct and obvious way of exposing yourself to ultraviolet light – but it's not just sunshine that delivers UV light.

There are two key kinds of ultraviolet rays. There's UVB, the kind which, in the UK, we only get in significant doses in summer sunshine, and which will burn the surface of our skin if we give it a chance. Then there's UVA, the longer-wavelength ultraviolet rays which reach deeper into the skin and help to break down the collagen and elastin that keep the skin firm and springy. UVA and UVB rays work together to produce a tan. UVA darkens existing pigment in the skin, while UVB prompts the melanocytes to produce more pigment. Both reactions are trying to protect the DNA in the skin from the damage that those UV rays are causing.

We only get decent amounts of UVB in the summer in the UK – in the sunshine, though it also finds its way through clouds. But UVA reaches us all day every day, not just in the summer or when it's sunny, but in boring old grey daylight, all year round. UVA rays also pass through glass, so if you are in the car a lot, or have a desk by the window, those damaging rays will reach you there, too, though you won't get a tan through glass.

It is the everyday, incidental exposure to UVA which slowly, gradually stacks up over a lifetime and which results in clusters of melanin (age spots) and broken-down collagen and elastin (wrinkles) and a damaged skin barrier (rough texture). Nothing dramatic or sexy about it, just life, slowly eroding the structure of the skin. This accumulated damage can also, over time, provoke skin cancer.

That is why dermatologists and skincare experts and beauty editors all bang on about wearing high-factor sunscreen the whole time, and why UV protection is fundamental to looking after your skin.

Sunscreens – SPF/UVA and 'Broad-Spectrum' Protection

Sunscreens are usually described by how much SPF they contain. Now, the SPF rating for a product tells us how much UVB light it can block, or absorb. What you also need to be interested in for preventing UV-related damage is blocking UVA rays, and most sunscreen products are formulated to offer 'broad spectrum' protection, with a certain proportion of UVA blockers. In general, the higher the SPF, the higher the UVA protection, too.

Sunscreens: Ones That Absorb the Rays, Ones That Reflect the Rays

The main choice with sunscreens (apart from picking a high enough SPF) is whether they are physical, reflective sunscreens, which literally shield the skin with a physical barrier of product and bounce back the sun and the UV rays away from the skin; or UV-absorbing sunscreens, which work by absorbing the UV light and preventing it affecting the skin.

Physical sunscreens are the type that used to be known as sunblock or mineral sunscreens; they contain finely milled titanium dioxide or zinc oxide. If you have tried these in the past and rejected them because they come up a bit chalky, it's worth taking another look at them, because every year the formulations get better, and the finish that the product gives improves.

UV-absorbing sunscreens are sometimes called 'chemical' sunscreens – an unfortunate term given the huge numbers of people who see the word 'chemical' as equivalent to 'evil'. These 'absorbing' sunscreens contain ingredients like oxybenzone (for UVB and some UVA), avobenzone (UVA), octisalate (UVB), or homosalate (UVB), which absorb the energy from UV rays and turn it into heat.

Most skins can tolerate these absorbing sunscreens well, but anyone who prefers to keep their skincare natural will have an instinctive aversion to this second group of ingredients. I'm big on using sunscreen of any sort, but I can see that absorbing sunscreens and their synthetic ingredients have their problems. Hawaii has recently banned the use of sunscreens containing oxybenzone and octisalate from use on its beaches, because these ingredients have been found to kill developing coral, bleach existing coral, and inflict genetic damage on coral, as well as having gender-bending effects on fish, feminising male fish.

Skin Cancer – What Are the Risks?

Sorry, it's a bit of a downer to introduce skin cancer when we were only talking about skin pigmentation, but I have to mention it.

The more exposure your skin has to UV light, whether that is the normal sort of exposure that you get in everyday life, or lying in the sun tanning your skin, the greater the chances are that you could develop skin cancer. I know that lying out in the sun feels fabulous, and most of us, me included, still think we look better with a tan than without. But tanned skin is damaged skin, and tanning has consequences in the form of wrinkles, pigmentation marks, rough skin texture and, possibly, skin cancer.

And I know that sounds like a crude scare tactic, but look at the figures. According to the latest statistics from Cancer Research UK, over 15,000 people in the UK are diagnosed each year with melanoma, the more rare but more dangerous type of skin cancer that kills around 2,400 people each year there. And over 136,000 people are diagnosed with non-melanoma skin cancers every year. That's a lot of people, enough to fill Wembley stadium one and a half times.

How likely are you to get skin cancer? Well, it all depends. If you have pale skin, you are more susceptible to sun damage. The Cancer Research website (www.cancerresearchuk.org) is good and matter-of-fact on this if you want to look further.

You might have genes that deal well with skin-related environmental stress like UV exposure, or you might not. How to tell? You can't. Dr Mark Birch-Machin is professor of molecular dermatology at the Newcastle University Institute of Cellular Medicine and a great expert in the damage that UV light does to our skin. The way he puts it is that the damage UV light creates in your skin stacks up over time; it is akin to building a Jenga-style tower of damaged DNA in your skin cells.

At what point does that DNA damage tip over into the sort of cellular mutations that can lead to skin cancer? It's hard to say. Think of it like throwing a pair of dice, says Prof Birch-Machin. When you get the double six, that's skin cancer. It might take a lifetime. But what you don't know is whether your genes have already thrown one of those sixes for you, in which case it may happen a lot faster.

It's hearing that sort of stuff repeatedly over the years that keeps me reapplying sunscreen and keeps me off the sun-lounger on holiday – or at least makes me drag the sun-lounger into the shade and bump up my skin colour with self-tan.

But Don't We Need Sunshine for the Vitamin D?

One big argument for lounging around in the sun – apart from the fact that it feels great – is that we all need more vitamin D.

It's a fair point, particularly if you live somewhere like northern Europe, where we have such a miserably small quota of sunshine that most of us are short of vitamin D by mid-winter, which is a serious issue. Wearing sunscreen, as you might suspect, blocks most of the production of vitamin D.

Vitamin D is a hormone rather than a vitamin. It has a role in regulating our immune system, and it helps keep bones strong because it is needed to help absorb calcium from the gut into the bloodstream; that's also why, if you have too little vitamin D, bone growth suffers. Oily fish, cow's milk, and dairy products are all good sources of vitamin D, but it is quite hard to pack in enough vitamin D just from your diet.

As with other vitamins, you can take supplements to increase the amount of vitamin D in the body. The latest government advice is that we should all take supplements; aim for 1,000–2,000 iU a day.

But the swiftest way for the body to acquire vitamin D is though exposure to UVB rays in sunshine. If you live anywhere north of 40 degrees latitude (that's anywhere north of Majorca, so most of Europe), the sun is only strong enough (or more precisely, only contains enough UVB light) to create vitamin D in the skin between April and September. You don't need to spend much time in the sun for the skin to start generating vitamin D. Around 10 minutes, two or three times a week, is enough, and because vitamin D is a fat-soluble vitamin, the body can store it.

The easiest parts of your body to expose to the sun are your face, neck, and hands, though of course they're also the ones most prone to wrinkling. So think laterally. When the sun is hot enough, bare your legs, or your back, or your arms for a few minutes to boost your vitamin D supplies before you slap on the sunscreen – but keep your face protected.

And take the supplements, too, just for backup. You can ask your GP for a blood test to see whether you need to be concerned about your vitamin D levels or not. I follow all the advice above, yet every time I have my vitamin D levels tested, I am told that they are too low, even when I have been on holiday and have diligently stuck my legs and back in the sun for 10 minutes every day without sunscreen.

Is It an Age Spot or Is It Skin Cancer?

If you're worried about particular marks, moles, or age spots, and are wondering whether they are ordinary pigmentation or potentially cancerous, glance over this list of warning signs from www.skincancer.org:

- **A – Asymmetric.** Is it a lopsided mark? That's a red flag.
- **B – Borders.** Are these smooth (which is fine) or ragged (which is not)?
- **C – Colour.** Is the mark all the same colour, which probably means it is harmless, or are there different colours within it?
- **D – Diameter.** Is the mark small? That usually, but not always, means it is less of a problem. Or is it bigger than the diameter of the end of a pencil?
- **E – Evolving.** Is the mark changing in shape and growing? If so, that is a warning sign.

There are a number of 'mole clinics' that offer to check over your body for abnormal pigmentation, but the best person to assess whether a mark or mole is problematic is a trained dermatologist who will know exactly what they are looking for, and what may be a problem and why. GPs don't usually know very much about pigmentation and moles, but they can refer you to a dermatologist.

If you are at all worried, get an expert opinion as soon as you can. Rates of incidence of skin cancer have more than doubled since the 1990s. As I mentioned, there are over 136,000 new cases of skin cancer in the UK every year, and the number is rising, even though we are theoretically much more sun- and skin-aware than in decades past. So it's not something we can ignore.

HOW SKINCARE CAN HELP WITH PIGMENTATION

Before you start contemplating tweakments to reduce pigmentation marks, take a look at what you could achieve with the right skincare.

Start with Sunscreen

There's a lot you can do for pigmentation with skincare, starting with sunscreen. Wearing sunscreen will not only prevent future damage but will stop the damage that has already been done from getting worse. Wearing sunglasses and a hat helps, too.

That means high-factor sunscreen, every day: SPF30 in winter, SPF50 in summer, and reapply it at lunchtime if you can, whatever your skin colour. And during and after any course of treatment for pigmentation, sunscreen is even more vital, to protect the newly cleared skin. So yes, it's a continuous process – once you start to notice pigmentation, and do something about it, it becomes a long-term commitment, as you can't give up on protecting your skin, or the pigmentation will all come rushing back.

'Generally, I will start treatment for pigmentation with skincare,' says consultant dermatologist and dermatological surgeon Dr Nis Sheth, from the St John's Institute of Dermatology in London. 'The first thing to use is sunscreen – and the right type. If you have melasma, for instance, it is important not just to protect against UVA and UVB rays, but to use some kind of physical protection, too.' That means a sunscreen containing titanium dioxide or zinc oxide, which will reflect back the light, rather than absorb it. Dr Sheth is keen on Heliocare 360 (see the section 'Physical and Absorbing Combined Sunscreens' on page 168) and Photoderm M by Bioderma with SPF50.

Fading Age Spots with Skincare

The right skincare can help to fade existing brown marks, but you need to use it consistently, every day, and with care (and, as mentioned above, commit to using sunscreen every day).

The key ingredients for fading pigment markings in the skin fall into different categories. First, there are the ones that stop the skin making so much pigment in the first place. These include vitamin C, arbutin (aka bearberry extract), liquorice, kojic acid, and azelaic acid. These all belong to a group of substances called tyrosinase inhibitors, and they work by blocking the action of tyrosinase, an enzyme used in the pigment-making process. (In a skin cell, tyrosinase oxidises an amino acid, tyrosine, to create the melanin pigment, if you want the detail.)

Then there's niacinamide, a version of vitamin B3 (niacin) which helps reduce pigmentation by blocking the transfer of melanin from the melanocytes that make it to the keratinocytes, the skin cells where it sits and shows up.

Alpha hydroxy acids can help reduce pigmentation marks in the skin, too. These exfoliating acids, which include glycolic acid and the gentler lactic acid, have a peeling action on the skin, encouraging the shedding of outer, pigmented layers so that fresher, clearer skin grows through from underneath.

'Retinol creams can help with pigmentation, too,' says Dr Sheth, 'and there are some over-the-counter products which have reasonable evidence to show that they work, such as No 7's Lift & Luminate range. They're not as good as prescription lightening agents, but they are not far off in their results, and they have less risk of irritation.'

THE PRESCRIPTION-ONLY PIGMENT BUSTER

The gold-standard treatment that a dermatologist can prescribe for tackling pigmentation is a cream containing 4 per cent hydroquinone, a well-proven pigment-buster. This cream should be applied as directed, just onto the actual pigmentation patches, morning and night; it will take around eight weeks to work.

ANTI-PIGMENTATION SKINCARE PROTOCOL

Dr Nick Lowe is a leading dermatologist based in Harley Street, London who has been treating pigmentation for decades.

This skincare protocol for anyone who comes to see him with any form of pigmentation problem goes as follows: a 4 per cent hydroquinone cream, just on the dark areas, followed by a good quality vitamin C serum, for its ability to inhibit pigment formation, all over the face, morning and night. In the morning, this should be followed by sunscreen.

'Whatever else you use, don't use pirated versions of high-strength depigmenting creams,' says Dr Lowe, 'because – ironically – they can bring on more hyperpigmentation.'

HIGH-STREET SKINCARE FOR MANAGING PIGMENTATION

Here is a list of high-street skincare products for managing pigmentation. With all these pigment-blockers and skin brighteners, you have to keep using them continuously to see constant results.

- **Olay Regenerist Luminous Skin Tone Perfecting Serum**, £29.99, www.boots.com
- **The Ordinary Niacinamide 10% + Zinc 1%**, £5, theordinary.com
- **No 7 Lift & Luminate Triple Action Serum**, £27, www.boots.com
- **iS Clinical White Lightening Serum**, £57, www.skincity.co.uk
- **Neostrata Enlighten Illuminating Serum**, £73, www.dermacaredirect.co.uk
- **Clinique Even Better Clinical Dark Spot Corrector & Optimizer**, £45, www.clinique.co.uk
- **Murad Rapid Age Spot Correcting Serum**, £70, www.murad.co.uk

VITAMIN C PRODUCTS FOR SKIN BRIGHTENING

See the list of vitamin C products for skin brightening on page 113.

HOW TO ADD BRIGHTENING SERUMS INTO YOUR SKINCARE ROUTINE.

Use your chosen serum after cleansing and before sunscreen in the morning. If you are using more than one serum, use the more lightweight, runnier one first.

PHYSICAL SUNSCREENS

Here are three physical sunscreens, ones that shield your skin with a physical barrier of product:

- **Exuviance Sheer Daily Protector SPF50**, £30, www.skincity.co.uk
- **Skinceuticals Sheer Mineral UV Defence SPF50** , £37, skinceuticals.co.uk

- **Avene Mineral Fluid, SPF50**, £16.50, www.boots.com

ABSORBING SUNSCREENS

Here are two absorbing sunscreens, ones that work by absorbing the UV light and preventing it affecting your skin. These are both lightweight creams, so they're good for normal-to-oily skin:

- **La Roche Posay Anthelios XL Ultra Light Fluid SPF50**, £16.50, laroche-posay.co.uk
- **Paula's Choice Clear Ultra Light Daily Mattifying Fluid, SPF30**, www.paulaschoice.co.uk

PHYSICAL AND ABSORBING COMBINED SUNSCREENS

Here are three absorbing sunscreens that also include physical protection:

- **Epionce Ultra Shield Lotion SPF50**, £29.50, epionce.co.uk
- **Heliocare 360 Fluid Cream SPF50**, £31, www.skincity.co.uk
- **Bioderma Photoderm M**, £16.10, bioderma.com

TWEAKMENTS FOR PIGMENTATION

When it comes to treating pigmentation at a skin clinic, the main ways are with light treatments – either lasers or IPL (intense pulsed light) – and with skin peels, backed up by specific skincare and sunscreen. A practitioner will need to assess what is going on with the pigmentation in your skin in order to decide how to treat you.

IPL and laser devices both use targeted light beams to break up clusters of pigment under the skin. The way they work is that the light is attracted to the pigment – the brown melanin – in the skin and shatters it into fragments that the body can clear away. These devices work most easily on paler skin tones; on darker skin, there is a greater risk that light treatments could cause hyperpigmentation, but some lasers can get good results on darker skin, too, so ask your chosen practitioner for more detail on this.

What Is IPL and How Is It Different to Laser?

IPL is a broad-spectrum light, a collection of different wavelengths of light, so they have a scattergun effect when they strike into the skin. IPL devices are less complex than lasers and also less expensive. Lasers use a specific wavelength to send beams of light that hit a precise depth in the skin. What the laser beam can do in the skin depends on its wavelength, its intensity, and the rate of the pulses at which it is generated.

Aren't These the Devices Used for Hair Removal?

Yes – IPL and laser are most commonly used for hair removal. But with IPL, you would use a different setting when tackling pigment in the skin; with laser, your practitioner will use a different kind of laser for dealing with pigmentation from the type they'd use for hair removal.

Does IPL Hurt More Than Laser, or Vice Versa?

It all depends. IPL treatment is usually very tolerable. The feeling of each IPL shot is most commonly compared to having an elastic band pinged against your skin – not nice, but not excruciating. Having said that, I've had some sessions of IPL where I've wondered if I'm just having a bad day, or whether they've turned the machine up extra high, because if someone pinged me with an elastic band that hard, I'd be tempted to take revenge on them.

Lasers are always thought of as being more painful, but of course it all depends on the energy levels that they are putting out. You can have a really easy, comfortable treatment with an Nd:YAG laser if it's on a low setting (as you would as part of the Skin Laundry laser facial; see page 66), but the higher the power is turned up, the more things are likely to hurt.

Most lasers have an inbuilt cooling system which both physically cools your skin to remove the heat that the laser is generating, and also distracts your brain from thinking about the impact of each zap. If a treatment is likely to be uncomfortable, you will be offered numbing cream beforehand. No practitioner wants deliberately to inflict pain, so they will do their best to make everything manageable for you.

> ## WHY LIGHT TREATMENTS ARE SEEN AS THE GOOD GUYS
>
> 'Light treatments' sounds gentle; friendly, even – and some of them can be. It all depends on the type of light and the intensity at which it is used. Once you concentrate light into a laser beam, it is capable of shattering the pigment within a tattoo or blasting the skin into vapour. Not so gentle.
>
> But one curious thing about light treatments is that they have come to be seen as the acceptable, clever route to managing ageing. In many people's minds, they're ok in a way that Botox and fillers just aren't.
>
> Well-known A-listers (Jennifer Aniston, Gwyneth Paltrow, and Tom Ford spring to mind) are happy to talk in interviews about having laser treatment, and people think 'Ooh, I must try some of that!' Yet celebs, as I've already grumbled, never mention Botox or fillers, unless it is to declare that they are so over them.
>
> I'm sure it's simply because light treatments don't involve using needles, so are totally non-invasive. Whatever the reason, it means that light treatments are, at least in many people's minds, the good guys when it comes to tweakments.

Does IPL Work Better Than Laser for Pigmentation and Age Spots? Which Should I Choose?

That depends on your practitioner and which machines they have at their disposal, since both methods can work very well. IPL technology has been widely available for 20 years and is a cheaper and less sophisticated technology than laser. For instance, beauty salons can often stretch to the price of an IPL machine, which cost up to £10,000, whereas lasers cost more like £40–£80,000.

As cosmetic procedures go, IPL is a relatively inexpensive treatment, so it will be cheaper, but you may need more sessions of it. Lasers offer a more hardcore approach to pigment-busting and are very effective. They are likely to cost more, depending on how much treatment you need, but you may need fewer sessions than you would of IPL.

You will get the best results if you find a practitioner who really knows their machine(s) and has many years' experience in how to get the best out of it. With light treatments, as with so many other areas of aesthetics, it is the expertise of the practitioner that really makes the difference to the outcome.

Is There Any Regulation over Who Uses Lasers and IPL Machines?

No. Shocking but true. Practitioners who use cosmetic lasers don't have to be regulated; nor do their clinics. Clinics that use lasers for cosmetic purposes used to be regulated by the Care Quality Commission (CQC), but the regulations changed in 2010.

As with other types of cosmetic procedures, practitioners may have impressive-looking certificates of competence on display on their walls – but unless you know how long and demanding each course was that produced those qualifications, they may not mean much.

IPL and Laser Treatments for Pigmentation and Age Spots

The best-known tweakments for clearing excess skin pigment use light in different ways.

TREATMENT REVIEW: CLEARING PIGMENTATION AND AGE SPOTS WITH IPL: LUMECCA IPL WITH DR DAVID JACK

An IPL machine produces flashes of intense light that shatter brown or red pigment in the skin, so that the fragments of pigment can be cleared away by the body's lymphatic system. IPL is different to laser light in that its beams land at slightly different depths in the skin, whereas a laser beam lands at one specific depth, so IPL has more of a 'scattergun' effect. The treated spots look darker for a few days before they start to disappear. To get the best results usually requires two or three rounds of treatment.

What It Is

'IPL is quick and simple and one of the most effective treatments available,' says cosmetic tweakment specialist Dr David Jack. 'I tend to be fairly aggressive with Lumecca to get the best results as quickly as possible – it is one of the most advanced IPL systems and can treat red marks such as thread veins and rosacea as well as age spots.' Lumecca can be used on pale, olive, or light-brown skin, but not on darker skins; after treatment, it is vital to protect the skin with high-factor SPF.

What It's Like
By Victoria Fisher

I used to have brown age spots across my face where I had had freckles as a child, but what made me seek treatment was my permanently red nose. I thought I was going to end up as one of those old ladies with a bright red nose, and I wore a ton of concealer to cover it up.

Dr Jack tells me it is just sun damage from the past, and the first treatment definitely calms down the redness. At the second appointment, a few weeks later, he zaps my nose again and also the brown spots all over my face.

Comfort Level

Moderately uncomfortable. Each burst of light from the machine feels like having elastic bands flicked at my face, but it's not as bad as going to the dental hygienist. The treatment usually started gently, then he would turn up the intensity as much as I could take.

Verdict

I'm obsessed with this treatment, because it really works. It has definitely calmed down my red nose, and I feel my skin is softer and fresher, too. My brown spots have gone, and I feel I have shed 10 years off my face. When I look at old photos, I can really see the difference. It's such a nice, gentle way of rewinding time on your skin. I hardly use concealer now. Will I go back every six months for maintenance? You bet! And yes, I use a cream with high-factor SPF every single day now to help keep up the results.

Cost and Location

From £150 per treatment; several treatments may be needed. Dr David Jack, London W1, www.drdavidjack.com. To find a practitioner in your area, go to www.thetweakmentsguide.com.

Would It Work for Me?

Yes. IPL is great for reducing pigmentation, and the intensity of the treatment can be dialled down if you find it all too much.

Potential Problems

IPL treatment manages the appearance of dark spots rather than eradicating them forever, so treatment needs to be repeated every six or 12 months. Because the treatment targets pigment in the skin, it works best on paler skins. After treatment, you must protect the skin with high-factor SPF. IPL treatment can't be done if you have a tan – after sun exposure, clinics should make you wait for four weeks before treatment.

TREATMENT REVIEW: CLEARING PIGMENTATION WITH LASER: FRAXEL TREATMENT WITH DR NICK LOWE

Whether you are looking to improve age spots or general damage, laser is one of the most effective tweakments to do the job.

> This is a review of Fraxel on my décolletage, rather than my face, but because I tried this in order to clear pigmentation, I have included it here.

What It Is

The best-known laser for reducing pigmentation is Fraxel. This is a 'fractional' laser, which means that its beam is fired at the skin through a grid with pinprick holes in it. Using the grid means that, rather than scorching all the skin beneath it, the light energy drills a mass of tiny holes into the skin. These minute wounds create a healing response in the skin tissue, which generates collagen and growth factors to repair the skin; as this happens, old damaged and pigmented skin is forced up and out of the skin, where it flakes off.

Healing is faster than with a non-fractionated laser, because the 'fractions' of skin left intact between the holes help the skin's surface to repair itself more swiftly. The whole process clears a good deal of brown pigmentation marks from the skin and leaves it tighter, smoother, and fresher.

This is a tweakment to save for after the summer. Lasers makes your skin extra-sensitive to the sun – for many months, in my experience – and you need three sessions, a few weeks apart, for best results.

What It's Like

Quite hot and stinging. There isn't much padding on the décolletage, and even with numbing cream, I can feel each pulse of the laser all too clearly. Turning down the intensity of the laser makes it more tolerable.

My skin looks red and stung-up after the treatment, like a moderate sunburn, and takes several days to calm down. The next week, it looks freckly as the old bits of dead skin and pigment flake away, after which it looks miles better – softer and smoother and more even in tone. As instructed, I look after it with particular care, applying hydrating serums and sunscreen every day, as it is very sensitive to light.

Comfort Level

Challenging, as above.

Verdict

A great result which smoothed away a good deal of pigmentation in one treatment, but I didn't have the commitment to go back for a second round. I hadn't realized how sensitive my skin would be afterwards: even six months later, sitting out in the sun for a few minutes, my skin felt that it was beginning to burn, despite wearing sunscreen – a reminder to keep out of the sun or keep it covered up.

Cost and Location

Fraxel, from £875 at Dr Nick Lowe, Cranley Clinic, 106 Harley Street, London W1; www.cranleyclinic.com. To find a practitioner in your area, go to www.thetweakmentsguide.com.

Would This Work for Me?

Yes. Fraxel is one of the best known and most popular lasers for clearing pigmentation for a good reason – it works very well. As with other light-based treatments, you need to be careful about protecting your skin with SPF50 after treatment and about avoiding sun exposure. And as with IPL treatment, it won't get rid of pigmentation for ever. Your skin will carry on busily pushing out melanin whenever it gets the chance. Fraxel can be used with darker skin tones, but it will need to be used at a lower intensity, and with treatment spread out over several sessions.

POTENTIAL PROBLEMS

Treatment may sting a bit, even with anaesthetic cream, depending on how sensitive you are and the intensity of the treatment. Your skin may be red afterwards, possibly for a few days. If the laser isn't used incorrectly, it has the potential to burn the skin.

While lasers can reduce pigment in the skin, it is possible that treated areas can afterwards become hyperpigmented (over-pigmented).

Skin Peels

Some doctors and dermatologists aren't keen on using peels for pigmentation, but for others, including Dr Stefanie Williams, peels are a crucial part of managing pigmentation.

In case you're squirming from even reading the phrase 'skin peel', I'll hasten to add that today's skin peels are much kinder and gentler than the ones that were popular 20 years ago, which would basically burn away the top layer of your skin.

Most of the newer peels work more cautiously. One worth trying is the PRX-T33 Peel, an incomprehensibly-named treatment more commonly known as the 'no-peeling peel'. You may have read about it in the previous chapter (see page 130), as it's great for improving skin texture; it is also very good for treating pigmentation.

And then there are serious peels, like the new MelaOut, which Dr Williams offers as part of a thorough and carefully planned strategy to soften and clear a patient's pigmentation. MelaOut works for all but the very darkest skin types. It comes as part of a package that includes a digital face scan with a Visia machine to assess the extent of pigmentation (and another scan at the end of treatment, to assess how well everything has worked), a consultation, a follow-up dermatology-grade facial, and a month's worth of specialised skincare to support the work that the peel is doing. Protecting the skin is, as ever with pigmentation issues, crucial: as Dr Williams points out on her website, a single day of excess sun can undo the work of months of treatment.

The MelaOut peel itself uses a combination of ingredients which are known as effective pigment-busters (such as kojic acid, azelaic acid, arbutine, and niacinamide) and is able to give up to a 50 per cent improvement, or up to 80 per cent if you are scrupulous with the recommended skincare, too. If you're thinking this sounds little short of miraculous and wondering where the catch is – it might be in the fact that you need to factor in 7–10 days downtime afterwards. 'There is redness and tightening for the first few days, for about a week,' says Dr Williams, 'then the flaking starts, and can last from one to three weeks. Most people are fine to resume their normal daily activities after one or two weeks, so most patients take a week or two off work.' Other potential drawbacks are the cost (£1,500) and the need for scrupulous aftercare.

The MelaOut package costs £1,500 from Eudelo, London SW8; eudelo.com.

Would MelaOut work for you? Yes, though you need to be committed. 'The combination of in-clinic treatment and vital maintenance at home for about a year is crucial,' says Dr Williams, 'as irregular pigmentation is a chronic skin condition, and a one-off treatment may improve the issue but would likely result in relapse some months later if we don't take proper care of maintenance afterwards.'

What about potential problems with MelaOut? If you are prone to cold sores or acne, you need to see a dermatologist before the treatment, in order to work on a strategy to prevent breakouts after treatment. You can't have this peel if you are using roaccutane, if you have rosacea, if you have cancer, or if you are pregnant or breast-feeding.

MELASMA

Another form of pigmentation is melasma, the often butterfly-shaped 'mask' of dark pigment which is triggered by hormonal changes in the body and which can show up during pregnancy, or when using birth control pills or hormone replacement therapy, and which gets worse with exposure to UV light.

Melasma is dreaded by sufferers and dermatologists alike because, even after treatment, it is likely to recur. So rather than 'fixing' melasma, treatment is more a question of managing it, and managing it carefully and consistently can be a slow and frustrating business. Light treatments can help with melasma, as can peels and appropriate skincare. As ever, the best bet for a good result is to find an experienced practitioner who can supervise your treatment, move cautiously, and work out what works best for you.

Dr Nick Lowe warns against using stronger skincare ingredients such as retinol when treating melasma, because they can irritate the skin, and irritation is one of the triggers that sets melasma off. 'Irritation is a big problem because the inflammation it causes almost masks the pigment,' he says. 'Then, when you stop using the product because of the irritation it's causing, you get the rebound melasma.'

Sunscreen Layering for Melasma

You may have heard of the idea of 'layering' skin serums – if not, all it means is using two or more skin treatment serums which deliver different benefits, not by mixing them all together, but by applying one, letting it sink in to the skin, then adding the next, and so on. Here's a technique for layering sunscreens, which Dr Lowe recommends for patients with melasma. This is what he says:

'I ask patients to apply a UV-absorbing sunscreen first and then, if they are feeling dedicated, a tinted reflecting sunscreen on top, because one of the things we know about melasma is that heat can cause inflammation in the skin, and that makes melasma worse. And, ironically, UV-absorbing sunscreens trap the heat and increase the temperature in the skin, hence the need for the reflective sunscreen on top.'

So why not simply use the reflective sunscreen? 'Because these don't always have as broad a spectrum of protection as UV-absorbing sunscreens,' says Dr Lowe, 'so they can let through some of the long-wavelength UVA, which is what causes the pigment-ation issues in the skin in the first place.'

Worth Trying for Melasma: Tranexamic Acid

One other thing worth trying if you are struggling with melasma, and which both Dr Sheth and Dr Lowe recommend, is tranexamic acid, which is available without prescription from UK pharmacies. 'It is an oestrogen receptor blocker,' says Dr Lowe, 'which is used for reducing heavy menstrual bleeding. There is some good evidence that if you use tranexamic acid for three months just before starting a treatment programme either with creams or creams plus clinic treatment, it helps stop extra pigmentation occurring.'

Dr Lowe suggests taking a 500mg tablet twice a day, in the morning and at lunchtime, so that it is there in the skin during the daylight hours. Any drawbacks? He points out that, as with any form of oral contraception, there is always a theoretical risk of deep-vein thrombosis.

And it's going to be very much more difficult to improve anyone's melasma if they are still taking an oral contraceptive or if they have a hormone IUD – because that's prompting ongoing pigmentation in the skin.

CHAPTER 9

Thread Veins, Rosacea and Redness, Large Pores, Acne

Aside from the lines and wrinkles, poor skin texture and pigmentation that I've talked about already, there are a few other things that stop your skin tone looking as clear and smooth as it might: thread veins, skin redness, large pores and acne. Most of us have an issue with one or other of them, and there is a lot that cosmetic practitioners can do to help you tackle each of them.

THREAD VEINS

These tiny veins, which show up as thin red lines on the face and which tend to congregate around the nose and across the cheeks, are another of the unwelcome marks that age leaves on the skin. Very unfairly, thread veins seem to be much more common among women than men, because hormonal changes seem to affect them. They're often referred to as 'broken veins', though really they're just minute veins which have become enlarged over the years, making them more visible.

Why Do I Have Thread Veins?

Getting thread veins is partly genetic, which is just bad luck, and partly due to lifestyle. Too much exposure to ultraviolet light (that's bright sunshine and/or just daylight), to wind, or to extremes of temperature all age the skin; and like the skin, thread veins lose their elasticity with age. If your skin flushes red easily, the repeated stretching of the veins means they can lose that elasticity faster; and once the veins stay enlarged, they become visible on your face.

Skincare can't help with thread veins, though depending on how obvious they are, you can cover them up with a well-pigmented concealer. The good news is that treating thread veins is not only straightforward but actually gets rid of them. The bad news? The skin will doubtless produce more thread veins as it gets older – but if it does, you'll know what to do about them.

Can Skincare Help Treat Thread Veins?

Not in any meaningful way. Some skincare products may temporarily shrink the thread veins a little, but they will not clear the veins.

Treatments to Get Rid of Thread Veins

Because thread veins present themselves with a handy bunch of visible pigment inside them – in this case, haemoglobin – they can be treated in the same way as you would treat pigmentation.

INTENSE PULSED LIGHT TREATMENT FOR THREAD VEINS

Intense pulsed light (IPL) is very effective on thread veins, because the light energy is attracted to the red haemoglobin pigment in the veins, and breaks it up, so that the body can disperse it. You will probably need more than one treatment, depending on the extent of the veins. To get an idea of the treatment experience, see page 171 for the case study who tried IPL for brown spots and found it also cleared her thread veins.

LASER TREATMENT FOR THREAD VEINS

Aesthetic practitioner Victoria Smith at the Whiteley Clinic in central London has three ways of tackling thread veins: 'I would classify the veins depending on their size, their location, and their colour, and would choose treatment accordingly,' she says.

The first means of treatment is electrosurgery, which, like electrolysis, involves using a fine needle and is best for bright red superficial veins around the nostrils and on the cheeks. The process uses diathermy, alternating currents of electricity and heat, so it is effectively cauterising the skin; because the veins are right on the surface, the needle is just placed on the skin rather than injected into the skin. You will get blanching for a few days after this, where the treated vein goes white, then a small crust forms in the area; when the crust falls off, which may take up to a week, the vein should already be gone.

If a client shows up with diffuse redness across the face, that is more likely to be rosacea, which Victoria would treat with the second means of treatment, IPL (see the section 'Treating Rosacea with Skincare and Light Treatments' on page 184). The third means of treatment is the Fotona laser, which she would use on broader red veins on the face; this is what she used on me to remove small veins around my nose.

TREATMENT REVIEW: REMOVING THREAD VEINS WITH FOTONA LASER

Lasering thread veins is a quick and effective way to clear them. If you're wondering where the catch is, it's not exactly pain-free.

What It Is

Lasers are calibrated to fire their concentrated beams of light at a certain wavelength to a certain depth in the skin. To disperse thread veins, aesthetic practitioner Victoria Smith uses a Fotona laser, which will hit the haemoglobin, the red pigment in my thread veins, and shatter it to smithereens. My thread veins are small but obvious, so they are easy prey for a laser. A few quick zaps, and they will be on their way to oblivion, though it may take a week for them to vanish.

What It's Like

I know this is going to be quick, and I also know that because the veins are around the sides of my nose, it is not going to be comfortable. Of all the areas of the face to stab with a needle or zap with a laser, the nose is the most sensitive. Victoria knows this too and is apologising in advance as she homes in on each tiny vein. 'I don't usually use numbing cream for this,' she explains, 'not because I am cruel, but because the treatment is so quick, and the majority of people can actually tolerate it without. Also, when using a laser, if there is cream on the skin it can increase the risk of burns or blisters, and I always try to do everything to minimise risks.'

There are four of these tiny veins, and each needs two or three zaps to despatch it. The first zap gives me such a jolt that I jump, and we both need to take a breath and steady ourselves before going on to the next ones. I get a grip on myself and hold still, and

Victoria leans in close and polishes each vein off in turn with a rapid-fire zap-zap-zap action, to get it over with. It's not fun, and my eyes are watering from the pain, but it is all over in a couple of minutes, and we both collapse laughing with relief when it's all done.

Comfort Level

Remarkably uncomfortable, but each zap of the laser is very, very quick.

Verdict

Very effective: the tiny veins gradually vanish as the broken pigment within them is dispersed by my body over the next week, so it is absolutely worth the very short-lived stabs of pain.

Cost and Location

Laser thread vein removal (or IPL, or electrosurgery) costs from £200 a session, depending on the extent of the treatment area, at The Whiteley Clinic, www.whiteleyclinics.co.uk. To find a practitioner in your area, go to www.thetweakmentsguide.com.

Would It Work for Me?

Yes. Laser is very effective on clearing thread veins.

Potential Problems

This treatment uses laser, which obviously can burn the skin if it's used inappropriately – so, as ever, make sure your practitioner knows what they are doing. Another potential problem is that if laser is overused, it can provoke rebound pigmentation in the skin.

The treated veins will take a while to vanish as the body clears away the debris of the shattered pigment, so have patience. One treatment should be enough, but it is possible you might need more than one.

ROSACEA AND SKIN REDNESS

When there is a little bit of redness across your nose and cheeks, maybe not always, but more often than not... how do you know whether it is a normal, healthy colour or whether it's a bit of a problem? It can be hard to tell, given that we have all grown up thinking that 'getting a bit of colour in our cheeks' is a good thing.

And skin just does go red when it's provoked. Exercise, sunshine, and heat will do the trick, as will stress and embarrassment. That sort of redness is normal. But if a flushed colour persists, or you get ruddy patches that flare up occasionally, or you get flare-ups accompanied by a rash of spots, here's the news: you might have rosacea.

What Is Rosacea?

Rosacea is an unfortunate skin problem known as 'the Curse of the Celts' because it is most obvious on pale skin. A cosmetic dermatologist will tell you that rosacea is a chronic condition that mainly affects the convex surfaces of the face – the cheeks, chin, nose, and forehead. They will also tell you that rather than being some kind of sensitivity in the skin, it is a disease of the oil glands, so it's similar to acne. The excess oil causes inflammation in the skin which leads to redness and spots.

What Does Rosacea Look Like?

One of the odd things about rosacea is that it can make the skin feel rough and dry rather than oily, and it is widely under-diagnosed. Then there's the way that not all rosacea looks the same. The tricky thing with identifying rosacea is that it shows up in many different forms. Apart from making the face look flushed, rosacea can show up as tiny raised red bumps or acne-type pustules, or an increased number of thread veins on the face. Add to that the way it tends to come and go, and you can see why it is tricky to spot, and why it isn't diagnosed as quickly or as often as it should be.

Rosacea can be very mild, where your skin just has the odd tendency to flush – or it can be very obvious and persistent. It tends not to be obvious before the age of 30, and it tends to get worse the older you get.

What Makes Rosacea Worse?

If this is starting to sound familiar, you will already know that it doesn't take much to make rosacea kick off. Common triggers include many of the normal things that make life fun, such as coffee, alcohol, spicy food, hot baths, and particularly sunshine – another reason for wearing an SPF every day.

What Can Be Done About Rosacea?

You might be wondering why I am including rosacea in this book when it is clearly a skin condition rather than anything to do with ageing. But as anyone who struggles with rosacea will know, it's not just maddening to have a red flush across your face, but those flushed capillaries can settle in and become persistently obvious thread veins, and the weathered look that those veins give to a face does make it look older. If the redness settles around the nose, it's a look that's – unfairly – associated with hardened drinkers; in fact, drinking too much alcohol doesn't cause the redness, but it does dilate the blood vessels that are there, so it makes an existing problem more obvious.

But using the right skincare can help you manage rosacea, and backing this up with redness-reducing light treatments can minimise the appearance of the rosacea. They're not a permanent fix, so the redness will come back, and you'll need to have treatment again, but least you'll get some respite.

Treating Rosacea with Skincare and Light Treatments

Cosmetic doctors concentrate on repairing the damaged skin barrier with specialized skincare and quelling redness with high-tech light treatments. Dr Mervyn Patterson of the Woodford Medical Clinic has a special interest in rosacea. He is keen on the Epionce Lytic skincare range, and backs this up with intense pulsed light (IPL) treatment, which reduces redness in the skin by destroying the tiny thread veins that appear on the skin's surface; fewer thread veins means that, when the skin does next flush red, it will be less obvious. It's the sort of treatment that's uncomfortable rather than acutely painful, and it's very effective.

'The best option is to have a course of IPL or laser treatment to reduce thread veins,' says Dr Patterson. 'Nothing in the past decade has emerged which is better than this for reducing the number of blood vessels in the skin – no skin cream can actually remove blood vessels from the face.' A course will mean three or more treatments, depending on how severe your problem is, done a month apart.

Here are two practitioners who specialise in treating rosacea:

- Dr Mervyn Patterson treats rosacea with laser or IPL treatment. From £195 per session (several will be needed), www.woodfordmedical.com.

- Similarly, Victoria Smith at the Whiteley Clinic in London combines specialised therapeutic skincare with light treatments. She recommends using a vitamin C serum and a specialised moisturiser such as Obagi Hydrate along with an SPF, and avoiding glycolic acid or salicylic acid, along with a course of IPL (from £150) or Dermalux or LED therapy (from £40 a session). For more on LED red light therapy, which is very comfortable, see page 123. A course of Dermalux involves four weeks of treatment with three 20-minute sessions a week; it's relaxing, but time-consuming. Victoria Smith, www.whiteleyclinics.co.uk.

Using Laser to Reduce Skin Redness

As you have probably grasped, laser light is also good for reducing redness in the skin, and not all lasers are uncomfortable. Here's a review of treatment with the VBeam Perfecta laser, which works well on a wide range of conditions including inflamed acne, thread veins, rosacea, port wine stain birthmarks, red stretch marks, and red raised scars.

TREATMENT REVIEW: REDUCING SKIN REDNESS WITH THE VBEAM
PERFECTA LASER

The VBeam Perfecta isn't a new laser – it's an old-style pulse-dye laser – but it has evolved over the past 20 years into such a reliable workhorse that one London cosmetic doctor, who has around 30 lasers to choose from in his practice, told me that if there was a fire, this was the one he would make sure to save, just because it was so very useful.

What It Is

Unlike most lasers, which use their concentrated beams of light to heat up the skin in various ways, the VBeam Perfecta uses a gentler wavelength of light that targets redness in the skin. The light breaks up and disperses the red blood cells – which are what is causing the redness on the surface of your face – without damaging the rest of the skin.

What It's Like

I am hustled under the VBeam after a previous skin treatment has left my skin looking horribly red and flushed. I can't believe that a laser wouldn't just do more harm. But Dr Sach Mohan explains that not only is the VBeam very gentle, but its raison d'être is to remove redness from the skin – and so it does, instantly and painlessly. Wherever he applies the head of the laser to my face, the redness vanishes, as if he had used an eraser. My skin, which had looked angry and red, is almost completely pale again after a quick 30-minute treatment.

Comfort Level

Completely comfortable. Phew.

Verdict

Little short of miraculous. I can see why it is so helpful in treating so many other conditions where redness is an issue. I'm told some people experience bruising from this treatment, but I certainly didn't. My skin only needed one session to bring it back to normal, but Dr Mohan explained that more persistent conditions may need several treatments to reduce redness.

Cost and Location

From £125, www.revereclinics.com. To find a practitioner in your area, go to www.thetweakmentsguide.com.

Would It Work for Me?

Almost certainly, yes, though treating rosacea is an inexact science. But it will certainly reduce the redness for a time.

Potential Problems

Few – VBeam is easy to tolerate, and its pulses calm the skin rather than inflaming it.

LARGE, OBVIOUS PORES AND WHAT TO DO ABOUT THEM

Some of us just do have large pores. Or pores that are much more visible than we'd like them to be. This isn't a health hazard, although if your pores, like mine, are bigger than average, big enough for facialists always to comment on them and set about cleaning them out, you're probably well aware of them and wish they were less obvious.

Why Do We Get Large Pores?

The size of your pores is determined by your genes, and if you feel your pores are on the larger side, particularly over your nose and chin and forehead, it is usually because you have oilier skin. If the sebum, the oil that your skin produces to help keep itself lubricated, flows freely out of your pores, all is fine. But it is when pores become blocked with a combination of old dead skin cells and oil, which oxidises into a black plug known as a blackhead, that's when you really start to notice them.

As so often with skin issues, things tend to get worse as you get older. The skin becomes less good at making collagen, the supportive protein that gives skin its structure, and that slight slackening means that pores dilate a fraction and appear bigger, so if you're getting older and you've been wondering whether your pores are larger than they used to be, or whether you're imagining it – I'm afraid you're not. Your pores really are growing, just a tiny bit but inexorably, by the year.

Managing Large Pores with Skincare

The key to managing large pores with skincare is to do your best to keep them clean, because when plugs of sebum build up in a pore, they tend to stretch the pore which, unsurprisingly, makes that pore more obvious. To help here, use products that reduce oiliness and then strengthen the skin with collagen-building treatments (see below) which will firm up your face and make pores appear smaller.

FIRST, EXFOLIATE

Gentle exfoliation is vital, to get rid of the dead skin cells that clutter up the skin's surface and to begin to wear away the surface of the blackheads. There are two ways to exfoliate, either physically or chemically.

A physical exfoliation uses a face scrub with small smooth particles – *not* microbeads, which are now by law being removed from skincare – such as Dr Levy's 3-Deep Cellular Renewal Microresurfacing Cleanser (£39, www.cultbeauty.co.uk). I like this particular cleanser because it also contains glycolic acid, the benefits of which I'll explain in a sec, and if you leave it on for five minutes, like a mask, it gives a deeper glycolic exfoliation. Any cheaper facial scrub will also do the trick, but please do be gentle with it so that you don't ruin your skin barrier. When you're using a scrub, use it lightly once or twice a week and think of it as polishing the surface of your face, rather than scrubbing. You don't want to scratch or tear the skin.

What I generally prefer is a chemical exfoliation of the face, partly because it avoids all the scrubbing or polishing, with a product based on glycolic or salicylic acid. These acids aren't as harsh as they might sound. Glycolic acid is an alpha-hydroxy acid (AHA), a water-soluble acid that gently dissolves the bonds that hold old dead skin cells onto the skin's surface, so wiping your face over with a glycolic product exfoliates it without scrubbing.

The following list gives four examples of chemical exfoliation products. Using any of these twice a week will do the trick.

- **Alpha-H Liquid Gold** (£33.50, www.marksandspencer.com)

- **31st State Overnight Clearing Pads** (£15.99, 31st-state.com). This is a range aimed at spotty teen boys, but it's just as good for their menopausal mums. The pads contain lactic acid, a milder sort of AHA than glycolic.
- **Pixi Glow Tonic** (£18.50, pixibeauty.co.uk)
- **Superdrug Naturally Radiant Glycolic Tonic** (£5.99 from Superdrug)

Face scrubs or alpha-hydroxy acids will sweep away dead cells on the skin's surface. That may be enough for you, but if you have an issue with oily skin, what you really need to do is to clean out the pores themselves, and the best home-use product for this is salicylic acid.

Salicylic acid is a beta-hydroxy acid (in fact, it's the only beta-hydroxy acid) and it is fat soluble, which means it can actually weasel its way into clogged, oily pores and clean them out while also exfoliating the surface of the skin. Here are two great salicylic acid products:

- **Paula's Choice Skin Perfecting 2% BHA Liquid Exfoliant** (£25, www.paulaschoice.co.uk). This is my go-to salicylic. There's also a 1% strength if you want to start gently.
- **Nip+Fab Teen Skin Breakout Rescue Pads** (£10 for 60, www.nipandfab.com). These pads are soaked in salicylic acid. They're easy to use and great value.

REDUCE SKIN OILINESS

One effective way to reduce oil-production at source is to use a retinol-based product (eg the ZO Instant Pore Refiner, £60, zo-skinhealth.co.uk). As well as slowing down the oil output, retinol-based products (I've mentioned some of these in the section 'Retinol Products to Try' on page 92) will also speed up the sluggish cell turnover in older skin, improve collagen production, and bring newer, stronger skin cells up to the surface.

KICK-START COLLAGEN PRODUCTION

The third thing to do to counteract middle-aged pores and the way they tend to spread out in mid-life is to try one of the many treatments that kick-starts collagen production. Needling treatments (or home-use needling), radiofrequency treatments, and lasers will all help here. With each of them, you will get an immediate improvement from the slight shrinking of the collagen that the treatment causes, followed by a further improvement over the next few months as the new collagen formed deep in the skin as a result of the trauma of the treatment is produced and rises to the surface. And that all means smaller, neater, less noticeable pores.

Managing Large Pores with Tweakments

There are plenty of facialists and skin clinics that offer deep-cleansing treatments that will really muck out the pores, after which your skin will look fresher and clearer. This is usually done with gentle steaming, which is not, as is popularly supposed, to dilate the pores (they're not like flowers, they don't open and close) but to soften the blocked oil that is stuck in them. After that the softened blackheads are extracted. The facialist either squeezes them out gently (it's not comfortable, but it is effective), or vacuums them out with a suction device.

Pore-shrinking tweakments take this to the next level, so that your pores will seem vanishingly tiny and you will feel you have given your skin a quick 'reset'. The following treatments can all help with this.

THE DEEP CLEANSING FACIAL WITH MICRONEEDLING

Mayfair-based celebrity facialist Chelseé Lewis has a low tolerance for blocked pores. She combines old-fashioned steaming and extraction techniques with wonderful lymph-draining, circulation-boosting massage, then uses a Dermapen, a microneedling device which oscillates 120 times a minute and with each oscillation, drives its tiny needles into the skin to stimulate a wound-healing process. The point of the needling is to boost collagen levels, strengthen the skin, and thus reduce pores.

This facial costs £425 from www.chelseelewis.co.uk.

SKIN LAUNDRY LIGHT AND LASER TREATMENT

This treatment (see page 66 for the full write-up) involves two 'passes' over the face using an Erbium YAG laser on a very low setting followed by one pass of intense pulsed light all over the face. The laser helps pores by vaporising the dirt, oil, and bacteria that get trapped in them. Vaporising? Yes, destroying them and turning them into vapour. There's a slightly queasy-making frying smell as this happens.

This treatment leaves pores cleaner and skin looking noticeably brighter and more refined in just 15 minutes. If you repeat the treatment regularly, you'll see the collagen-building effects of the laser and IPL at work strengthening skin and pores, too.

The Skin Laundry treatment costs £60 (though the first treatment is free), at Liberty, London W1, skinlaundry.com.

TREATMENT REVIEW: DR JONEY DE SOUZA'S PORE PATROL

Alternatively, you could Botox your pores into submission with this no-holds-barred pore-blasting treatment, which first gives your skin and your pores a deep cleaning like they never knew was possible, then adds in Botox for an oil-reduction finale.

What It Is

A deep-cleansing peel combined with microdermabrasion, radiofrequency, IPL, and Botox injections. Botoxing your pores sounds like overkill, but for people who are really concerned about their complexions, Botox adds an extra dimension to the task of pore management by reducing the oiliness of the skin where it is injected. These injections aren't the deeper sort that are usually done in the face muscles to stop frowning, but the really shallow sort that are used for treating excessive sweating (a condition called hyperhidrosis). Those injections work by preventing the nerves that tell the sweat glands to perspire from communicating their message and, though the precise mechanism by which shallow injections of Botox reduce oiliness in the skin isn't yet fully understood, it is known to be one of its effects.

It was when Dr Joney de Souza found that patients, whose foreheads he was injecting to reduce sweatiness, told him that their foreheads were much less oily, too, that he had the idea of injecting the oilier areas of the face to help reduce pore blockages.

What It's Like

Before Dr Joney will Botox my oily nose, he wants the pores to be super-clean, so I spend a happy hour with his aesthetic nurse and laser expert, who paints on a salicylic acid mask to soften the blockages (it doesn't sting), then uses a gentle microdermabrasion device to vacuum out the debris. Next, she gives my whole face a once-over with a radiofrequency (RF) device which heats up the skin tissue until it gets to the point (42 degrees) where the collagen contracts and tightens. Because the skin thinks it is being injured, a repair process is kick-started, which will gradually produce more supportive collagen over the next couple of months.

The RF feels warm but not uncomfortable, and the intense pulsed light (IPL) that comes afterwards, for more skin-strengthening and collagen boosting, is a bit like having my face flicked, but not painful. Then the nurse drapes a cloth mask saturated with hydrating serum over my face and switches on a canopy of red LED lights, which have a soothing effect and a (small) collagen-boosting effect too.

Finally, it is time for Dr Joney to administer the Botox, which he does quickly and neatly, landing his needle right into the worst offenders among the pores on my nose. Yes, it hurts a bit – enough to make my eyes water – but it is mercifully quick. Dr Joney recommends that I start using the ZO Instant Pore Refiner (see the section 'Reduce Skin Oiliness' on page 189) at home to make my skin generally less oily.

Comfort Level

Most of the treatment is very comfortable. If you have Botox injections on the nose, as I did, these are definitely not comfortable, but they are very quick.

Verdict

Very impressive. My pores are cleaner – and less visible – than I have ever seen them. Over the next few weeks, they stay much less obvious and are also much less prone to becoming clogged with gunk, which must mean that the Botox has reduced the prodigious oil output from my nose. This could prove addictive.

Cost and Location

£300, Dr Joney de Souza, London W1, www.drjoneydesouza.com.

Would This Work for Me?

Probably – and the oilier your skin is in the area that is being injected with Botox, the more of a result you should see. What I really loved was the pore-cleansing preparation. That will surely work for anyone.

Potential Problems

Few likely problems. If you find the masks stings, it can be whisked off, or if the RF treatment is uncomfortable, the intensity can be turned down. You are unlikely to get a bruise from injections into the nose, but you might get a bruise if you are having your forehead injected.

SPOTS: ADULT ACNE

Why oh why? If you're one of the many women who finds that spots are still a problem as you move through your thirties, forties, and fifties, and wonders how Mother Nature can be so bitter as to make it possible to still have acne-type blemishes when you are closer to the menopause than you are to puberty – well, it's not much comfort, but you are not alone.

Adult acne – doctors class it all as acne, whether it's a few occasional spots or a mass of inflamed pustules – is on the increase, and doctors and dermatologists tend to point the finger at many contributing factors in our modern lifestyles.

Spots are at root a hormonal problem, and they are most likely to emerge when your hormone levels fluctuate, as they do every month, or when starting or stopping taking contraceptive pills, or in the run-up to menopause, or when you start taking hormone replacement therapy (HRT) or bio-identical hormones (BHRT).

Stress doesn't help, nor does going short on sleep, which both ramp up levels of cortisol (the stress hormone) and androgens (male hormones), making your skin produce more oil – and making it more likely that pores will become blocked and inflamed.

Eating too much sugar will make a tendency for spottiness worse, too, since digesting sugar leads to spikes in insulin levels, which in turn prompts the release of more androgens. Drinking too much sugar, either as fizzy drinks or in the form of alcohol, has much the same effect.

Keep those thoughts in mind as you look at the more direct, topical ways you can tackle blemishes.

Skincare to Reduce Spots

There's a great deal you can do to reduce spots with skincare, and the following advice is just the tip of the iceberg, as this book is more about treatments. Whether you favour all-natural products or prefer to go straight to the sort of heavy hitters that dermatologists recommend, the aim is the same: to reduce levels of skin oiliness, keep pores clear, and not clog them up with the wrong sort of products.

I've still got skin that is on the oily side, at least down the centre panel of my face, where the more obvious pores congregate. The following sections explain the things that I find most helpful.

FACE WASH

Use a face wash that removes excess oil without stripping the skin, such as one of these:

- **Neostrata Foaming Glycolic Wash** (£23, www.skincity.co.uk
- **Nip & Fab Glycolic Fix Foaming Facial Cleanser** (£7.95, www.nipandfab.com)
- **Alex Steinherr Pore Balance Cleanser** (£4, Primark)

These will give your skin a mini exfoliation whenever you use them. If you prefer a creamy cleanser, I find Liz Earle's Hot Cloth Cleanse & Polish (£16.50, uk.lizearle.com) does a great job, works on all skin types, and helps to balance troublesome skin. You massage this cleanser on and wipe it off with a rinsed-out (clean!) flannel.

SALICYLIC ACID TONER OR SERUM

Experiment with a salicylic acid toner or serum – my favourite is Paula's Choice Skin Perfecting 2% BHA Liquid Exfoliant (£25, www.paulaschoice.co.uk). Or you might fancy Estee Lauder's Clear Difference Advanced Blemish Serum (£63, esteelauder.co.uk).

I said it above but I'll say it again: why I'm so keen on salicylic acid is that it is 'lipophilic', ie it dissolves in oil, and so it is the only skincare ingredient that reaches into pores and cleans them out, so it is hugely helpful for managing blemishes and skin oiliness and stopping pores from becoming clogged.

Another product worth trying is La Roche Posay Serozinc solution, which contains spot-calming zinc sulphate (£5, larocheposay.co.uk).

HYDRATING SERUM

Consider adding a hydrating serum to your skincare regime – because even if your skin is producing too much oil, it still needs moisture. It might sound unlikely, but it is quite possible to have skin that is both oily and dehydrated at the same time, because skin that is short on moisture and feels dry will start producing more oil to try to hold onto what little water there is within it.

Any light serum based on hyaluronic acid (HA), which is superhydrating and adds no oil to skin, will do the trick. Here are four suggestions:

- **Garden of Wisdom Hyaluronic Acid Serum** (£9, www.victoriahealth.com)
- **Beaskincare Vitamin C and Hyaluronic Acid Serum** (£49, www.bea-skincare.com)
- **Indeed Labs Hydraluron Moisture Booster Face Serum** (£24.95, www.boots.com)
- **Dr Sebagh Serum Repair** (£69, www.drsebagh.com)

SUNSCREEN

Finish off with sunscreen – you really need a sunscreen, too, because acne is an inflammatory skin condition and, guess what, all inflammatory skin conditions are made worse by exposing them to ultraviolet light. When you have skin with a tendency to break out, you need to find a sunscreen that is light enough not to clog pores and make things worse. These ones are some of my favourites:

- **Effaclar Duo SPF30** (£16, www.laroche-posay.co.uk)
- **Paula's Choice Resist Anti-Ageing Skin Restoring Moisturiser SPF50** (£33, www.paulaschoice.co.uk)
- **Exuviance Sheer Daily Protector SPF50** (£30, www.skincity.co.uk)

NIGHT TREATMENT WITH RETINOL

Using a vitamin-A derivative such as retinol at night can really help skin that is prone to spots. Retinol and other retinoids help by reducing the oiliness of the skin and preventing pores from becoming clogged, as well as stimulating the growth of new collagen that will help heal blemishes. See the section 'Add a Vitamin A Cream for Regeneration' on page 88 for more detail and for product suggestions.

LIGHT TREATMENTS

Blue LED light can be very helpful for reducing spottiness in the skin, because this has an antibacterial effect: the light denatures the proteins that bind the bacteria together. A 20-minute session will kill most of the *Propionibacterium acnes* bacteria on the skin which cause acne. Red LED light is great for acne, too, as it calms inflammation in the skin and helps promote healing.

This treatment is effective, but it needs to be done consistently; a dermatologist will offer sessions two or three times a week, and this is a hard schedule to stick to unless you live close to the clinic. I've tried this in the past and found it effective – all you have to do is turn up, lie on the treatment couch, and relax while the light glows at your face. It's a cool light, so it doesn't even feel warm.

There are home-use blue-light devices that can help with acne. Neutrogena's Visibly Clear Light Therapy Acne mask offers blue and red light combined, along with claims that 98% of the participants in a study who used it for 10 minutes a day for 30 days all saw reductions in acne. The device is a very reasonable £59.99, but you need to buy a new 'activator' battery pack every month (around £15). See page 80 for a review of the Visibly Clear Light Therapy Acne Mask. The Foreo Espada device (£129) homes in on individual spots with focussed blue light, so you need to apply it spot by spot, and do it regularly, but also has good data showing that it gets results.

While blue light will bring down bacteria levels on the skin, it won't help remove the underlying, usually hormonal issues that are making your spots kick off in the first place.

SALICYLIC ACID PEEL

A peel sounds aggressive and the last thing that you would want to do to irritable, blemished skin, but a salicylic acid peel is more of a deep-cleansing mask than a peel. Because salicylic acid is fat-soluble, it can melt its way into blocked pores and gently exfoliate the dead skin cells at the surface that are provoking the blockages. It's also anti-inflammatory, so helps to calm down the redness that comes with spots. Clinics like Sk:nclinics (www.sknclinics.co.uk) offer salicylic peels from £120.

ACNE SCARS AND POST-INFLAMMATORY HYPERPIGMENTATION

More aggressive light treatments such as lasers can be useful for repairing skin that has been left with pitted scars as a result of acne. Here, you need to take the advice of an expert practitioner who has assessed your skin and who can explain how their particular laser can work to stimulate the growth of new collagen and elastin in the skin below the scar, to soften its appearance.

Here are two other tweakments that can help with pigmentation left by acne scarring:

- Microneedling (see page 58)
- Skin peeling (see page 62)

CHAPTER 10

Reshaping the Face with Fillers

When your face starts losing its youthful volume, it's such a slow and stealthy process that you tend not to notice it until someone else remarks on it, or you look in the mirror and have what one friend described as 'a horror moment' of realising that everything seems to have has changed.

I had originally called this chapter 'Reviving a tired face', but that seemed too euphemistic, though being too direct and calling it 'Plumping up a gaunt or hollow face' sounds hideous. It is somewhere between the two. But to get to the point, it is all about what you can do for the face with facial fillers, both to restore lost volume and to improve its proportions, and why I'm shilly-shallying around like this is that most people who are considering tweakments are deeply wary of fillers.

So what I'm going to do in this chapter is, first, explain why older faces start to look gaunt and how facial fillers can make a huge difference. I also give you the entire lowdown on facial fillers, because it is essential you understand fully before you commit to any treatments with them.

Once you know how to choose suitable fillers and how they're used, the next section takes a look at the filler-based tweakments available for different problem areas of the face. I've written these up as a series of one-off treatments – treating hollow eyes, replumping cheeks, softening thinning lips, and so on – in order to give an idea of what each particular treatment is like. But I also explain how leading practitioners now treat the face as a whole in order to create harmony in it. So even if you go for a consultation with one very specific aim, it is worth keeping an open mind to your practitioner's suggestions, because they may be able to achieve the result you want in various ways.

WHY DO OLDER FACES START TO LOOK GAUNT?

You don't suddenly start looking all gaunt and hollow-cheeked overnight, but like many other aspects of ageing, this one creeps up on you gradually as the fat pads that have been filling out your face start shrinking, usually in your early 40s.

Why Losing Your Fat Pads Hurts Your Face

Even if you don't have a particularly plump face, you have around 20 of these useful fat pads in the cheeks, under the eyes, around the temples, and down to the chin. The ones under the eyes are the first to go, which makes the eyes a bit sunken; then the cheeks begin to look less full, which is the point at which you start noticing the change. To add insult to injury, some of these pads, maybe those ones under the eyes or the ones around the jaw, may drift south a bit from their original moorings, leading to pouchy bags under the eyes or a jowly jaw.

What makes the whole process more noticeable is that these shrinking fat pads lead to less volume in the face (imagine the fat pads as a series of tiny balloons holding up your skin, but balloons from which the air is slowly escaping), which makes the skin appear looser and more likely to sag and crease into folds. If your younger face was on the solid side, as mine was, the reduction in volume is not always a bad thing; I was amazed to discover some cheekbone definition in my forties, though now that I'm halfway through my fifties, I definitely have a tendency to look gaunt. If nature has just given you a fatter face, you may yet have the last laugh, as all that padding will last longer. But losing volume around the eyes and the chin is less amusing.

Why Bone Loss Is a Bother, Too

Another aspect of ageing that doesn't help is the way that we also lose bone mass in the face as we age – from the temples, around the eye sockets, along the jaw and chin, and around the mouth. The result is that everything in the face gradually starts to collapse inwards.

This is all very natural, but it's not great, is it? And all this loss of volume and support is exacerbated by any mid-life dieting or strenuous exercise regimes designed to reduce fat levels all over the body. Stripping back your fat percentage may be great for your waistline, but it isn't so kind on your midface. This is what lies behind the old maxim that once a woman reaches 40, she has to choose between her face and her figure. Hang on to a few extra pounds, and your face should look softer; diet them away, and it will swiftly look older.

WHAT CAN SKINCARE DO?

Skincare can't help to revolumise a face that is starting to look gaunt. Even if creams or make-up promise a 'plumping' effect, what they are talking about is plumping up the skin. For sure, that will make the skin look softer and less wrinkly, but even plumped-up skin cells are only fractions of a millimetre thick and won't do anything to replace the volume that has been lost beneath the surface.

WHAT ABOUT FACE EXERCISES?

Facial exercises may help by keeping the face muscles firmer and springier, which in turn stop the face getting that look of imminent collapse. I say 'may' because, for every beauty expert who advocates face exercise, from Eva Fraser and Carole Maggio to Danielle Collins with her face yoga and Carme Ferre with her facial pilates, there's an equally vociferous expert who feels the exact opposite.

The anti–face-exercisers (including skincare expert Paula Begoun and cosmetic surgery expert Wendy Lewis) feel that over-working the face muscles will only increase the likelihood of wrinkles from stretching and pulling the skin, which is in any case losing elasticity as it ages. And besides, they say, it's loss of volumising fat and loss of supportive collagen that is making the face look old, not loss of muscle definition.

Leading London cosmetic surgeon Rajiv Grover says that from entirely unscientific observations over the course of his career, it seems to him that the people who do facial exercises look better as they age than the ones who don't. Me? I really don't know. The exercise evangelists are very persuasive, but I have never been able to properly learn or stick to any of their regimes. I'll leave you to make your own decision.

BUT BACK TO WHAT *CAN* BE DONE – WITH FACIAL FILLERS

Revolumising the face can work wonders to restore a bit of youthful softness, and this is where facial fillers, gels that are injected into the face, come in. If you hear talk of people having 'liquid face lifts', it will be facial fillers (which are technically gels, rather than liquids) that are doing the lifting.

If you want to get straight to the treatment reviews of different types of filler treatments for different areas of the face, they start on page 222, but I'd strongly recommend you read the following pages before you move on to that.

Why You Might Be Scared of Fillers

Fillers! They are the f-word when it comes to non-surgical procedures. Having written about this whole area for a long time, and having had treatment with fillers over this time, I didn't think that they were such a big deal. But over the past few years, cosmetic doctors have told me that when new patients come to see them, the one thing that scares those patients witless is not Botox, but fillers.

Why? Because we've all seen what happens when a face has too much filler injected into it. The hamster-cheeked celebs and actresses suffering a bad case of 'pillow face' – where the face looks like an overstuffed pillow. Duck-bill lips, injected so much that they project forwards in a bizarre way. Slug-like lips that have simply been over-filled. These horrors and more are fodder for TV programmes like Botched! and the Instagram videos of doctors who repair badly done work with fillers.

Little wonder that people are wary. What is it about fillers that makes people so scared of them? I spoke to Dr Tracy Mountford of the Cosmetic Skin Clinic, who has been injecting faces for 25 years and who has perfected the art of reassuring patients, as well as getting optimum results.

'Patients tend to be scared of fillers because they are frightened of looking too puffy or overfilled,' says Dr Mountford. 'Also, they don't understand the new concepts of strategic multiple syringe filling which helps to generate lift, not "puff", in the face.

'People still see celebrities who look weird and overdone, and therefore they just don't believe treatments can look natural. Once they see our before-and-after case study pictures, they understand what we are doing, and how we achieve natural results.

'And once they try a filler, and it is done the right way – they love it!'

Why You Shouldn't Be Scared of Fillers

Because the right fillers, in the right hands, can give fabulous results. I'm a big fan of what can be done with fillers. There's no need to be scared as long as you choose the right sorts of products and have the work done by an experienced, super-competent practitioner. Not just someone who knows technically how to use the stuff, but someone who can work with it like an artist, re-sculpting your face to add the softness, volume, or structure that it needs, so that afterwards, you just look like yourself, but fresher. And that is what this chapter is all about. It will tell you what you need to know to navigate the somewhat swamp-like world of fillers so that you can find a practitioner and products that will best suit your face and your needs.

What Are Fillers, Anyway?

Facial fillers (or dermal – ie 'in the skin' – fillers, as they are more correctly known), are gel-like substances that can be used to physically give structure to the face. They are available in different densities, or thicknesses, depending on what they are for – it takes a firmer, denser filler to contour the cheeks, whereas you would want a more lightweight, pliable filler to give a gentle boost to the lips.

To get fillers where they need to be to, say, replace lost volume in the cheeks, or to add more definition to a jawline, they need to be injected below the skin, so they must have a fine enough consistency to be able to pass through either a needle or a cannula (a kind of blunt needle which some practitioners prefer; see the section 'Needles or Cannulas?' on page 222). Fillers usually come in 1ml syringes, and practitioners charge according to how much filler they are using on you, as well as for the time that the procedure takes.

Aren't Fillers Much the Same as Botox?

No. They're utterly different substances, injected into different parts of the face to do different things. Botox is a nerve toxin that is injected into the muscles to reduce their ability to contract. A filler is a gel made (usually) from hyaluronic acid which is injected to add volume or structure in the face. The confusion comes about because people often use the phrase, 'Botox and fillers' as a kind of shorthand to describe non-surgical tweakments – and perhaps also because practitioners often give patients both Botox and fillers in the same treatment session.

Botox is most commonly injected in the forehead, to soften frown lines. Fillers are most commonly injected into the cheeks and lips, to stop them looking deflated.

If you wonder why I'm spelling out something as basic as this at this stage of the book – well, it's just because I know that people confuse the two, even people who know quite a bit about aesthetics. One friend told me that she had been for treatment, and had had Botox in her lips. When I said that I thought it was filler she'd had in her lips, not Botox, she got quite shirty. I hadn't been there, she pointed out… (She was wrong; I checked with the doctor, but the point is she had got as far as having treatment with Botox and fillers but still hadn't understood what went where or did what.)

So just to be clear, Botox and fillers are two very different substances, though they are often used in the same treatment, but to achieve different results.

What Are Facial Fillers Made From?

There are three main categories of fillers:

* Temporary fillers made from hyaluronic acid gels
* Temporary but longer-lasting 'stimulating' fillers

- Permanent fillers

The following sections explain what you need to know about them.

TEMPORARY HYALURONIC ACID (HA) FILLERS

Most temporary fillers on offer in UK clinics are made from different types of hyaluronic acid gel. The best-known, best accredited, and most commonly used brands of filler are Juvederm and Restylane and they both fall in this category, as do other well-known but less widely used products such as Teosyal, Hylaform, and Belotero.

Saying that Juvederm and Restylane are 'best-known' may be correct, but it is probably overstating the case, as most people who have had fillers injected don't seem to have asked – or been told, or remembered – what brand of filler was used. I'll get onto why it matters in a minute.

If you have heard of hyaluronic acid (HA) as a moisturising ingredient and are wondering whether fillers are made from the same stuff, the answer is yes, up to a point.

But the hyaluronic acid in the form that it's used in moisturising serums would quickly be absorbed into the body and vanish. So in most hyaluronic acid filler gels, the molecules of hyaluronic acid are first stabilised and then 'crosslinked' into a kind of lattice to make them hang around for longer in the skin. The crosslinked gel holds onto moisture as well as hyaluronic acid does in a serum, and that moisture helps give the filler its structure and plumps up the skin from beneath.

Interestingly, there have been studies that show how using fillers benefits the skin above the treated area. This is because the presence of the hyaluronic acid filler improves the levels of collagen and elastin in the surface skin. This is the same effect as you get with the beneath-the-skin moisturising injectables such as Volite, Skinboosters, and Profhilo, which are now being described more as 'skin tissue stimulators' rather than just dilute fillers, because of the way they can help the skin regenerate itself, grow more collagen and elastin, and hydrate itself better. See the section 'Under-the-

Skin Moisturisers That Give the Face a Complete Reboot' on page 148 for more information on these injectables.

Many of these hyaluronic acid fillers come with a built-in anaesthetic in the form of lidocaine, to make the injection process more comfortable.

WHAT DO THESE HYALURONIC ACID FILLERS DO, AND WHERE ARE THEY USED?

These fillers just fill – so they can be used to replace lost volume in the cheeks and lips, the hollows under the eyes (the 'tear trough'), and the temples (it's not an area that most of us notice, but it becomes more hollow as we age). They sit where they are placed beneath the skin, and attract water which helps them hold their shape and, over the following weeks, integrate with your skin's tissues and become part of your face. Fillers can also reshape a bumpy nose (see the section 'Nose Reshaping/Non-Surgical Nose Job' on page 251), lift the eyebrows a touch if they are carefully injected just under the arch of the brow, or add structure to a face by strengthening an ageing jawline.

They're also useful for balancing up asymmetry all over the face. I had no idea my chin was a bit asymmetric until this was pointed out to me by a doctor who then kindly added a spot of filler in the right place to even things out. For men, fillers are increasingly popular for strengthening a weak jawline or making a feminine jaw more square and masculine-looking.

Fillers will last for between six months and 18 months before they are broken down by the body, depending on the sort of filler that was used. Exactly how long fillers last depends on how much was injected in the first place and also on the metabolism of the person who's had them; some people's bodies appear to break fillers down much faster than others.

Hyaluronic acid fillers come in different densities depending on what they are designed to do – and that affects how long they last, too. A thin, runny gel that works well in the lips doesn't have the staying power of a thicker gel designed to build up volume in the midface or strengthen the jawline.

PROS AND CONS OF HYALURONIC ACID FILLERS

The good, the bad, and the one drawback of hyaluronic acid fillers:

- Hyaluronic acid fillers are the most readily available and most straightforward type of filler. All the brands above give reliable results, though obviously the precise results that you get, and how happy you are with them, depends on your practitioner, their skill, your particular concerns, and how clearly you have both discussed what the treatment is trying to achieve before you start.

- If you don't like the results, or have been over-treated, it is possible to reverse the treatment by injecting the filler with Hyalase, an enzyme (hyaluronidase) that works like magic and dissolves the injected hyaluronic acid. In theory, it does not dissolve your own hyaluronic acid, the stuff that is naturally present in your skin, as that is being broken down and replaced every day while the skin goes about its own structural housekeeping. But in practice? I have heard people grumble that, after having Hyalase to undo fillers that have gone wrong, they have ended up looking more hollow than before, because the Hyalase appears to have dissolved rather more than just the injected filler. As I said, technically, it doesn't do that, but some people suspect it does.

The main disadvantage of hyaluronic acid fillers is that they don't last that long (between six and 18 months, depending on the sort of filler that was used), so to keep up the results, the work will need repeating in due course.

'STIMULATING' FILLERS

Then there are other fillers, such as Sculptra, Ellansé, and Radiesse, which are also temporary but which are longer lasting than hyaluronic acid fillers, and which work in two ways. Like the hyaluronic acid fillers, these 'stimulating' fillers come in the form of injectable gels that plump out the area where they are placed, but also, each contains a second substance that stimulates the skin to create more of its own supportive collagen, which develops over the course of the next six months and lasts for two years.

What are these extra, second substances?

- In Sculptra, it is tiny particles of poly-L-lactic acid, a synthetic substance that has been safely used in medicine, in dissolvable sutures/stitches, since the 1980s. The poly-L-lactic acid takes around six months to be absorbed by the skin, by which time it has built new collagen that will last for two years.

- In Ellansé, it's minute round particles of polycaprolactone (a bioabsorbable material that is also used in sutures for stitches) that slowly get absorbed by the body but in the meantime are busy stimulating collagen growth.

- In Radiesse, it's particles of calcium hydroxylapatite (a bone-like substance that also eventually gets absorbed) which form a kind of miniature scaffold within the skin, around which a network of new collagen forms.

PROS AND CONS OF 'STIMULATING' FILLERS

The advantage of stimulating fillers is that they last longer than hyaluronic acid fillers, so they are a more economical option in the long term. The disadvantage is that, if you don't like the results, all you can do is wait until the filler is all absorbed by the body.

PERMANENT FILLERS

If someone tries to offer you permanent fillers, please, just say no. Why? Because you really don't want anything injected into your face that is going to stay there for good.

Permanent fillers might sound like a great idea – no need to go back every year for a top up! So much cheaper! – but the potential problems are huge. Liquid silicone is popular in the USA for, say, filling out old acne scars, but with anything that is injected into your face, there is always a risk that the body will at some point in the future decide that it doesn't like this foreign material and 'encapsulate' it, growing collagen around it in a hard lump to shut it off from the rest of your skin tissue. If that happens, the only way to remove the growth, and the original filler, it to have it surgically removed.

Encapsulation isn't the only problem. As your face changes over the years, and some parts of it sag and descend, the blob of permanent filler may no longer be exactly where you want it to be. So just don't try permanent fillers. Particularly not in your lips.

OTHER WAYS: OTHER SUBSTANCES THAT ARE USED FOR RESTORING VOLUME IN THE FACE

Instead of the fillers discussed in the previous section, there are several other substances that can restore volume in your face. These substances include collagen, your own blood, and your own fat.

Collagen Fillers

Before hyaluronic acid fillers and all the rest came into being, the only material for filling out deep lines and lips and replacing lost volume was collagen. This worked well enough, but because most collagen was made from cowhide, you had to have a patch test before using them to check for allergic reactions. There may be a few practitioners out there who are still using collagen, but they are a rarity.

Your Own Blood

No, you didn't misread that. There is even a technique for creating a volumising filler from your own blood. This is not the same as PRP, the 'Vampire Facial' technique which uses your own blood to create Platelet Rich Plasma (PRP), a liquid which is reinjected into the skin on your face to reinvigorate the skin. The Plasma Filler is different. More on page 235.

Your Own Fat and Stem Cells

Your own fat makes a good and long-lasting filler, though it's a good deal more of a palaver to use it: first, it has to be extracted from your stomach or thighs, where you have some to spare, processed until it is liquid enough to pass through a fine needle, and then reinjected into your face. It can give great results and lasts longer than temporary fillers since, once it has 'taken' (grown its own blood supply and established itself in its new location), it should be there for good.

Fat grafting in the face has been done for many years, but it has never been a simple procedure, particularly because if you just pile a bunch of fat into the face, up to 50 per cent of it will die off and be reabsorbed by the body before it manages to establish the new blood supply to keep it alive in its new location.

You may have heard the term 'pillow face' used to describe celebs who have gone overboard on fillers and have the chipmunk cheeks to show for it. This was the result of some doctors, mostly in the USA, using fat to build up their patients' midface area, but overcorrecting, ie putting in too much volume, to allow for the fact that a proportion of it would not last.

Fat on its own isn't such a popular choice these days, but there are various techniques which combine fat with other substances which do look exciting. One promising technique is 'stem cell' fat transfer, which mixes extra stem cells extracted from your own fat with the fat that is being reinjected in the face, greatly increasing the proportion of fat that survives the transfer.

Stem cells? Yes, the extraordinary repair-cells that can grow into any type of cell in the human body, and which are found in umbilical cords and in bone marrow. Stem cells are also found in fat, so most people have a good supply of them ready and waiting for harvesting. Combining these 'adipose-derived mesenchymal stem cells', to give them their full name) with fat before reinjecting it into the face helps the fat to bed down wherever it is placed and grow the blood supply it needs to keep it healthy.

Still, fat transfer has been a minority interest for the past decade, certainly in the UK, but thanks to further new developments in fat-working techniques, this area is starting to look very exciting.

There's more on treatments involving fat and stem cells in the treatments section of this chapter. See the following sections:

- See page 228 for coverage of the SVF face makeover created by consultant plastic surgeon Mr Kambiz Golchin.
- See page 227 for details on the nano-fat technique by consultant plastic surgeon Dr Olivier Amar.
- See page 234 for information on the Angel PRP Fat Transfer with Dr Aamer Khan.

How Safe Are Fillers, and Do I Really Need to Know All This?

I realise I've given you a lot to consider. All this information is here to give you a grounding in the subject. Because if you *do* decide to try fillers, you want to be very sure of what you are having injected into your face. Why? Because if anything were to go wrong (see the section 'What Can Go Wrong? Potential Problems with Fillers' on page 215), the action you can take to remedy the problem depends on what you had injected in the first place, and if you don't know, that's no help at all.

YES – FOR YOUR OWN SAFETY!

The other reason that you really ought to do yourself a favour and read all of this if you are even vaguely considering facial fillers is this:

Because of the appalling lack of regulation in the whole area of aesthetic medicine in the UK, anyone can legally inject you with anything when it comes to fillers.

Maybe read that sentence again if it hasn't sunk in yet. Yes, there are many brilliant, ethical cosmetic practitioners doing terrific work, but there are also many who are less scrupulous, undertrained, and using products that have not been put through rigorous tests to see how safe and effective they are. Which is terrifying. And even more terrifying, it's perfectly legal. You or I could go and set ourselves up as aesthetic practitioners tomorrow, and there would be nothing in law to stop us. That's why the UK is seen by the rest of the world as the 'Wild West' as far as facial fillers are concerned.

Whereas Botox and other wrinkle-relaxing toxins are prescription medicines and can (in theory) only be obtained by an appropriately qualified medical professional (a doctor, a surgeon, a dentist, or a nurse-prescriber) and can only be injected by that professional or someone they are supervising, there are no such restrictions on fillers. Anyone can take a training course in how to inject fillers, and some of these courses are very short – a day or two. After which, they can inject you with whatever they fancy.

WHAT IS REGULATED AND WHAT ISN'T?

Anything invasive, where medical instruments like scalpels are inserted into the body, is closely regulated. So all cosmetic surgery, such as face-lifts, tummy tucks, and liposuction is regulated.

Botox, as I've said above, is a prescription medicine. But other non-surgical procedures – which includes all injectable dermal fillers, lasers, and peels – are not regulated.

There's often a bit of confusion over this because people often refer to having anything done to their faces as 'cosmetic surgery'. Just to be clear, surgery involves scalpels. Everything else comes under 'non-surgical procedures'.

SO HOW DO I FIND A BRILLIANT, EXPERIENCED PRACTITIONER?

By doing your homework and asking the right questions. There's a whole chapter on this (see Chapter 3, starting on page 39) because it applies to every treatment in the book.

IF THERE ARE SO FEW RESTRICTIONS, HOW DO I KNOW WHICH FACIAL FILLERS ARE SAFE?

While all the best known and most widely used fillers have been put through lengthy and specific tests to assess their safety and how well they work, there are scores of others that haven't. Many of these newcomers sound like fascinating, innovative products made from unusual ingredients like, say, seaweed, and some of them may well be the big new names of the future. But until they have been around for a few years and been shown to be safe and effective (and, have at least acquired a CE mark and, preferably, have also attained the gold standard of approval from the American Food and Drug Administration, the FDA – more on which in a minute), it is hard to know whether or not they may be problematic.

In the USA, facial fillers are classed as 'cosmetic devices' and are regulated by the Food and Drug Administration (FDA). Only the specific fillers that get through the lengthy FDA approval procedure can be used, and then only by medical doctors.

A CAUTIONARY STORY ABOUT FILLERS

Back in 2008, I jumped at the chance to be one of the first people in the UK to have a 'non-surgical breast enhancement' using a substance called Macrolane, a thicker version of the well-accredited (and FDA-approved) fillers Restylane and Perlane, which were all made by a well-known and well-respected company called Q-Med. It worked, but I found that the product didn't last the 18 months that had been promised, and also had a tendency to harden into lumps, which needed aggressive, painful massage to soften them up.

Why should one product that at first glance didn't seem hugely different from the rest of its product family start throwing up problems? It's impossible to say, but eventually Macrolane was taken off the market, having never achieved FDA approval.

It taught me, not for the first time, that it isn't wise to offer myself up as a guinea-pig for new treatments. I am none the worse for it, thank goodness, but I still get occasional emails from women who tried the treatment around the same time and were left with persistent lumps in their breasts that wouldn't go away.

In the UK, facial fillers are regulated as 'medical devices' under European Regulations and must have a CE mark, which says that the product does what it claims to do. A CE mark is much easier to obtain than FDA approval, but it does offer some reassurance that a product is fit for purpose (more details on page 214).

After the PIP breast implant scandal of 2010, Professor Sir Bruce Keogh led a team that surveyed and reported on the whole area of aesthetic medicine as well as cosmetic surgery. One of the strong recommendations of the 2013 Keogh report was that face-fillers should be reclassified as prescription-only medical devices, but this hasn't happened. Another recommendation was that there should be a central register of all surgical and non-surgical practitioners; yes, it's a scandal that there still isn't one.

WHAT THE KEOGH REPORT SAID ABOUT FACIAL (DERMAL) FILLERS

'Dermal fillers are a particular cause for concern as anyone can set themselves up as a practitioner, with no requirement for knowledge, training or previous experience. Nor are there sufficient checks in place with regard to product quality – most dermal fillers have no more controls than a bottle of floor cleaner. There has been explosive growth in this market, driven by a combination of high demand and high profits in an era when all other commercial income is stalling. *It is our view that dermal fillers are a crisis waiting to happen.*'

SO WHICH FILLERS ARE SAFEST?

You can start with the FDA and search on their website (www.fda.gov, look for *medical devices, dermal fillers, approval*).

On that list, you'll see two major lines:

- Lots of hyaluronic acid–based products in the Juvederm range (from medical giant Allergan, which also makes most of the world's breast implants and all the Botox)
- Many products in the Restylane family (now owned by the dermatology specialists Galderma)

You'll also find a handful of others:

- Teoxane's hyaluronic acid fillers, which joined the list last year
- Belotero Balance, a hyaluronic acid gel (owned by Merz Aesthetics)
- Radiesse (calcium hydroxylapatite; also owned by Merz Aesthetics)
- Sculptra (poly-L-lactic acid; owned by Galderma)
- Elevess (hyaluronic acid–based filler that is rarely used in the UK)

- Artefill, which used to be called Artecoll in the UK, though since 2015 it has been renamed Bellafill (still with me?). It is also a very long-lasting filler, combining collagen with microbeads of polymethyl methacrylate. (Why fill your face with plastic microbeads? To stimulate the growth of new collagen. You don't fancy that? No, me neither.)

But in terms of what's FDA approved – *that's it*. Ellansé, which I've mentioned above as it's an interesting filler with a lot of safety studies behind it, and its sister-product, a hyaluronic-acid filler called Perfectha, don't yet have FDA approval but they are working their way through the lengthy process towards accreditation. Does that mean you shouldn't use them? No – they seem very good, and plenty of great practitioners rate them highly.

AND AS FOR ALL THE REST...

And yet, what about all the other fillers that can be found in the market in the UK? There are many. The Keogh report estimated that there were between 140 and 190, and that was years ago.

In the UK, the Medicines and Healthcare products Regulatory Agency (MHRA) classifies dermal fillers as 'medical devices' rather than as prescription medicines. If you ask what safety data there is to support them, you'll be told they have a CE mark, which companies can self-certify for, or use independent laboratories to gain.

WHAT A CE MARK MEANS AND WHETHER YOU CAN TRUST IT

Can you put much trust in a CE mark? I spoke to Rajiv Grover, a leading cosmetic surgeon and former president of the British Association of Aesthetic Plastic Surgeons (BAAPS) about this. He says: 'Dermal fillers are classified as medical devices which only require a CE mark. A CE mark can be obtained by treating a handful of patients with a 6–12 month follow-up. Often the real issues with medical devices take longer than this to emerge.'

Often, companies will suggest, as I mentioned earlier, that the more novel types of injectable filler will be the big new names in the business within a decade. That's always possible, but in the meantime, it is the UK consumers who are being used as guinea pigs by the companies who want to try out new products but are prevented by law from using them in other countries.

What the Keogh report called for back in 2013, and what all reputable cosmetic practitioners have been asking for, is to have dermal fillers classified as prescription medicines rather than simply as 'medical devices'. That would mean fillers could only be obtained, and given to patients, by registered medical professionals (doctors, surgeons, dentists, and nurse-prescribers).

There was a flurry of excitement on social media early in 2018 that this might be able to happen because the MHRA is currently introducing new regulations around medical devices, which will have an impact on the filler market. But they're not going as far as reclassifying fillers as prescription medicines.

Instead, what is happening is that, following the Medical Devices Regulations (MDR), which came into force in 2017, all dermal fillers will need a CE mark in order to be sold in the UK, whether they are 'medical' fillers or 'aesthetic' fillers. There's a three-year transition period for companies to comply with this new ruling, and it's still a long way short of what most cosmetic practitioners want to see. However, it is a move in the right direction and it should lead to some tightening up within the aesthetics industry.

SO HOW SAFE ARE FACIAL FILLERS?

In a nutshell? The good ones – the ones with FDA approval, or a CE mark – are safe, in the right hands – that is, in the experienced hands of medically trained professionals who are following the correct protocols for treatment. The flipside of that sentence is that there are an awful lot of dodgy fillers around, and an awful lot of less-than-brilliant practitioners, which means there is huge potential for problems.

WHAT CAN GO WRONG? POTENTIAL PROBLEMS WITH FILLERS

It's a long list. I've put all these points in order of how likely they are to happen and how serious they are.

- **Bruising.** Any injection carries a risk of bruising, which will be temporary but which may take a fortnight to fade. Bruising is very common. Some people just do bruise more than others. Taking exercise, which speeds up the blood circulation, or drinking alcohol, which temporarily thins the blood, soon after the procedure may make any bruising worse.

  What to do: Bruises are easy enough to cover with concealer – I prefer the sort of product that is strong enough to cover tattoos.

- **Swelling and skin redness**. It is very likely that there will be swelling around the injection site, and that the skin will be red, simply from the fact that a needle was sunk into your skin. The swelling will go down, which may take a few hours, or a few days. There may also be swelling of the area that has been injected, though it can be hard to tell how much of this is due to the volume of the product that has been put in and how much is due to your face protesting at being injected. Again, this may take a few days to settle.

  What to do: Swelling can be reduced by holding an ice-pack wrapped in a clean cloth to the area every few hours. A latex glove, filled with water, tied, and frozen, makes a quick ice-pack.

- **Rashes, swelling, or itching** caused by an allergy to the particular substance used – this is rare, given that most fillers are made of substances like hyaluronic acid with minimal potential for causing reactions, but not unheard of.

  What to do: Swelling that seems more like an allergic reaction may respond to an antihistamine.

- **Acne-like skin eruptions.** These can result from bacteria getting into the holes left by needles on your face.

  What to do: Wash your face with care, swab it with a salicylic acid toner, and don't pick at the spots.

- **Infection at the injection site** – again, this can be caused by bacteria getting into the injection site and needs swift treatment.

  What to do: Consult your practitioner and send them photographs; you may need antibiotics.

- **Blistering of the skin.** This is rare but has been reported, around the injection sites.

  What to do: Consult your practitioner at once for advice.

- **Asymmetric result.** The only way you would end up asymmetric after a treatment is if your practitioner had a poor sense of proportion. But once the filler is in there, your choices are limited.

  What to do: Either you can have the filler dissolved (with Hyalase) or you can have more filler injected in the appropriate place to balance things up. You might want the corrective work to be done by a different practitioner.

- **Filler moving away from the intended treatment area over time.** Filler 'migrating' away from the site where it is injected is not common, but it can happen.

  What to do: The only solution is to have the misplaced filler dissolved with Hyalase, and start again.

- **Filler forming lumps under the skin** (1). Fillers, particularly hyaluronic acid fillers, don't often provoke reactions in the skin, and integrate quickly and smoothly with the skin's tissues. There are two ways they form lumps under the skin. The first is simply if the filler has been misplaced, or badly positioned, and not smoothed into shape, which practitioners will usually do with a firm, gentle pressure and massage after injecting the fillers.

  What to do: If these lumps are obvious and you can't live with them, you'll need to have them dissolved with Hyalase.

- **Filling forming lumpy granulomas** (2). The second type of lumps are more of a problem. However well tested fillers are, they are still a foreign substance that has been introduced to your body, and your body may, in its wisdom, at any point suddenly decide that it objects to having them there, and start to form a 'granuloma' around the filler. It's not an allergic reaction, more of an inflammatory reaction, but the net result is that you end up with a lumpy growth with the filler encapsulated inside it.

What to do: The best way to treat these is with steroid injections, which interfere with the way the fibroblasts within the skin cells are enablinSg the growth. The other option is to cut the growth out, surgically, but *a)* it can be hard to get the entire growth that way, and *b)* it will leave a scar.

- **Filler injected into a blood vessel.** This is rare but extremely serious. It is rare because one of the first things all injectors are taught is, once they have put the needle through the skin, to 'aspirate', ie to pull the plunger back a fraction, just to check that they are not in a blood vessel (so if they aspirate and blood comes into the syringe, they know they need to stop, get out of that area, and reposition). Because if filler is injected into a blood vessel, it can block that vessel and kill the surrounding skin tissues (necrosis), or that blockage can travel back to the tiny blood vessels that supply the eye, which can lead to blindness. The first signs that something is wrong are usually pain and skin blanching or discolouration at the injection site and, if it happens, your practitioner needs to treat it as an emergency.

  What to do: Contact your practitioner immediately if you think this is happening. You need treatment straight away to try to shift the blockage.

When you've seen this list, you can see why it is vital to choose a practitioner who not only knows how to use fillers, but what to do if any problems arise, and it is one reason why the aesthetics industry is so keen that non-surgical treatments are perceived as the medical procedures that they are. This is something you should ask about at your consultation before treatment (see page 45 for more advice on consultations and what to expect), and this is where medically trained practitioners clearly have the edge over others. Because if you have a problem and your practitioner is not helpful, or is dismissive of your problem, you will need to seek help elsewhere.

Understanding How Fillers Are Used

In this section, I'll explain quickly what you need to know about the ways that practitioners currently use fillers to restore volume to the face. I'll also explain the difference between needles and cannulas, the two devices that practitioners use to inject the fillers.

THE WAY FILLERS ARE USED HAS EVOLVED – FROM FILLING LINES...

The way that the leading practitioners use fillers is evolving all the time. Twenty years ago, it was about focussing on obvious lines in the face – say, the nose-to-mouth (nasolabial) lines – and putting filler directly into those lines to bulk them out and soften them. Then, 10 years ago, the aim shifted towards softening the face by replacing lost volume, particularly in the cheeks and lips. At this point, practitioners stopped injecting the nose-to-mouth lines because they'd worked out that if you put a spot of volume back in the upper outer cheek area, it hoists up the skin a fraction, and that softens the appearance of those nose-to-mouth lines without doing anything to them. And besides, just injecting the lines without putting volume back into the midface can give it a weird, froggy look.

TO REPLACING LOST VOLUME IN THE FACE...

More recently, practitioners have preferred to look at the face not just as an assembly of parts – lips to boost, cheeks to fill – but as a whole, and to take a more thoughtful approach as to what might make that whole face look fresher and softer. Allergan, the pharma company behind Juvederm, the best-known and most widely used range of facial fillers, began to introduce training concepts for doctors who used its products.

There's the '8-point lift' and the 'MD Codes', both of which suggest specific spots on the face where doctors should consider injecting small amounts of filler in order to give a natural-looking all-over lift. (Obviously, each patient's face needs something different, but these protocols give doctors a framework for reference.)

Both the 8-point lift and the MD Codes were created by a Brazilian plastic surgeon called Mauricio de Maio, who is the undisputed rock-god of the injectables world, and who has been leading Allergan's treatment programme for several years. His status is legendary as much thanks to his ability to charm a lecture-hall audience as his skills with a syringe of filler.

TO IMPROVING FACIAL STRUCTURE AND SYMMETRY...

In the past couple of years, the focus has changed again. Along with subtle revolumising, doctors have been focussing on what fillers can do to add structure to the face, say by adding definition to the jawline (really helpful when that jawline is starting to soften thanks to mid-life bone resorption), or to give a man a squarer, more manly-looking jaw. There's a lot that can be done for the chin, too, by adjusting its proportions subtly (more on this on page 250). And using fillers for non-surgical nose-jobs, to make a hooked or bumpy nose appear straight, has been a huge hit with clinic-goers.

TO BEAUTIFYING THE FACE...

And then there's the way that fillers can now be used to enhance a face that many would argue is already lovely and needs no 'work', particularly when that face is young. This book started off as a guide for how tweakments work for older faces, but it is impossible to avoid the issue that many younger women, often still in their teens, now feel that they would look much better with just a spot of filler in their lips, or want to amplify their cheekbones and add drama to their faces.

You can blame this trend on TV series like The Only Way Is Essex and Love Island; you can blame Kylie Jenner, the youngest of the Kardashian clan, who had her lips boosted with filler when she was 17, denied it, then eventually admitted that they had been 'helped'. But then you'll also find that companies such as Allergan are promoting their fillers directly at this 'beautification' market.

I feel hugely conflicted about this. I spend much of my time explaining non-surgical procedures and tweakments to people, but want to shout 'NO!' every time anyone under the age of 30 asks me if I think they should try fillers in their lips. That's partly because I'm old enough to be their mum, and just think they shouldn't, at least not yet, particularly because they can't see just how lovely they are already. But partly because however much people pretend this whole area of starting treatment isn't a slippery slope, for many, it is. One thing leads to another and, before you know it, lovely young faces start looking a tad odd, then decidedly 'done'. So it's all going on, but no, I don't approve of it. Except perhaps for non-surgical nose-reshaping (see page 251), because that gives lovely, subtle results and can be a good way to gauge whether it would be worth saving up for a surgical procedure.

AND THEN ADDING EVEN MORE FILLER...

Until this year, all these treatments have focussed on making the maximum impact with minimal doses of filler. But now, even that has changed.

Dr de Maio's latest approach to creating harmony in any face is to use really rather a lot of filler. That sounds like a recipe for pillow face, not to mention very expensive – but when the filler is used thoughtfully and skilfully, the results are fabulous.

Dr Tapan Patel, who is director of the PHI Clinic in Harley Street, and who helps Dr de Maio teach the latest techniques to other doctors around the globe, explains: 'Originally, fillers were used to fill lines. But over time, as practitioners developed a better understanding of the ageing process, it was clear that volume loss was a major factor, so we started using fillers to address volume loss. Because doctors and patients were used to treatments comprising one or two 1ml syringes, we were trying to use the same quantity to restore volume.'

'We now know that volume loss isn't limited to one area. In any one patient, we may need to treat the temple, cheekbone, mouth region, chin, and jawline – so we need more product. It is now not unusual for us to use up to 16 syringes of product in one treatment plan.'

It's worth noting that this 'more is more' approach is being promoted by Allergan, the company behind Juvederm facial fillers, and obviously it helps sell more filler. And it may not suit everyone.

So while I've written these treatments up as one-offs addressing one part of the face (cheeks, lips, nose, etc.), just to give you an idea of what each is like, seeing your face as an assembly of parts isn't really the best way forward.

When you go for a consultation with a cosmetic practitioner, he or she is likely to suggest a number of options. Not so much in order to sell you more product, but with the aim of trying to create overall softness and freshness in your face. Also, if there are a number of options on the table, you don't have to do them at once, but a coherent plan which can be carried out slowly and stealthily will give the best results.

I've also tried the whole-face-redesign-with-lots-of-fillers, too, so I've included that for good measure, at the end of the chapter.

NEEDLES OR CANNULAS?

There are two ways of getting dermal fillers into the face: either through the tip of a sharp needle or through a cannula, which is like a blunt needle. A blunt needle may sound like a terrible idea, but in fact a cannula can nose its way along between the layers of the skin, pushing out of the way fibrous bands, or blood vessels, which a needle could just stab through, so it is gentler on the skin tissues. The practitioner begins by making a hole in the skin with a needle, then inserts the cannula through the hole. It feels a bit peculiar, having a cannula stealthily burrowing its way across your face, or running just below the surface of the lips, but it's not painful. Which is best? It's a matter of personal choice for practitioners. Some like cannulas, others always prefer to work with needles.

TREATMENTS FOR HOLLOW EYES

Eyes may be viewed as the windows of the soul, but for the middle-aged woman, they're a giveaway of her age. Not only is the skin around the eyes thin and delicate and dry, but it is continually stretched and scrunched by facial expressions, so it wrinkles easily. Add to this the way that when the fat pads beneath the skin shrink and the eye sockets enlarge, as they do in our forties, when the bone in our skulls starts to be reabsorbed, the eye area starts to look either hollow or pouchy. Either way, it's not a pretty picture. If you're wondering whether your eyes are sinking further back in your head as you get older or whether you're just imagining it, I'm afraid it's for real.

Skincare can brighten and smooth the skin around the eye, but it can do absolutely nothing for hollowness, so you really have only two options. First, you can blame your genes and find a good-quality light-reflecting concealer, or second, you can try one of the treatments described below that can counteract hollowing. The main treatment is having carefully placed filler injected into the 'tear trough', the curved groove that tears follow as they slide out of the inner corner of your eye.

Tear-trough work is all about creating a smooth junction between the lower eyelid and the cheek. It sounds like a simple enough thing to do, to pop in a spot of filler to blur this boundary between cheek and lower lid, but it is a tricky treatment to pull off. Leading oculoplastic surgeon Sabrina Shah-Desai does a great deal of work in the eye area with both surgical and non-surgical procedures and says that working around the eye with needles 'is like putting your hand in a snake pit'. There are a bunch of nerves, a lot of tiny blood vessels, and then there's the fact that not all tear-trough issues are the same.

Some tear troughs go hollow, some have bulges of fat; these can both be treated. Some have dark circles from hyper-pigmentation, which really doesn't respond well to filler. Nor, adds Mrs Shah-Desai, do you want to put fillers into under-eye areas where there is masses of loose skin, because the problem there is with the sagging eye muscle, not hollowness. Likewise where there's lots of cheek sagginess, because that's a problem with the cheek; nor do you want to inject where you've got a ring of fluid under the eye, because that's thanks to a weak lymphatic system. It's a fiendishly difficult area for practitioners, and Mrs Shah-Desai's lectures on this topic at aesthetics conferences are always packed with doctors and surgeons keen to learn from her experience.

It's also very easy for inexperienced practitioners to stick the filler in slightly the wrong place. If the injections are too near the surface, or in fractionally the wrong spot, you get something called the Tyndall effect, where the bulge of the filler can be seen through the skin and looks bluish where the light hits it. And then there's the way that filler placed incorrectly between the ligament that supports the eye socket and the eye muscles gets bunched and rolled like a blob of dough every time those muscles contract, and ends up in a lumpy sausage shape that shows up when you smile.

'The trouble with tear-trough injections is that they often create 'speed bumps' of filler beneath the eye,' says Mrs Shah-Desai. 'More than half of my non-surgical work is treating botched tear-trough procedures.' This she does by dissolving the offending speed bumps with Hyalase before she can set about correcting the original problems.

Now that I've said all that and probably put you off ever trying this particular procedure, here's a review of how treatment goes when it works really well.

TREATMENT REVIEW: UNDER-EYE FILLERS FOR HOLLOW EYES

I've always had shadows under my eyes, and they have become more obvious with the years. When I heard, 10 years ago, about tear-trough injections to correct these hollows under my eyes, I leapt at the chance to try them.

I've had tear-trough work a few times since then, but it hasn't always been a huge success. There was the time when I foolishly went for a facial a couple of days after treatment, and the facialist's strong fingers moved the filler away from where it should have been. Another time, the filler was injected in what seemed the right place, along the lower rim of the eye socket, but the small ridge it raised had the unfortunate effect of making the hollow bit of my eye look even more hollow. By the time I saw eye surgeon Sabrina Shah-Desai for an assessment, I hadn't risked further tear-trough work for four years.

What It Is

The basic idea is that filler is used – in tiny doses – around the edge of the eye socket, to minimise hollowness around the eyes. However, everyone's eyes are different so treatment needs to be customised accordingly.

Mrs Shah-Desai says that injecting filler in the tear trough isn't necessarily the answer, since it often creates bumps beneath the eye. She realised that the problem arises at the inner corner of the lower eyelid, where it meets the thicker skin of the cheek. 'It creates the optical illusion of a hollow, like a hammock,' she says. To overcome this, her Eye Boost treatment involves injecting the thinning skin of the lower eyelid area right up to my lower eyelashes not with a thicker filler usually used for tear-trough work, but with a thin, runny filler called Restylane Vital Light. The aim is to plump up, hydrate, and thicken this delicate skin and smooth the hollow between lid and cheek, which will help the under-eye area look less tired.

'It's a layering technique,' says Mrs Shah-Desai. 'My Eye Boost technique works well, but it's not a magic wand. People think they will look photoshopped afterwards, but they have to be prepared for some downtime.'

That means that there will be swelling after the injections, and possibly bruising – there are so many tiny blood vessels in the area that it is hard not to catch any of them. More noticeable, though, are the bumps of filler under the eyes, which will take up to two weeks to be fully absorbed into the skin. She shows me a worst-case scenario picture, of a patient with many small lumps, each the size of a fat sunflower seed, beneath his eyes (yes, it's a popular treatment with men, too) and with a scattering of tiny dark bruises among them. I refuse to be deterred.

What It's Like

Being in my fifties, I'm on the old side for Mrs Shah-Desai's treatment – many of her patients are in their thirties – but she thinks it will work well for me, as I have hollowing beneath the eyes but no loose skin (that would need tightening up – say, with radiofrequency treatment, or a lower-eye-lift – beforehand). For her younger patients, the treatment helps to get rid of sunken-looking eyes and dark circles.

Because, at my consultation, Mrs Shah-Desai discovers old 'speed bumps' of filler trapped around my eye from the last procedure I had, four years earlier, she injects these with Hyalase to dissolve them, and books me in for the Eye Boost treatment the following week. The bumps dissolve almost instantly, but this leaves my eyes looking more hollow than ever.

When we finally get to the actual treatment, it is a breeze. Anaesthetic cream is applied beforehand, so I can barely feel the injections, which are done with a very fine needle. There are about 15 injections in all, each dispensing droplets of 10 microlitres of product – that's one-hundredth of a millilitre at a time.

After five minutes, the first eye is done, and I'm given an ice pack for the treated area (to reduce swelling and bruising) while she moves onto the second. After dealing with the lower eyelids, she layers a little filler around my tear-trough ligament – not so deeply that there is the danger it will be rolled into a sausage – in order to smooth out the dip between my lower lid and my cheek.

The purpose of these tiny injections is to stimulate the 'dermal matrix' where the skin cells are formed. The filler is made of hyaluronic acid which has the ability to hold 1,000 times its own weight in water. This will hydrate the skin and plump it up so that it looks thicker.

Right after the procedure, the area under my eyes looks rather bumpy, like an unusual outcrop of spots with the odd little bruise among them. But the swellings go down within five days, and my lower-eye area starts to look much fresher, less hollow and, crucially, less tired. As billed, it's not been airbrushed perfectly smooth, but it is a definite improvement.

Comfort Level

Thanks to the anaesthetic cream, the injections are almost painless.

Verdict

Terrific. There is an obvious improvement which I notice every time I look in the mirror, which brings with it a huge psychological boost – it's such a heartsink when, every time you see your face, you think, 'Oh dear, do I really look that tired?' Even better, it looks completely natural. These effects should last for eight months, particularly if I look after my skin. In terms of how big a difference it makes to my face and how I feel, this has to be one of my favourite treatments.

Cost and Location

Eye Boost procedure with Mrs Sabrina Shah-Desai, from £750, www.perfecteyesltd.com. To find a practitioner in your area who treats hollow eyes with filler, go to www.thetweakmentsguide.com.

Would It Work for You?

Yes, brilliantly, if you have the right sort of tear-trough hollow (see above) and are treated by a practitioner who is expert enough to know their way with confidence around the 'snake-pit' of the eye socket.

Potential Problems

See the section 'What Can Go Wrong? Potential Problems with Fillers' on page 215.

Using Fat to Treat Hollow Eyes

These two innovative tweakments use a patient's own fat and can be used more widely in the face – as well as around the eyes.

NANO-FAT INJECTIONS

Mr Olivier Amar, an aesthetic plastic surgeon based in Sloane Street, Chelsea, is renowned for his light touch with eye surgery. He has pioneered face- and body-sculpting techniques with liposuction and fat transfer (extracting fat from one part of the body, purifying it, then reinjecting it where it is more needed).

Mr Amar is a huge advocate of using our own body tissues for regenerating our faces. 'We have this wonderful tissue available to us, in the form of our own fat,' he says. 'You can think of tissue transfer – taking fat from one part of the body to another – like recycling.' While he is not against the use of hyaluronic acid fillers just into the surface of the skin, for deeper, more restorative work, he prefers to use your own fat and stem cells.

The other advantage of fat over filler, as Mr Amar explains, is that it is rich in adipose-derived mesenchymal cells (stay with me), particularly after repeated filtering. These cells are the ones that contain within them stem cells which can develop into whatever sort of tissue is needed. ('They are like the super-player who can sit on the bench, and then take any place on the field where they are needed,' enthuses Mr Amar.)

To restore a youthful look to hollowing eyes, he recommends 'nano-fat' injections. This involves having a small amount of fat – between 5 and 10cc – extracted from your body wherever you have a surplus, under local anaesthetic. This fat is then repeatedly forced through a fine filter to emulsify it to an injectable fluid state, before it is reinjected into the area around the eye, where the skin layer is close to the bone, filling out any hollows or depressions. Because the injected mixture is so fluid, it reduces the risks of lumps and swelling, so if you are someone who experiences puffy eyes or swelling around the eyes after hyaluronic acid fillers (which can happen because it is so good at attracting and holding water), then nano-fat can be a good alternative.

Due to those adipose-derived mesenchymal cells, nano-fat is more than just a filler alternative – it has a variety of uses all over the face, and because it heals and plumps 'from the inside out', Mr Amar says it gives fantastic results for those struggling with crepey skin or superficial fine lines around the face and mouth. 'Nano-fat gives an all-round, subtle, and natural softening effect in the areas that it treats, as it builds on your own internal tissue structures, creating a healing response from deep within the facial tissues so your skin continues to regenerate and restore from the inside out,' he says. You'll continue to see improvements for around three months before it settles.

Nano-fat isn't the best answer if you need a lot of volume adding to your face, nor if you want more obvious face sculpting and contouring. However, if your focus is on improving and plumping your skin from the inside out, and you prefer the idea of using your own stem cells instead of a foreign product, then nano-fat is a natural bespoke alternative to the traditional filler.

Nano-fat injections, from £2,500, with Olivier Amar, www.cadoganclinic.com.

SVF FACE REPAIR

More of a facial makeover than a facial, this is a new technique that is being pioneered by Mr Kambiz Golchin, a consultant plastic surgeon who practices in London and Dublin.

This technique is right at the cutting edge of the face repair and enhancement, a 'grow-your-own-facelift' type of treatment that uses your own fat to provide a regenerative cocktail for your face.

Once some fat has been extracted from your stomach or thighs, it is treated to separate out a particular part of it, the 'stromal vascular fraction' (SVF), which is a cocktail of mesenchymal stem cells and growth factors. If this SVF cocktail is injected into skin that has been lightly damaged by laser treatment, 'the stem cells will go to work and act as building blocks. They can regenerate as fat cells, muscle, or skin cells, whatever is needed,' says Mr Golchin. That is what is behind the extraordinary, regrow-your-own-face effect, the fact that the SVF cocktail enables the body to rebuild what it is missing.

Most surgeons who are up to date with fat grafting have now switched from transferring plain fat to using fat that has this SVF stem cell cocktail mixed in, because it makes the fat much more likely to 'take' in its new location.

Where Mr Golchin's work is leading the field is by using the laser before SVF fat transfer; he is one of only two people in Europe to offer this procedure. 'The key point about SVF and stem cells,' he says, 'is that you have to give them something to do, something to repair. If you don't, they will just sit there quietly. But if you create trauma in the skin, which I do with laser, then they will go to work.'

It's a lengthy and expensive procedure which takes around three hours, but the results are similar to a facelift and will last around five years.

Would SVF Face Repair work for you? Very probably, if you have the budget. It is early days for this procedure, but there is immense worldwide interest in it, and so far the results look extremely promising.

The cost varies but may be more than £10,000. For details, go to www.kambizgolchin.com.

TREATMENTS FOR PUFFY BAGS BENEATH THE EYE

Puffiness can result from the lymph channels around the eyes not draining properly, or from eating lots of salty food, which makes the skin hold onto fluid, which shows up around the eyes. Or it could come as part and parcel of allergies such as hay fever. Or it could be because the fat that sits behind the rim of the eye socket when we are younger splurges forwards into a visible puff of fat in our late 30s (the technical term would be 'prolapses', but you know what I mean).

Can Skincare Help?

Not much, despite all the suggested promises you'll see on the packaging of eye creams. As ever, using antioxidants such as vitamin C and rejuvenating potions containing retinol will keep the skin in the best possible condition. Some rejuvenating potions are specially formulated for use around the eyes, including Olay Eyes Pro Retinol (£29.99, www.boots.com) and Kate Somerville's +Retinal Firming Eye Wrinkle Cream (£72, www.katesomerville.co.uk).

Don't be tempted to load heavy creams onto the eye area in the hope that they will be extra-moisturising. The thin skin in this area responds better to light serums and gels for more hydration, whereas heavy creams can clog up the skin and make it go puffy.

What Treatments Can Do

Bagginess is the result of skin becoming slacker with age (and losing the supporting fat beneath it), so it is best tackled with treatments that tighten up the skin – or possibly a surgical lower eye lift. See the section on Tixel on page 106 and the section on Plexr on page 261 for what non-surgical tweakments can offer.

As for puffiness: every puffy eye is a bit different, so you need an expert practitioner's opinion on what is causing yours; but briefly, some puffy-looking eyes can be treated with injectable fillers and some can't. Two practitioners who consistently get great results treating puffy under-eyes with dermal filler are Dr Maryam Zamani (drmaryamzamani.com) and Dr Nick Milojevic (www.miloclinic.com).

TREATMENTS FOR CHEEKS AND NOSE-TO-MOUTH LINES

Some time in your forties, your face starts to flatten and lose volume. As with most other aspects of ageing, it's something we hardly notice at first; and it's just what happens as those balloon-like fat pads that have been supporting your face and holding up the skin nice and taut all these years start gradually to deflate. As they do so, your cheeks start to look a bit flatter, or possibly a bit hollow, and the skin starts to hang over the lines between your nose and mouth. Those creases have always been there – how else can you smile, without creating folds in your face? – but we tend not to notice them until the volume starts to fall out from underneath them.

TREATMENT REVIEW: INSTANT CHEEK VOLUMISING TO REDUCE NOSE-TO-MOUTH LINES

The nose-to-mouth lines – the naso-labial lines, as your practitioner may call them – are one of the biggest bugbears for most ageing faces. Rather than being nice little creases that dimple up as you smile, they become well-worn grooves with a bit of overhang that sags forwards towards your mouth. Your first instinct will be that to improve them, you need to fill in these grooves, and that is what cosmetic doctors used to do. But then they worked out that the reason you get these grooves is because the cheek pads have flattened, so if you perk the cheeks back up with a spot of filler, it both raises the curve of the cheek in a flattering way and also lifts and softens that nose-to-mouth groove.

What It Is

Adding a judicious amount of filler – just 1ml, maybe less – at the right spot in each cheek creates the small amount of lift needed to soften the nose-to-mouth lines and gently redefines the curve of the cheek, too.

What It's Like

There's no need for anaesthetic cream, so this tweakment is very quick. All I need is a dab of ice on the injection site towards the upper part of my cheekbone on either side. And all I can feel is the small scratch as Dr Patel makes each injection, followed by the strange sensation of pressure beneath the skin as the facial filler is slowly injected into position. Dr Patel then massages the gel to make sure it is in the right position, and that's it.

Comfort Level

Very comfortable and manageable.

Verdict

Lovely. My cheekbones were never obvious when I was younger, but they've emerged with age, and with this added definition on top of them, my face is starting to look really quite sculpted. Who would have thought that was possible? And yes, my nose-to-mouth lines have lifted and softened in response, which makes me look years less tired.

Cost and Location

Juvederm Voluma with Dr Tapan Patel, PHI Clinic, from £750, www.phiclinic.com. To find a practitioner in your area, go to www.thetweakmentsguide.com.

Would It Work for You?

Yes, as long as your practitioner can make the right call about where to place the filler on your cheeks – the location will rather depend on the shape of your face and your bone structure.

Potential Problems

See the section 'What Can Go Wrong? Potential Problems with Fillers' on page 215.

TREATMENT REVIEW: GRADUAL CHEEK REVOLUMISING WITH SCULPTRA

Dermal fillers made with hyaluronic acid give you an immediate, what-you-see-is-what-you-get effect. You have them injected, they take up a certain amount of space under the skin and hold onto water to keep themselves firm, and there is your result. Sculptra, on the other hand, is a slow-burn injectable for revolumising the face.

What It Is

Sculptra is made not from hyaluronic acid, but from a gel of poly-L-lactic acid, the same substance that is used for absorbable stitches. When this is injected into the skin, it stimulates your body to produce more of its own collagen. So Sculptra provides little bulk by itself, but the main results come three to six months after the first treatment (you will need two or three treatments, a month or six weeks apart) and last for up to two years.

What It's Like

I have my Sculptra injections done by Dr Tracy Mountford, who likes the product for its ability to restore volume to the face slowly and gradually ('It's an excellent biostimulator,' she says). She uses the product in my midface and cheeks, placing the injections in the areas where I am losing the padding in my face, to pad these areas back out again, and massaging the product into the correct position. I don't have anaesthetic cream beforehand, as there aren't that many injections, and they aren't painful.

I can see a small change immediately after the injections, and go home and follow Dr Mountford's instructions to massage my face for a minute morning and evening for a week. My face looks a little red on the injection sites, but there isn't any noticeable swelling afterwards, so it's not the sort of treatment that other people are going to notice. I go back for a second round of treatment five weeks later, then a third treatment a month after that, by which time I can see that my face is losing the gaunt look that had been creeping up on me.

Comfort Level

Reasonably comfortable.

Verdict

The results looked very good and natural, and I loved the way this treatment was a slow builder, so there were no sudden surprises. Building up the padding around my cheekbones softened my nose-to-mouth lines, too, without injecting them directly. And it certainly lasted. It was years before I had my cheeks injected again.

Cost and Location

£450 per vial, www.cosmeticskinclinic.com. To find a practitioner in your area, go to www.thetweakmentsguide.com.

Would It Work for You?

Sculptra works well on faces that need subtle volumising but it is also particularly good for faces that need a lot of building up (it has for many years been used for people with HIV, who had suffered lipodystrophy – a marked hollowing of the face – which was one of the side effects of the older type of antiretroviral drugs used to treat the condition). Because it takes a while to reach its full volume, it is good for people who prefer to do things gradually where their faces are concerned.

Potential Problems

Here, too, see the section 'What Can Go Wrong? Potential Problems with Fillers' on page 215.

USING FAT AND PRP AS A FILLER FOR CHEEK REVOLUMISING

As mentioned earlier in this chapter, your own fat makes an alternative filler for padding out your face. It is more of a palaver than using hyaluronic acid filler, clearly, as the fat has to be extracted from somewhere where you have plenty of it – say, your tummy or your thighs, via a minor but obviously invasive liposuction procedure – then purified, mixed with PRP (that's platelet-rich plasma, extracted from a vial of your own blood), and reinjected where you need it.

Once it has been put in place, the fat will take a while to settle, and the PRP, which is rich in growth factors, will help blood vessels to grow through the fat to help keep it alive in its new location, so that it will then last in a way that hyaluronic acid fillers won't. Think of it as repurposing your body's own surplus…

The Angel PRP Fat Transfer with Dr Aamer Khan costs from £3,500, www.harleystreetskinclinic.com.

Would this treatment work for you? Very likely. Dr Khan has been doing this procedure for a decade, so he has great expertise in getting very nice results. As you can see from the company website, he uses the process for sculpting the body as well as the face.

PLASMA FILLERS MADE FROM YOUR OWN BLOOD

If revolumising your face with your own fat isn't enough to make your brain spin, what about the idea of fillers made from your own blood? Before you even start wondering whether that's just another way of describing PRP (the aforementioned 'Dracula' treatments) – yes, this starts off in a similar way; but no, it's not the same.

Dr Nick Milojevic, who has started offering the treatment at his clinic in London, explains how it works. First, he extracts 8ml of blood from a patient (in the same way that a blood sample is taken from a vein in the forearm), and puts it in the special centrifuge device that extracts the plasma. Doing this produces two 'fractions' of plasma, with Fraction 1 being a slightly thicker liquid than Fraction 2.

Usually, it's just Fraction 2 that is used for PRP; but Dr Milojevic heats up Fraction 1 in a special (purpose-made, clinically approved) device until it solidifies, which takes up to 16 minutes, depending on how thick a filler he is looking to use. He then mixes this solidified Fraction 1 into a gel by combining it with Fraction 2, the PRP mix, then reinjects it where it is needed. He says it doesn't work for the tear trough or for nose-sculpting, but it's great on the cheeks. Once it has been injected, it will have a stimulating effect on your skin, so it helps to rejuvenate the skin as well as give it a lift.

'It's a new technology and it's exciting,' says Dr Milojevic. 'To obtain 3ml of gel, I need to extract about 8ml of blood, so not too much, and the patient needs to set aside an hour in the clinic. You will get a good lift in, say, your cheeks, but not as big a lift as you would get with a hyaluronic acid filler such as Juvederm Voluma, and it won't last as long.'

It's clearly not one for the needle-phobic nor for people who shy away from blood. Why on earth would you want to go to all this palaver for a filler that doesn't last as long as a hyaluronic acid gel? It's a good deal cheaper than hyaluronic acid fillers and, as Dr Milojevic points out, for people who don't want any sort of foreign substance – however good its safety profile – injected into their faces, this could count as an organic, home-grown treatment. Perhaps this sounds mad, but that's Dr Milojevic's view, and he has plenty of patients who like the treatment.

Plasma fillers cost from £800, www.miloclinic.com.

Would plasma fillers work for you? Yes, but as explained above, you won't get as much of a result as you would from other types of filler.

TREATMENTS FOR THINNING LIPS AND UNEVEN LIPS

Lips seem to lose their stuffing with age, and get thinner and drier with age, and it's for all the same reasons as with other parts of the face. The collagen that plumps lips up gets gradually broken down, because the delicate skin on the lips suffers the same gradual daily aggressions of daylight. On top of that, drying wind and being licked too much wears away at the skin barrier, which makes lips feel dry, and less able to retain the remaining moisture within them.

Plump lips are one of those eternally appealing, youthful looks, hence the massive appeal of lip injections – both to the older person whose lips are thinning and to the younger ones who just want their lips to be that bit bigger, poutier, and sexier. Since last summer's TV series of Love Island, where several of the young contestants had had lip fillers and discussed them freely, practitioners who specialise in lip work, such as Dr Tijion Esho, have seen a surge in under-25s asking for treatment. Alarmingly, there is no minimum legal age for treatment with injectable fillers, but most responsible practitioners, Esho included, are reluctant to treat anyone under 25.

How Do Lip Injections Work?

Lip injections are pretty straightforward. First, your chosen practitioner assesses your lips and discusses your concerns: What is it about your lips that bothers you? Are you looking for bigger lips? Or better defined lips? Or both? Or simply more hydration in your lips? You and your practitioner then decide on a treatment plan.

Next, your practitioner will take a very fine needle and a syringe of an appropriate filler and inject the filler into your lips. Depending on their preferred technique, they may make a series of tiny injections along the border of the lips to put the product in place, and again in the fleshy part of the lip, or they may slide the needle into the lip border and the whole way along to the cupid's bow, then gradually pull it back to where they started, injecting a tiny line of product along the border as they go.

Or they could use a cannula (which is like a blunt needle) to ease its way along under the skin of your lips, distributing the product as they move it along.

WHAT IS INJECTED INTO THE LIPS?

The lips are soft and flexible, so you need a filler that will sit happily within them, and you're best off with a hyaluronic acid filler designed for the lip area, such as Juvederm's Volbella, Restylane's Kysse or Lyps, or Teoxane's Kiss. Once in the lip, the filler will integrate with the lip tissue and hold onto moisture, because that's what hyaluronic acid does, and this will provide the extra plumpness in your lips.

HOW WELL DOES IT WORK?

Lip fillers can work a treat – but oh boy, can they go wrong! I'm all for a touch of lip-filler but wince when I spot overblown ones which are clearly out of proportion with the face around them.

Seeing what happened to actress Leslie Ash's lovely lips when they were over-inflated in 2002 put many women off lip fillers for good. The really unfortunate thing for her was that her lips were injected with silicone, which settles permanently in the lip tissues and can't be removed.

DOES IT HURT?

A bit, but much less than you would expect. Below, I've written up my experiences with the full range of anaesthetic options, from a full dental block, via numbing cream and a vibrating distraction device, to having no pain prevention at all (which, oddly, didn't hurt). What does hurt is that afterwards, your lips tend to feel a little stiff and ache where they have been injected. You only notice this when you move your mouth, but since we all do that quite a lot, you can't avoid feeling this.

WOULD LIP FILLERS WORK FOR YOU?

It really depends on your lips. Are they a good size but just a bit flatter with age? Then a bit of volumising might be in order. Do they need defining rather than enlarging? In that case, a bit of filler in the border of the lip could do the trick.

If your mouth is small, or your lips are thin, be cautious. There is only so much filler that your lips can take before they will look distorted. As I've said above, your lips need to stay in proportion to the rest of your face, otherwise they will look bizarre.

Also, beware the urge to have just your top lip injected. Lots of people seem to think this is exactly what they need, but once your top lip becomes the same size as your lower lip, it will make your mouth look unbalanced. What looks better is to stick with that golden ratio, phi, so that the proportions of the upper lip to the lower lip are 1:1.6. As ever, find a good practitioner and discuss what is realistic for you. And in case it needs saying again, you only want a temporary filler, one based on hyaluronic acid, in your lips.

If you want a really temporary tweakment just to see how lip fillers might work, you could always try Dr David Jack's Cinderella Lips treatment. He injects lips with saline solution, which gives an idea of what your mouth would look like with extra volume in the lips, but will be reabsorbed by your body by the next day. He came up with this idea as an alternative to treating younger patients with lip filler, rather than sending away empty-handed, but of course it works just fine on older lips, too (£50, drdavidjack.com).

I've written up four very different lip-injection treatments that I've had over the years, but first, here are a couple of things you can try that don't involve needles.

No-Needle Lip Treatments

If you want to try something for your lips which involves no needles of any sort, here are a couple of suggestions. The first is a high-tech lip gel, and the second is a non-invasive, in-clinic treatment.

FILLERINA LIP PLUMPING GEL

A lip gel with plumping powers? I had to give it a whirl to see if it really could live up to its promises.

What It Is

This no-needle lip booster is a home-use product. It's a tube of gel with a click-dispenser device at one end and a rollerball tip at the other, so all you have to do is apply the product and let it sink in.

The gel contains hyaluronic acid molecules of six different molecular weights which are small enough to penetrate the thin tissues of the lips and plump them up. Once inside the lip, these molecules attract and hold onto moisture, which is what creates the gentle swelling in your lips. (Pop a bit of balm over the top, to seal the moisture in.) The gel also delivers an assortment of peptides, which are good for tackling wrinkles such as the 'bar-code' wrinkles above the upper lip.

What It's Like

Very easy to use – except that you are meant to use it five times a day for at least a month, to consolidate the effect, and I find it really difficult to remember to use it this much. And if you drink as many cups of tea as I do, you too may feel that every sip of hot liquid is washing some of the product off your lips.

Verdict

I had had low expectations of this, but after a few days of reasonably obsessive use, I notice my lips are more hydrated and don't need anywhere near as much reapplication of lipstick as usual. They are just a little plumper. I'm not bowled over by the results, but I can see there is a small improvement.

Fillerina Lip Volume, 5ml, from £40, marksandspencer.com.

TREATMENT REVIEW: LIP PERK – THE NON-INVASIVE LIP TREATMENT

This unusual in-clinic treatment offers a novel way of giving lips a temporary, plumping boost.

What It Is

The Perk device was created to fill the gap between plumping lip gels and injectable treatments. It is a pen-like device and it works by giving the lips a thorough, mechanical exfoliation while at the same time soaking the newly scoured skin with a special solution of lip-plumping ingredients including peppermint oil and wheat proteins.

Dr Rita Rakus, who has long been known as London's lip queen for her expertise when injecting lips, and at whose clinic I am trying the Perk treatment, says that it will give my lips a short-term boost. So while it won't in any way give the sort of results I could expect from lip filler, it will definitely make my lips look plumper, and there won't be the risk of any needle marks.

What It's Like

The device uses suction to get a grip on my top lip as it starts its exfoliating business, which makes me want to pull away, except then I have visions of my lip stretching out like a strand of spaghetti. It's a really strange feeling as, chunk by chunk, sections of my lips are vacuumed up, gently exfoliated, and at the same time drenched in the plumping solution. It's quick, too – the treatment takes less than 10 minutes. The Perk device is one that can be used alone, but because it's so quick, many of Dr Rakus's clients use it as an add-on to the Hydrafacial (see page 51).

Comfort Level

Disconcerting, because it's such a strange feeling, but not actually uncomfortable.

Verdict

My lips are definitely softer and plumper, not least because of the effects of the suction and the slight tingling from the peppermint oil in the mix. I am given the rest of the tube of solution that was used on them, and told to apply this at least twice a day, to keep up the volume. Despite doing this, my lips quickly deflate to their normal proportions over the next couple of days. Worth a try for a short-term fix, perhaps before a party, but don't expect lasting results.

Cost and Location

Lip Perk, £65, www.drritarakus.co.uk. To find a practitioner in your area, go to www.thetweakmentsguide.com.

Would It Work for You?

Yes. But not for long.

Potential Problems

None, unless the peppermint oil in the plumping solution irritates your lips.

Injectable Treatments for Re-Shaping and Enhancing the Lips

I have been having my lips injected on and off for nearly 15 years. That makes it sound casual, but it is the procedure I'm most cautious about, just because the lips are so delicate and so much on show that having injections in them feels more of a big deal than other tweakments.

The first time I had my lips done, back in August 2004, I had to stop off in the park on the way home and take 15 minutes just to sit down and process what had happened. It hadn't been painful but, oof, I felt I had had a major shock to the system. It didn't help that I had been anxious about the procedure beforehand, even though I had been thinking about having it done for at least a year. I was worried what I would look like afterwards – memories of Leslie Ash's trout pout were fresh back then – and I hadn't told my husband what I was up to. Also, my lips were a good deal larger than I had bargained for.

That's the thing – the delicate tissues of the lips swell in protest if you stick needles in them. That swelling will go down in due course, but it may take a few days. Then there is the swelling that the dental block (the numbing injections, the same that dentists use when working on the teeth) causes. This swelling will disappear in an hour or so, but it does mean that you will inevitably leave the clinic with lips larger than you had expected, wondering if you have made a terrible mistake. What I have learned since then is that, first, you just need not to panic, because that swelling will subside; and second, it helps to use an ice pack on your lips every hour to help bring down the swelling.

Four Ways with Lip Injections

I am constantly amazed by the different ways in which practitioners adjust and augment lips. You might think that putting fillers into the lips is a straightforward procedure, but it seems more to be an evolving art, and many practitioners develop their own particular methods.

Some like to inject the vermillion border, the thin line of tissue where the lips join the face. Others prefer to work in the body of the lip. Some like to dispense microdroplets of filler throughout the lips with a needle. Others prefer to lay a seam of product using a cannula. Some inject just above the lip line, to make the upper rim of the lip flip out (some people like that look).

Here are four very different lip enhancements, all done with hyaluronic acid fillers, which I have tried over the years.

- First, a full lip enhancement
- Second, a minimal treatment to improve the symmetry of my lips
- Third, an 'anti-ageing' lip treatment
- Fourth, a lip hydration treatment using a cannula

POTENTIAL PROBLEMS WITH LIP INJECTIONS

Swelling is a given – but what you can't tell until you try lip injections is whether you are a person where the swelling will last for hours or one where it will last for days. Bruising is always a possibility. Lumpiness and asymmetry are less likely to be a problem if your practitioner has lots of experience.

For other potential problems, see the full list in the section 'What Can Go Wrong? Potential Problems with Fillers' on page 215.

TREATMENT REVIEW: FULL LIP ENHANCEMENT

The first people I went to for lip enhancement were Fiona Collins and Marie Duckett, two brilliant aesthetic nurses who worked together in Harley Street at the time. They are now in separate practices but are still doing fab work.

What It is

Straightforward lip injections to strengthen and balance the outline of the lips – mine are slightly asymmetrical – along with gentle revolumising.

What It's Like

After giving me a dental block – the sort of injection that completely numbs your mouth when you're at the dentist, which means that you won't feel a thing in your lips (hallelujah!) – Marie injects my lips with tiny drops of Restylane filler. She works along the border of the lips first, to define, enhance, and balance the shape of my lips, before adding a little filler into the body of my lips.

Comfort Level

Very good. Because of that dental block, I can barely feel a thing.

Verdict

At first my lips look simply huge, especially as I have been sent away with a slick of Carmex lip balm which makes them tingle and shine and look even larger than they in fact are. As the swelling subsides, I find I only have two tiny bruises on my lips that look like small inkblots, and my lips are transformed. It only takes a day for the extra swelling to go down, but it takes weeks for me to get used to the enhanced size. But they look lovely and aren't so startling that anybody else is moved to comment. So yes, I was very pleased with the result.

Cost and Location

Lip augmentation treatment with Marie Duckett, from £370, www.marieduckett.co.uk.

Would It Work for You?

Yes. It takes a fair bit of trust to let someone work on your lips, so make sure you have seen pictures of their work beforehand, and discussed the sort of results you want to achieve before you let them loose with a needle.

Potential Problems

See the section 'Potential Problems with Lip Injections' on page 242. To find a practitioner who offers lip enhancement in your area, go to www.thetweakmentsguide.com.

TREATMENT REVIEW: MINIMAL TREATMENT TO IMPROVE LIP SYMMETRY

Dr Tapan Patel is known for his conservative approach to treatments, and although he has agreed to treat my lips, he doesn't really think they need any bulking up with added volume. However, he can see that they're not very symmetrical, and he's happy to work on that.

What It is

The most minimal lip treatment I've ever had, just to correct the asymmetric outline of my lips, which are smaller on the left-hand side.

What It's Like

I'm given numbing cream on my lips for 20 minutes before the injections, but I'm still apprehensive that it may hurt – and even though I'm quite used to injections of all sorts and have a reasonably high pain threshold, I'm not a masochist, and have only ever had lip injections with the aid of a full dental block.

But then Dr Patel produces a small, pen-shaped device with a metallic T-bar on the end. It's called a Nuevibe, and when he switches it on, it vibrates gently. When he places the device on my upper lip, my brain is so bemused by the vibration that it simply doesn't have the bandwidth to notice that he has slipped in the needle and done the injections already. What a relief! My whole mouth is done within five minutes.

Comfort Level

Strangely enough, this was perfectly comfortable. Thanks to not having a dental block, the whole treatment is far quicker, and my lips haven't swollen up noticeably either.

Verdict

Super quick and easy. This treatment was only addressing the borders of my lips, but it has balanced them up beautifully so that they are much more symmetrical. I'm delighted with the results.

Cost and Location

Lip injections with Dr Tapan Patel, PHI Clinic, from £750, www.phiclinic.com. To find a practitioner in your area, go to www.thetweakmentsguide.com.

Would It Work for You?

Yes. If your practitioner proposes injecting with only a Nuevibe for pain relief, it's well worth a try. And sometimes tiny corrections like this can have disproportionally pleasing results.

Potential Problems

See the section 'Potential Problems with Lip Injections' on page 242.

TREATMENT REVIEW: ANTI-AGEING LIP TREATMENT

Yvette Newman has been injecting lips for longer than she cares to admit, so I know I'm in good hands. After a close examination of my mouth, she decides that what my lips need is rejuvenation rather than augmentation.

My lips are very dehydrated, Yvette says, but they're a decent shape and they really don't need lots of extra volume, as that can look odd on an ageing face (I love her honesty). The golden rule, she says, is to maintain balance and harmony in the whole face, to make sure that the outcome is aesthetically pleasing and you don't end up looking like a blowfish.

What It is

Straightforward, thoughtful lip work to make my lips look a touch less like dessicated earthworms, without looking overdone.

What It's Like

Before she starts, Yvette gives my lips a dose of numbing cream. There is also local anaesthetic in the product – Restylane Vitale –

that she is using. The key to keeping the treatment comfortable, she says, is to inject slowly, because then the local anaesthetic in the gel kicks in at the same time. Rather than working on the borders of the lips, Yvette concentrates on the body of each lip, to give them a small boost. She uses more product on the left side, to make it more symmetrical, and more of a match with the right-hand side.

Comfort Level

Apart from the pinpricks each time the needle goes through the skin of my lips, it really doesn't hurt at all, which is a great relief. It helps that Yvette is very calm and clearly knows exactly what she is doing, which is reassuring.

Verdict

Immediately afterwards, my lips look great. The dry look is gone, as they are now subtly plumped out with filler. Yvette has warned me that they will swell up overnight, and so they do, enough that I would have worried if I hadn't been told not to panic when this happened. It takes a day for the swelling to go down.

Given how fluid Restylane Vitale is, I was pleased by how well it lasted. My lips seemed much better hydrated, as well as a more impressive size, for the following six months.

Cost and Location

Lip treatment with Yvette Newman, from £225 for 0.5ml at The Lip Lounge at The Whiteley Clinics, www.whiteleyclinics.co.uk. To find a practitioner in your area, use the tools on my website, www.thetweakmentsguide.com.

Would It Work for You?

Yes. Particularly if you find a practitioner as skilled and experienced as Yvette.

Potential Problems

See the section 'Potential Problems with Lip Injections' on page 242.

As part of a full-face-filler treatment that Dr Tapan Patel did for me in 2018 (see the 'Facial Redesign with 10ml of Filler' treatment review on page 253), he decided my lips needed a boost. Not to make them bigger, but to give them extra hydration.

What It Is

To soften and hydrate my lips without adding extra volume, Dr Patel uses 1ml of Juvederm Volite, a particularly soft and fluid form of hyaluronic acid gel which is more often used as a 'moisture jab' injection to condition the skin from the inside. To flood the tissues of my lips with this hydrating mixture, Dr Patel uses a cannula, a blunt type of needle, to place the product via four tiny holes, in the 'corners' of my lips (upper left, upper right, lower left, and lower right).

What It's Like

I can feel the pinprick as Dr Patel makes the hole for the cannula, then it is the strangest feeling as the cannula noses its way along just beneath the skin of my lips, dispensing product as it goes. This is all very quick, too – it must take all of five minutes.

Comfort Level

To my amazement, completely comfortable, without any sort of anaesthetic apart from a dab of ice at the injection sites where the pinprick holes for the cannula are made.

Verdict

No bruising, no swelling, but lovely soft hydrated lips which barely need lip balm for the next three months.

Cost and Location

Lip injections with Dr Tapan Patel, PHI Clinic, from £750, www.phiclinic.com. To find a practitioner in your area, go to www.thetweakmentsguide.com.

Would It Work for You?

Yes, if your lips are like mine and need hydration more than volume.

Potential Problems

See the section 'Potential Problems with Lip Injections' on page 242.

TREATMENTS FOR 'BARCODE' LIP LINES

The little vertical lines above the upper lip are the ones that are known as the 'barcode' lines, because they run vertically downwards into the top lip. You start to notice them as the skin ages, the collagen degrades, and the levels of elastin in the skin drop, so that that patch of skin above the upper lip, which is always being stretched when we open our mouths or smile, becomes less able to spring back into shape and starts to collapse into tiny wrinkles.

Barcode lines are much more obvious in smokers, because smoking is appallingly bad for directly ageing the skin. Smoking will affect the skin all over your body, but these lines are some of the first to show up on the face, which is why they're often thought of as smoker's lines.

Barcode lines also show up more as lip volume decreases, because the body of the lip is no longer holding the skin taut, so it sags a little. For that reason, lip enhancement of any sort in the upper lip usually softens the look of these tiny vertical lines.

Injecting these lines directly with fillers doesn't work satisfactorily. The lines are so small that anything other than the thinnest type of filler will show up as a bump under the skin, which you clearly don't want, and because so little product is required in each line, it won't last very long either.

You'll get a better result here with a treatment designed to kickstart production of collagen within the skin, such as a laser treatment or Tixel, which uses heat to prompt collagen growth (see page 106 for more details on Tixel).

TREATMENTS FOR MARIONETTE LINES

And then there are the so-called marionette lines, which run down vertically from the corners of the mouth – so-called because if you imagine a wooden puppet or ventriloquist's dummy, those are the lines where the mouth block would drop when it is 'talking'.

Marionette lines settle in for all the same reasons as any other lines – the loss of underlying fat and bone; the ageing, stretching, and wrinkling of the skin – but they are a particular menace, because once they are etched on your face, they give it a permanently grumpy look and drag the corners of your mouth downward.

How to Soften Marionette Lines

You can have dermal filler injected into this area – not directly into the lines (unless they're really deep) but at the corners of the mouth, to lift this area a little, and beneath the lines, to push them back out. But the treatment I've found very helpful for marionette lines is Botox; here's my review.

TREATMENT REVIEW: BOTOX FOR THE MARIONETTE LINES THAT PULL THE FACE DOWN

Botox is best-known for relaxing muscle activity in the upper face, but it can work a treat in the lower face, too.

What It Is

There are no two ways about it: the 'marionette' lines are ageing. And, I found, if you are in the habit of pulling faces, you can easily make them worse. Dr Tapan Patel points this out to me while we are having a chat about fine-tuning my face. 'Have you noticed?' he asks brightly, 'You do this a lot,' and pulls the corners of his own mouth down. He says it nicely but nonetheless, I'm taken aback. Good grief, do I really? I must do if it is something he has picked up on.

I know that a drop of filler at the corners of the mouth can help prevent those corners from being permanently drooped, but hadn't thought about how Botox can help. Dr Patel enlightens me. A touch of Botox in the muscle that pull the corners of my mouth down will damp down this expression and reduce my marionette lines into the bargain.

What It's Like

Very quick, and the injections are barely noticeable. I think there is only one per side. That's it.

Verdict

As the next week goes by, I am of course uncomfortably aware of my habit of pulling the corners of my mouth down, and consequently find I am doing it the whole time. I do it in the mirror, too, to see if and when it changes. Between four and 10 days after treatment, it does. First, one side won't pull down properly, then the other falls in line to match it. I can still make the dratted expression, but it's a ghost of its former self.

Cost and Location

PHI Clinic (www.phiclinic.com), Botox, from £150; with Dr Patel, from £250. To find a practitioner who offers Botox in your area, go to www.thetweakmentsguide.com.

Would This Work for You?

Absolutely, if you are someone who has a habit of pulling this sort of face. It's a nifty trick which any experienced practitioner should be able to do for you.

Potential Problems

Possible bruising at injection sites, and possibly greater loss of expression than you wanted, if your practitioner injects too much – though, as with most Botox injections, reduction of expression is the main aim.

WEAK CHINS: USING FILLER TO IMPROVE THE LOOK OF THE CHIN

The chin seems an unlikely place to inject fillers – it has no wrinkles, and doesn't lose volume in the way the upper face does as it ages – but this is an area to which cosmetic doctors are increasingly turning their attention in order to improve the structure and balance of the face.

Using filler in the lower part of a weak or receding chin can make the chin project further forward and improve the side profile.

This works for both men and women, and it is also a useful trick for counteracting the bone resorption in the chin that creeps in with age. For men, reshaping the chin and jawline with filler is popular for making a face look more masculine.

Clever placement of filler in the middle of the chin can even make a long face look shorter; it's an optical illusion, because of the way the light catches the new slight projection of the chin. As treatments go, it's the icing on the cake, but it's increasingly popular.

I have had my chin injected and reshaped as part of a wider face-remodelling treatment, so I have included it in that review. See the section 'Facial Redesign with 10ml of Filler' on page 253 for details.

NOSE RESHAPING/NON-SURGICAL NOSE JOB

You might not think that there is much that can be done to change the appearance of a nose by adding dermal filler to it – but then you may not have looked at the astonishing before and after pictures from the doctors who do this sort of work.

A quick trawl through the website and Instagram of Dr Ayad Harb, who runs a clinic called Qosmetic in Bicester and London, will show that he can make hooked or bumpy noses appear straight, and adjust the appearance of noses that tip down at the end, all in a matter of minutes. It's a question of rebalancing the proportions rather than an optical illusion, but his grateful patients feel that what he does is akin to magic.

TREATMENT REVIEW: NON-SURGICAL NOSE RESHAPING

If there is something about your nose that you don't like, but you'd never go as far as the palaver and expense of surgical rhinoplasty, this procedure is well worth looking into. Hooked nose? A nose with a bump in the middle? A nose with a droopy tip? Or a nose that looks too big? Their appearance can be adjusted with injectable fillers.

What It Is

Injecting small amounts of filler at strategic points on the nose makes an amazing difference to the way it looks. Dr Ayad Harb calls this procedure the '3-point rhino' – rhino referring of course not to how you'll look after the treatment, but to a surgeon's shorthand name for a rhinoplasty, as a 'nose job' is more properly known.

Dr Harb has the largest non-surgical rhinoplasty practice in the world and does around 2,000 of these a year – and clearly loves doing them, too, whether it's improving what he calls 'family' noses, working on brides-to-be, or sorting out surgical rhinoplasties that haven't had the desired result. The three points where he injects are at the top of the nose, in the middle, and at the tip.

What It's Like
By Helen Nuttall

I've always had a big nose. I don't hate it, but it's a bit droopy and looks a bit 'witchy' from the side. After following Dr Harb's work on Instagram for a while, I realise he might be able to lift the tip of my nose – and if he can, it will look a lot nicer, so I book in. I am just so curious to see what he can do for me.

I tell Dr Harb what I don't like about my nose and can see he completely understands, which is reassuring, as I really don't know what to expect from the treatment. The actual injections are super-quick – the whole procedure only takes 15 minutes. There is no numbing cream, but I don't need it even though I'm a bit of a wimp. There are just three injections, one between my eyes, one in the middle of the nose, and one at the tip to upholster it. That last one really stings, but it is done fast, and I can see the difference immediately.

Comfort Level

It's reasonably comfortable – less painful than having your upper lip waxed.

Verdict

I'm really happy with it. It's a subtle change that friends only notice when I point it out to them. When I see my parents, they don't comment; they just say I'm looking well. This should last me for up to a year, and I'll definitely have it done again; next time, I might ask for the tip to be perked up even more.

Cost and Location

From £575 with Dr Ayad Harb in Bicester or Harley Street, www.qosmetic.co.uk. To find a practitioner in your area, go to www.thetweakmentsguide.com.

Would It Work for You?

It all depends on what your nose looks like to start with, but given the amazing changes that a skilled doctor can make, it is worth having a look at before-and-after shots on their websites or social media. Bumps can be smoothed away, droopy tips lifted, proportions subtly altered.

Potential Problems

Possible bruising at the injection sites. If your practitioner is not skilled at this procedure and doesn't place the filler correctly, the filler might look lumpy, and you might not get the correction you were looking for.

FULL FACE REDESIGN

If you have deep pockets, plus the confidence and trust in your practitioner to let them loose on your face with multiple syringes of filler, the results can be transformative.

TREATMENT REVIEW: FACIAL REDESIGN WITH 10ML OF FILLER

Dr Patel has been doing my fillers (and Botox) for the past few years, and one of the reasons I love his work is because it tends of be on the understated side, which suits me very well, as I much prefer to look normal, rather than 'done'. He has tended to use very little filler – just one or two millilitres, at strategic points in my face; but recently, the thinking behind the use of fillers has changed, as I mentioned earlier in this chapter.

What It Is

The new filler paradigm is that, to create balance and harmony in the face, you may need quite a lot of filler – perhaps even 15ml or 20ml of it. Alongside his role as medical director of the PHI Clinic in Harley Street, Dr Patel is one of the top global trainers for Allergan, the pharma giant that makes Juvederm, the leading brand of facial fillers, so I had an early chance to try out the new look for myself.

At the time I was treated (March 2018), I hadn't had any fillers – apart from a lip treatment (see the section 'Full Lip Enhancement' on page 242) – for well over a year; and I know that if Dr Patel had suggested using so much filler on me even six months before, I would have run away, fast. But I have seen the results that this sort of treatment can give and have done a 180-degree turn in my opinions. Besides, I have every confidence that Dr Patel won't leave me looking a fright.

What It's Like

It's peaceful in the all-white treatment room at the PHI Clinic and so quiet I can hear the slight hiss as each syringe of filler slowly empties. Dr Patel uses Juvederm Voluma, a sturdy gel that is good for providing support and structure, in my temples (0.7ml of filler each side). This is an area that doesn't get much attention, but the temples become hollow as the face ages, so filling them out a bit helps soften the whole look of the face. Filler in this area also helps lift up the tails of the eyebrows, which tend to droop downwards with age.

My cheeks are given 1ml on the right, 1.6ml on the left, to even them up and to gently boost the outer curve of the cheek and soften my nose-to-mouth lines.

A good deal of product (3ml) goes into my chin, which is marked up for treatment with two long rectangles below my lower lip and three round spots along my jawline – an area known as the pre-jowl sulcus. The long patches are treated with a cannula, the spots with a needle, to build up my chin and give it better definition. I know my chin is asymmetric, so one side receives more than the other. Another 1ml goes into each corner of my jawline.

My lips, as usual, are in need of hydration, so rather than adding volume with a more resilient sort of filler, Dr Patel uses a cannula to dispense 1ml of super-runny Juvederm Volite beneath the surface. It feels incredibly strange as the cannula noses its way along just beneath the surface of my skin.

Comfort Level

Apart from the small scratch each time the needle goes in, all I can feel is a strange sensation of pressure as the filler gel eases its way into my face. There's no pain – Dr Patel's assistant, Sarah, gently dabs ice on my skin each time before the needle slips in. The ice numbs the skin and also constricts the blood vessels so there is less chance that they will be nicked and bleed – and the Voluma filler contains local anaesthetic, so it numbs as it goes. Even when my lips are being done, it doesn't hurt – which seems astonishing, given how much anaesthetic I have usually had whenever I have had them treated. Perhaps I have slipped into some sort of treatment trance.

Dr Patel does keep sitting me upright – to check how everything is looking, but also to check that I haven't gone and zoned out altogether. He wouldn't normally do this much treatment in one go – to spread the cost, as well as the number of injections – but he knows I can manage it and am not likely to suddenly develop needle fatigue and call a halt.

Verdict

Amazing. Straight away, I can see the difference in my cheeks, which look a little lifted, and my lips, which look much softer. My chin looks stronger, though I don't notice the huge improvement in my jawline until I am photographed from the side. Now it is more defined. The fillers settle in quickly in my cheeks, temples, and lips, more slowly along my jawline, and my chin goes on feeling as if it has had an implant for about a month, until the filler integrates with the tissues around it. The main fillers should last for up to 18 months; the lip treatment with Volite will need refreshing in six months' time.

Altogether, a real improvement, yet there is nothing about it that looks startling or out of place. You can see all the clinical pictures on my blog at www.alicehartdavis.com.

I had fantastic results with this treatment but feel I should point out that, as well as being expensive, this 'use-more-filler' approach may not suit everyone. It's a treatment strategy that is being promoted energetically by Allergan – naturally, because then they sell more filler – but other doctors have told me that is very easy to upset the balance of a face by simply piling in more and more filler.

Cost and Location

10ml filler facial redesign with Dr Tapan Patel, £3,995, www.phiclinic.com.

Would This Work for You?

It would depend on what your face looks like, and which bits could benefit from adjusting with dermal filler. I was a good candidate for this procedure because of the way my face has lost volume in all the obvious places like the temples and the cheeks.

One question I've been asked a lot since is whether my face will be 'worse' afterwards, in a couple of years when all this filler has been reabsorbed – will it be left looking hollow and collapsed like a deflated balloon? In short, no – it will just go back to how it was looking before, though there will be the effects of a couple of years of the normal ageing process to contend with, too. It won't look collapsed, because the treatment isn't stretching the skin – it is just gently propping it up from the inside.

Another question I've been asked is, given the expense of this, wouldn't it be better to wait, save up, and have surgery. Well, possibly – but I was discussing this point with top plastic surgeon Rajiv Grover, who pointed out that a face lift can only tighten the skin over the existing bone structure. So while a face lift would make the lower face and jawline more taut, it couldn't create this same remodelling-from-the-inside effect that Dr Patel has achieved with filler, which has managed to give me a better jawline, lift my cheekbones, and improve the look of my chin.

CHAPTER 11

Tightening Sagging Skin

Can you shrink-wrap sagging skin? Yes, you can – up to a point – and these are the tweakments that can do it.

WHY DOES SKIN SAG?

By this stage of the book, I'm sure you've grasped the reasons why our skin starts to sag as it ages, but in case you've been skipping around from section to section, I'll spell it out again. First, the skin loses its firmness and elasticity with age, and the collagen and elastin in it becomes depleted. Then there's the way the fat pads – which give the face its lovely youthful curves – shrink as we get older, and the bones in the skull start to recede a fraction. Also, the facial muscles tend to slacken with age, like worn elastic bands. So you end up – to be brutal – with floppier skin draped over a shrunken frame.

CAN SKINCARE HELP?

Skincare really isn't much help here. Collagen-boosting vitamin C serums, retinoids, and well-proven high-street anti-agers like No7's Protect & Perfect line can help up freshen and firm skin – but can't tighten the skin as effectively as tweakments.

WHAT YOU CAN DO WITH INJECTABLES

You can reduce some of the sagging with dermal fillers (see the previous chapter). But to tighten the skin itself, what is needed is more aggressive treatment with micro-needling or with energy-based devices that use radiofrequency, heat, laser, or ultrasound energy. These both shrink the existing skin and encourage it to renew and strengthen itself from the inside out.

Having said all that, most practitioners will point out to you that skin tightening works really well in combination with injectables, because one is lifting and propping up the sagging from below, while the other is shrink-wrapping it from above.

HOODED EYES AND SAGGING UPPER EYELIDS

Saggy eyelids and hooded eyes are one of the commonest complaints among the ageing. First, you notice that your eyeliner starts blotting itself onto your brow bone, when you had no idea they were so close together; and then it becomes pointless applying eye shadow, as it all vanishes into folds of skin and can't be seen – unless you close one eye, when you notice it has migrated into the creases of the eyelid.

It's not hard to see why this happens. Along with the rest of the face, the eye area gets exposed to ultraviolet light, which, over the years, speeds up the breakdown of the collagen that keeps skin firm and the elastin that keeps skin bouncy. When that starts to happen, the skin becomes floppier; and it's all the more marked on the eyelids, because they are one of the most mobile parts of the face, constantly opening and shutting and stretching.

As the skin becomes less elastic, it is less able to ping back into shape when it is stretched. The skin on the eyelids is also thinner than on the rest of the face, so the effects are more pronounced; and there are precious few sebaceous glands in the area, so the skin gets dry very easily, and dry skin wrinkles more swiftly than oily or well moisturised skin. Put all that together, and it's a wonder we don't all have eyelids drooping down to our noses by the time we're 55.

So what can be done? It very much depends on the extent of the hooding and sagging, but you will get the best and swiftest results with cosmetic surgery. An upper-eyelid blepharoplasty (surgery to the eyelid, to remove excess skin) is quick, neat, and a relatively straightforward procedure; but I know that surgery is a no-go area for most people, and it's not what this book is about.

Skincare can make small improvements in hydrating and tensing the skin around the eyes; and a regime that includes decent vitamin C products and retinoids will keep your skin as fresh as it can; but still, neither will achieve any shrinking of excess skin on the upper eyelids.

Until very recently, that was about it. But even in the time since I've been writing this book, a couple of new treatments have arrived in the UK that can give impressive improvements in tightening loose skin on the upper eyelid.

Skin Tightening with the Hot-Iron Treatment

The Tixel treatment was introduced to me as being 'like a waffle-iron for your wrinkles' – which sounded intriguing but alarming. What that phrase meant was that instead of using a high-tech source such as laser, ultrasound, or plasma energy to cause an injury to the skin, which would stimulate a wound-healing response and tighten up the skin tissue, the Tixel device uses heat. It gives a good result and I've mentioned it here because unlike a laser, the device can be used directly on the skin of the eyelids. For a full treatment review, see 'Tixel Skin Tightening and Resurfacing' on page 106.

Tixel, from £495 per treatment (three are recommended), PHI Clinic, 102 Harley Street, W1; www.phiclinic.com.

The Shrink-Wrap Treatment: Radiofrequency

Radiofrequency (RF) devices offer a useful type of technology for tightening up the skin. Radiofrequency is commonly referred to as a tweakment that can have a 'shrink-wrapping' effect. Radio-frequency devices heat up the lower layers of the skin (the dermis) to 42 degrees C, at which point the existing collagen contracts, giving an immediate tightening effect.

The radiofrequency energy also makes the skin think it is injured, so it starts throwing out growth factors and new collagen to heal the perceived wounds; in due course, these show up on the surface of the skin as smoother, firmer, tighter skin.

There's more detail on how radiofrequency devices work on page 144, including details of potential problems, which include redness and swelling because of the heat generated.

TREATMENT REVIEW: PING RADIOFREQUENCY EYE-LIFT

Ping is a treatment just for the eye area, created by Dr Sach Mohan at his Revere Clinics. Ping uses EndyMed FSR, so it both tightens and smooths the treatment area. Other doctors also use radiofrequency for lifting the eye area – see the tweakment finder tool on www.thetweakmentsguide.com.

What It Is

This treatment is described as a non-surgical eye lift treatment. Ping uses focused radio frequency treatment (FSR – Fractional Skin Resurfacing) to create thousands of microscopic holes in the upper layer of the skin to initiate what Dr Mohan calls 'hyper healing', causing skin cells to interlock and stimulating collagen production to leave the skin smoother, tighter, and brighter. Its main aim is to do enough tightening to give a lift to the upper eyelid, and it is also meant to soften fine lines and even to improve dark circles.

What It's Like
By Karen Heath

My eyelids could certainly do with a lift, so I am keen to try this treatment; and I know that radiofrequency energy is clinically proven for tightening the skin, so I have high hopes. I have numbing cream applied for 45 minutes before the procedure, and then Dr Sach Mohan applies the radiofrequency device in short bursts, working over the skin all around my eyes.

Even with all the numbing cream, I can still feel a slight burning 'ping' with each pass of the device (that's where the name came from). It isn't too painful, but it does feel sore, and it is difficult not to flinch. Fortunately each eye takes less than 10 minutes.

Afterwards, when the numbing cream wears off, my eye area feels hot and looks red, but worse is the smell of burning flesh – I keep getting wafts of it all that night. For the next two days, my eyes just look a bit swollen, as if I've been crying (I use a soothing cream on them, as advised), and they are fine after a week.

Comfort Levels

Uncomfortable – but mercifully quick.

Verdict

After a couple of weeks, I could definitely see changes in the skin around my eyes. It was just that bit softer and smoother and less crepey, and when I went back to the clinic for the 'after' pictures, I was startled by how much 'lift' had taken place in my upper lids. Impressive.

Cost and Location

£550 per treatment (three are recommended), Revere Clinics, Harley Street and Northwood, www.revereclinics.com.

Would It Work for You?

Probably. How much tightening and skin renewal can be achieved depends on the quality of your skin. If there is too much wrinkling and sagging of the eyelid, it won't work that well, and you'll be better off with an upper eyelid lift (though yes, that means surgery).

Potential Problems

Possible redness and scorching if the skin is overtreated.

Skin Tightening with 'Plasma' Energy: Plexr 'Soft Surgery'

The newest and most eye-catching way of lifting upper eyelids without going under the knife is done using 'plasma' energy, which burns away tiny patches of skin along the creases of the excess skin below the browbone, thus abruptly shrinking it back up into a neater shape.

You'll be wondering what plasma energy is (I am still getting my head around this, and it is two years since I first saw this machine in action). We are all familiar with solids, liquids, and gases; plasma is one step beyond this, a different state of matter. The machine ionises gases in the air to create a small electrical spark similar to a tiny lightning bolt, which vaporises a minute patch of the skin. When you watch it being done, the tip of the wireless, pen-like device is a small metal prong that appears to be zapping the skin with these miniature lightning bolts.

Each zap leaves a small burn mark and causes an instant tightening in the skin. The technique is to create a pattern of these little marks along a crease of excess skin, which is what gives the instant shrinking effect.

If you're thinking this sounds quite a hardcore option, you're right. Those burn marks make the eyes puff up for a few days as scabs grow over them; then after a week or so, the scabs fall off, leaving fragile new skin beneath, which needs to be well protected from UV light. Practitioners who are keen on this system include two well-known eye surgeons, Sabrina Shah-Desai (www.perfecteyesltd.com) and Maryam Zamani (www.drmaryamzamani.com), who find it is a good intermediary step for patients who don't yet need a full blepharoplasty, and also cosmetic practitioners including Dr David Jack (www.drdavidjack.com) and Dr Frances Prenna Jones (www.drfrancesprennajones.com).

The website of GT Fusion, the company behind the treatment, points out that the treatment also works well on other areas of the body too, and even on acne scarring.

POTENTIAL PROBLEMS WITH PLEXR

The Plexr device can only be used by trained medical specialists; even so, if you're interested in this, look for a practitioner who has as much experience as possible with the technique. Because it is basically creating burns on the skin, there is the potential for scarring with each of those tiny lightning-bolt marks; and because three rounds of treatment are advised for the maximum result, that's potentially a lot of scarring.

That said, various practitioners, including all the ones mentioned above, have told me that their patients have never experienced scarring problems with Plexr. I'd suspect that is because of the expert and light-handed way in which they are using it; other doctors tell me they have seen less happy results.

Despite these practitioners' reassurances, I am wary of this device and am keeping an eye on the Mk II version of it, which is called FELC. This was invented by Professor Giorgio Fippi, who came up with Plexr, and delivers a less aggressive form of plasma treatment.

I find the idea very intriguing but am too concerned about the potential for scarring (see below) to want to try it. There are various other forms of 'plasma machine' that offer a similar treatment: the Medicetics clinic (www.medicetics.com) has Plasma IQ, and Dr Nick Milojevic (www.miloclinic.com) has a machine called Plasmage.

TREATMENT REVIEW: TIGHTENING WRINKLED, SAGGING LOWER EYE LIDS WITH PLEXR

As well as lifting the skin on hooded eyes, Plexr can also be used on the lower eyelids, to lift and tighten wrinkled eye bags.

What It Is

As explained earlier in this chapter, the Plexr plasma device is used to vaporise tiny pin-prick-sized holes in the skin, without damaging surrounding skin or muscle. This results in a superficial burn-like injury to the skin, which creates new collagen to tighten the area and give a smooth, even result.

What It's Like
By Karen Heath

Under the protective goggles and with the anaesthetic cream on, I have to ask Dr Dev Patel whether he has actually started the treatment, as initially I can't feel a single thing. As he reaches the outer edges of the treatment area, I become aware of a hot pin-pricking sensation, which is bearable because each pulse from the machine only lasts a millisecond. A nurse is also using a fan directed on the area to help cool the skin. It takes less than 30 minutes to treat both eyes, and afterwards it takes a few hours for the anaesthetic to wear off.

Initially the area is just red – it isn't painful at all – but I have been told to take Ibuprofen if I need to, which I don't. Two days later, hundreds of tiny pin-prick scabs have developed under each eye to form an unsightly crust, and they remain there for six days before they start to fall off. They aren't painful and don't itch, either. I go about my daily business, with a pair of sunglasses on as much as I can, and just ignore any strange stares. As anyone who sees them close up likes to tell me, they look horrific, especially as the concealer that I have been told to put on them just sinks into the cracks between the scabs and makes them look all the more obvious.

Verdict

After nine days, most scabs have fallen off (mostly on my pillow – yuck!), and my under-eye area is red, but this can be easily covered with the SPF 50 foundation the clinic has given me. It doesn't bother me in the least, because I can see that already my under-eyes look smoother and considerably less crepe-y. This continues, much to my delight, even once the swelling subsides.

Cost and Location

£650 for lower or upper lids or crow's feet, £895 for both upper and lower lids, and £995 for all three. Dr Dev Patel, perfectskinsolutions.co.uk; up to three treatments needed. To find a practitioner in your area, go to www.thetweakmentsguide.com.

Would It Work for You?

Before opting to try this treatment, sit down for a proper, honest discussion with your practitioner about whether they really think it is the best option for you.

Potential Problems

As above, there is potential for scarring if the skin is overtreated and burned.

MIDFACE SAGGING: LOOSE SKIN ON THE CHEEKS

The midface – that's everything below your eyes and above your jaw – is another area where sagging skin becomes all too obvious as the fat pads that have been holding up the skin start to shrivel. Given that this is such a normal and common problem, it's not surprising that there are so many treatments available that aim to help out in this particular area, all by tightening the skin in one way or another.

The main types of technology used for tightening treatments are radiofrequency, focussed ultrasound, laser, and heat.

Radiofrequency Treatments for Midface Sagging

These treatments use radiofrequency (RF) energy (see the sidebar 'How Radiofrequency Works' on page 144 for details) to boost collagen production in the lower layers of the skin by heating the skin to the point where the skin thinks it is being injured and sets in motion the healing response that produces collagen. As with all the other energy-based technologies, treatments range from 'light' to 'intensive'.

THE GENTLE OPTIONS

For the curious who don't want to commit themselves to anything intensive, there are salon-type treatments (as opposed to clinic-type treatments) that use radiofrequency energy to give the face a spot of gentle tautening. There's Venus Freeze, which I've written up in Chapter 4 (see page 56; www.venustreatments.com), and Collagen Wave Therapy (www.lisaharrisskinscience.co.uk and elsewhere), which works in much the same way. These treatments cost around £120 each. They're swift, comfortable and, though you might be left a tiny bit pink afterwards, there is no actual 'downtime' as such. Also, because the treatment works is done at a low intensity, you will need to do a whole course of treatments in order to sustain and prolong the results.

THE INTENSIVE OPTIONS

If you are prepared to undergo more intensive radiofrequency skin tightening, you have several treatment options, such as Thermage and Intracel.

TREATMENT REVIEW: THERMAGE RADIOFREQUENCY SKIN TIGHTENING

This treatment uses radiofrequency energy for a shrink-wrapping effect. At the Dr Rita Rakus clinic, they call this treatment 'face ironing' because of the smoothing effect it can achieve on saggy skin. It works well to help hooded eyes, too.

What It Is

Rather than using a hot, smooth-ended device that is kept constantly moving around the face in contact with the skin, the

Thermage handpiece delivers a precise dose of RF energy in one spot. Then it is moved to the next patch of skin, where another precise dose is delivered, and in this way it is worked slowly across the cheeks and the neck, to bring each area up to the required temperature (42 degrees C).

The heat damages the existing collagen in the skin, which shrinks in protest (which is what gives the immediate lifting effect), then starts to repair itself. That repairing part takes time, so best results will be seen three to six months after treatment. Also, Thermage is a one-off treatment.

What It's Like

My face is marked out into squares with a grid-like transfer for the doctor to use as a guide. Unlike laser light, radiofrequency energy isn't drawn to dark pigment, so the grid doesn't get in the way of the treatment; this difference also means the treatment is good for all skin colours.

Each pulse from the treatment device feels firm and hot but not unbearable – the 'comfort pulse' device tip buzzes slightly when it meets the skin, which distracts my brain from noticing any pain, and the device tip also cools the skin as it goes. It's less comfortable around the jaw but otherwise, it is perfectly bearable.

Comfort Levels

Comfortable to moderately uncomfortable around the jaw.

Verdict

Even though my skin was red immediately afterwards, I could see it already looked tighter and a bit lifted, which was very exciting. The redness calmed down during the afternoon, and I had to wait a few months to see further improvements, but these have been good – there is a subtle smoothing and lifting all across my cheeks, and my neck looks more taut, too.

Cost and Location

£2,900 for the lower face and neck, Dr Rita Rakus, London SW1 and clinics around the country; www.drritarakus.co.uk. To find a practitioner in your area, go to www.thetweakmentsguide.com.

Would It Work for You?

Yes, it probably would, particularly if your practitioner is experienced in how to get the best out of the treatment.

Potential Problems

Minimal – this is an FDA-approved technology, though there is the potential for burns if it is done incorrectly. There may be some redness, swelling and tingling in the treatment area but this is temporary and unlikely to persist for longer than a day.

ENDYMED PRO 3DEEP SKIN TIGHTENING

EndyMed is another treatment system that uses radiofrequency (RF) energy to tighten the skin. As well as the usual radiofrequency trick of deep-heating the dermis to tighten the collagen and stimulate the fibroblasts, EndyMed Pro has two other treatment modes.

- **FSR.** FSR stands for Fractional Skin Resurfacing (as described in the section 'Ping Radiofrequency Eye-Lift' on page 260), which burns microscopic channels of damage into the skin, so it improves texture and pigmentation as well as providing the basic tightening.

- **Intensif.** This mode deploys an oscillating treatment head packed with microneedles, which can be adjusted between 0.5mm and 5mm (yeow!), so you get a microneedling treatment at the same time as a radiofrequency boost. Yes, both of these treatments are quite challenging and will leave you looking a little pink and sore for a day or two, but they certainly work.

My review of this treatment at the Waterhouse Young clinic in London is on page 145. I put it there because it also did a great job of smoothing and improving the surface of my skin.

Would this treatment work for you? Yes, probably, as long as you complete the course and also use the skincare that they recommend alongside the treatments.

TREATMENT REVIEW: INTRACEL

Another form of radiofrequency treatment is Intracel, which combines radiofrequency tightening with microneedling.

What It Is

The Intracel machine has a treatment head which incorporates heated needles as well as electrodes that dispense radiofrequency. The needles can be adjusted between 0.5mm and 2.5mm, depending on which bit of the face is being treated. This treatment head has a squarish end, which is carefully stamped across the face and forehead, with each 'pulse' or 'zap' delivering radiofrequency and needling together.

This is the sort of treatment that needs 30 minutes of numbing cream beforehand. It is quite intensive enough to generate good results, both in boosting collagen in the lower layers of the skin and in smoothing and resurfacing on the surface, thanks to the microneedling. And it is one of the few treatments that can be used on active acne.

What It's Like

Not as bad as I had feared. Radiofrequency treatments can feel as biting as laser; but this treatment, done by Dr Sarah Tonks, was manageable, which was good, because it took around 40 minutes. My face went quite red afterwards and took a day to calm down.

Comfort Level

I needed the anaesthetic cream. With it, each blast from the device tingled a bit, but wasn't actively painful.

Verdict

My face looked a little tighter immediately, and would have improved further if I had gone back for the recommended follow-up treatments. All the needling helped reduce the look of the pores on my nose and chin, too.

Cost and Location

From £800 with Dr Sarah Tonks, thelovelyclinic.co.uk. To find a practitioner in your area, go to www.thetweakmentsguide.com.

Would It Work for You?

Yes, though it's not as much of a result, nor as noticeable, as you would get with other radiofrequency treatments that are more expensive and more intensive.

Potential Problems

Few, unless you are over-treated, which could potentially leave the skin scorched.

THE FOCUSED ULTRASOUND LIFT

I can hear you thinking: 'Ultrasound? Which is nice and gentle and used for looking at babies in the womb? How can that...?' – to which the answer is, it's a different sort of ultrasound. Focused, high-intensity ultrasound, which narrows its sound-energy waves in to a single point. These don't hit the surface of the skin, as a laser would, but a predetermined spot up to 4.5mm beneath the skin's surface.

What each jolt of ultrasound is aiming to do is strike deep into the skin in order to make the collagen contract, and to stimulate the formation of new collagen and elastin over the next few months, which further tightens up the skin. It can do this at different depths (1.5mm, 3mm and 4.5mm) below the surface, for greater tightening.

At 4.5mm below the skin's surface, the ultrasound can reach the superficial muscular aponeurotic system (SMAS). The SMAS is the layer of muscular tissue in the face that surgeons manipulate when they are performing a face lift.

Again, there are different types of focused ultrasound treatment on offer, some of which are branded. Any of them can be called HIFU (High Intensity Focused Ultrasound), as this is the type of treatment rather than a brand, in the way that not all vacuum cleaners are Hoovers. So if two different clinics offer 'HIFU', it may not be the same treatment at each. Of the branded ones, the best known are Ultracel, which combines HIFU with radiofrequency and microneedling (so it's like Intracel, discussed above, with added ultrasound), and Ultherapy, which is the only ultrasound-based treatment device to have achieved FDA clearance for its stated claim of lifting the skin. Even though this is

ULTHERAPY BACKGROUND AND POTENTIAL PROBLEMS

If you've heard anything about Ultherapy, it is probably that it hurts like anything. I know I'm partly to blame for that, having written a story for the Daily Mail when the treatment was launched in the UK in 2013, which was headlined 'Is this the world's most agonizing facial?'. (Not my choice of headline; obviously this treatment is a good deal more serious than a 'facial' and – although it was certainly uncomfortable – it wasn't 'agony'.)

But people love scare stories, particularly in this business, and it was true that one of my beauty-journalist colleagues had quit the treatment halfway through the week before I went, unable to take the pain; it was also true that, in the USA, practitioners routinely gave patients Valium before starting the treatment – as they now do in this country. And although the treatment was extremely effective – the muscles of my face and neck ached for three weeks afterwards, and showed a considerable lifting and tightening effect over the next year – I wouldn't have been in a hurry to do it again; but then, luckily, it's a one-off treatment.

The second version of the Ultherapy machine, which emerged two years later, found a way to dial down the intensity of the treatment considerably while still gaining most of the results. I tried that too, and found it gave good, if not quite so remarkable, results without as much discomfort as the original; the effects of the treatment last for 18 months or so. I've since had the treatment a third time, in 2017, and found it much more tolerable.

The other thing that you may have gleaned about Ultherapy if you have searched online is that there are enough horror stories on the web about the way it 'melts fat' in faces (look on realself.com) to prevent you wanting to consider it. It worried me – I don't want to lose any of the remaining fat in my face – so I have investigated further and spoken to the manufacturers of the machine and to top practitioners such as Dr Tracy Mountford, whose clinic does more Ultherapy treatments than anywhere else in Europe.

(continued)

ULTHERAPY BACKGROUND AND POTENTIAL PROBLEMS
(continued)

The manufacturers (and the practitioners) say that if a practitioner is scrupulous about following the treatment guidelines, uses the machine correctly and, above all, as long as they are using a genuine Ultherapy machine, all will be absolutely fine. Because it is a new, effective, and FDA-approved technology, there are already many copies of the Ultherapy machine in the market. Many of these are (illegally) advertised using Ultherapy branding but don't have its safety and efficacy data, and there are also apparently fake machines around. In aesthetics, as in other luxury industries, there is a great deal of counterfeiting.

Even having been reassured by all that and having been fine myself with three rounds of treatment over the past five years, from which I have seen good results, I find there are still questions over this treatment. Some people – as with any treatment – just don't respond. And some have visibly negative results, with fat loss beneath the skin that leaves it droopier than before. This isn't new news to the company. If you burrow into the far reaches of the Ultherapy practitioner website, you will find the section that lists problems reported during the clinical trials – mostly short-lived redness, swelling, and pain – but also fat and volume loss, skin sagging or drooping, and hyperpigmentation.

So it obviously does happen, and the company acknowledges it happens. As I said before, I've been fine with the treatment, as are most people, but others haven't.

---

an impressive claim to be able to make, Ultherapy is not without its detractors – see the nearby sidebar.

TREATMENT REVIEW: ULTHERAPY SKIN LIFTING AND TIGHTENING

'Ultherapy is the only FDA-cleared technology to lift the face in a single treatment,' says Dr Tracy Mountford, who runs the Cosmetic Skin Clinic, the top provider of Ultherapy treatments in the UK. 'It also gives swift, durable, and impressive results.'

What It Is

Just to recap, Ultherapy uses high-intensity focused ultrasound waves which pass deep into the skin, targeting collagen as deep as the SMAS layer, which lies below the skin and the fat. The SMAS layer is at different depths on different areas of the face, and the usual procedure with Ultherapy is to do two 'passes' at varying depths, in order to catch the SMAS and a layer of tissue above it. (How does the therapist know where to aim? Because there's a handy visualizer pane on the device, which uses what we'd think of as 'normal' ultrasound to show the layers of the skin, so that the therapist can focus the treatment in exactly the right spot).

Ultherapy can tighten and lift the face – or the eyebrow, or the skin under the jaw – because the treatment is targeting and tightening the skin so deeply. The ultrasound energy also boosts the formation of new collagen and elastin over the next few months, which is what really tightens up the skin.

What It's Like

Fascinating. I have a couple of Ibuprofen before the treatment as a precaution (see the 'Comfort Level' section, next), then relax and let aesthetician Esther Loughran get on with it. She marks out the treatment area in white pencil – a swathe across each cheek and then down over my jawline into my neck – on each side, then begins working the treatment head of the Ultherapy machine methodically over these. Whereas lasers bite, and radiofrequency treatments feel hot, each blast of ultrasound delivers a zinging little pulse.

It takes about 45 minutes to treat my whole neck-to-jaw area. Esther goes over each area twice, focusing the ultrasound waves to different depths, and advises me not to chatter but to concentrate on calm, deep breathing.

Comfort Level

Mildly-to-moderately uncomfortable – mild on the neck, moderate when the treatment head is working over the jawbone.

Because the treatment area lies well below the skin, numbing cream is no help (because that only numbs the surface of the skin). Ibuprofen will take the edge off, and the Cosmetic Skincare Clinic offers ibuprofen before the treatment, along with diazepam (Valium) if you want it. Having tried both the original and the adapted versions of Ultherapy without the benefit of diazepam, I can tell you that Ultherapy 2.0 is less painful than the original, but not pain-free. At least it is a one-off treatment.

Verdict

I can see an instant lifting and tightening along my jawline and down my neck. I know that is just from the initial hit from the immediate collagen shrinkage, but still, it is good to see. And I know the main results will take three months to show up as the new collagen is formed. I've had this treatment three times over the past five years and find it has really helped to counteract the way that my lower face and jawline were descending into a middle-aged droop.

Cost and Location

From £1,200, Cosmetic Skin Clinic, London and Stoke Poges, www.cosmeticskinclinic.com. To find a practitioner in your area, go to www.thetweakmentsguide.com.

Would It Work for You?

Probably. It really ought to, and has better data on the results that it achieves than other HIFU systems.

Potential Problems

See the sidebar 'Ultherapy Background and Potential Problems' on page 270 for coverage of potential problems.

TREATMENT REVIEW: ULTRACEL

Like Intracel and Ultherapy, this treatment offers high-intensity focused ultrasound, but it also wraps in two other tightening and lifting technologies to give the face an instant boost and also a longer-term lifting effect through all layers, from the lowest right up to the surface. (If you're wondering whether you didn't just read all this – you almost did. Ultracel is the big sister of Intracel, and adds ultrasound into the mix.)

What It Is

Three technologies used together, a triple-whammy if you like, delivered by three separate handpieces. There's focused ultrasound for deep muscular lifting, radiofrequency to tighten the skin in the dermis (the lower layers), and microneedling for a resurfacing effect on the skin's surface.

What It's Like

By Karen Heath

The treatment begins with radiofrequency, done with a device which is kept moving around my face. It just feels a bit warm on the first pass, but then the temperature is turned up on the second pass to a point where I feel it is going to burn, but it is moved just before it does. This is followed by focused ultrasound using a handpiece with a nib about 2x1cm, which isn't particularly painful but feels like it is creating an ache deep inside my skin.

After Dr Galyna Selezneva, who is doing the treatment, has finished one side, she shows me how tight my jawline is compared to the untreated side, where I can grab a good wedge of skin under my jaw. I escape without part 3, the microneedling, as Dr Galyna says I don't need it. Some people end up red and slightly swollen in the face after treatment – I look perfectly normal, maybe because I didn't have the needling, so I am able to get on with my life with absolutely zero downtime. A week later, I can still slightly feel it if I touch my face, just a slight reassuring soreness (it's strange, the way you think once you start to do these treatments), which should mean great results.

Comfort Level

Fine to moderately uncomfortable.

Verdict

There was a small instant result – from the way the collagen is forced to contract – and now, a month on, there is a little less slackness which I pinch the skin under my jaw. I found it an easy treatment with minimal to no downtime, and it gives reasonable results – but it is eye-wateringly expensive, bearing in mind it needs topping up every 18 months.

Cost and Location

From £3,500, Dr Rita Rakus, www.drritarakus.co.uk. To find a practitioner in your area, go to www.thetweakmentsguide.com.

Would It Work for You?

It should do – if you have the budget.

Potential Problems

Temporary redness, swelling and tingling of the treatment area. Potential damage to the nerves in the temple and jawline if the area above them is treated by accident, which may take a few weeks to resolve.

Laser Skin Tightening

And then there are lasers which can help tighten the skin. 'Lasers' is such a broad term and covers so many different machines that it is hard to generalise. Some lasers work on the surface of the skin and can 'ablate' or burn it away – good for resurfacing the skin, but a hardcore treatment that hardly anyone wants any more. Other lasers are non-ablative, and reach a little deeper into the skin.

POTENTIAL PROBLEMS WITH LASER SKIN TIGHTENING

If you're looking into laser treatments, check carefully on the make of machine the clinic is using, what that machine is promising to do, and whether it has any safety or efficacy data to show that it can do what it is claiming. Also, check how long the laser technician has been using the machine for.

Clinics using cosmetic lasers in the UK no longer need to have a CQC (Care Quality Commission) certification, nor do cosmetic laser operators – so, as with fillers, anyone can offer the treatment. It goes without saying that lasers are powerful tools and need to be used with immense care lest they burn or scorch the skin; any over-treatment can cause hyperpigmentation.

Mostly, clinics use lasers on a 'fractional' setting. That means firing the laser through a grid of minute holes, to create tiny channels of damage in the skin, which will prompt a wound-healing response in the skin. This response makes for newer, tighter collagen, and therefore firmer skin.

TREATMENT REVIEW: DEBBIE THOMAS SIGNATURE DNA LASER

Debbie Thomas's philosophy is to provide bespoke treatments for each client using proven technologies to get optimum results – and lasers tick all the boxes when you know how to wield a laser as skilfully as she does. Most facialists who use lasers have only a single laser, but Debbie has many, and finds that 'layering' several - different laser procedures within one treatment session gives better results than traumatising the skin with a heavier treatment from a single laser. Exactly what she'll use depends on what your face needs.

What It Is

Debbie decides to use three lasers on me. First, a Dual Yellow laser with a short wavelength to reduce discolouration and uneven pigmentation on the skin's surface. Second, a longer-wavelength Fotona laser to stimulate collagen and elastin production in the skin and produce a tightening effect. This same laser is then used inside the mouth, for an extra face-lifting effect. That might sound bonkers, but lasers are widely used for tightening mucous membranes – both in the mouth, to reduce snoring, and in the vagina, to help treat stress incontinence – so it makes sense. And thirdly, a fractional Erbium laser to resurface the top layers of the skin and stimulate yet more collagen production. 'Fractional' means that the laser is fired through a grid of tiny holes into the skin. This leaves tiny patches of intact skin between the minute holes drilled by the laser, for faster healing.

What It's Like

Before starting the treatment, Debbie gives my face a light peel with glycolic acid (prickly, but not intolerable) to loosen dead skin cells that clutter the surface and will get in the way of the lasers. Then she covers my eyes with tiny solid blackout goggles, and brings on the lasers.

The Dual Yellow Laser feels warm and comfortable. Next, the Fotona laser, which Debbie uses in 'smooth' mode, feels no worse than a strong blast of hot air. After this, she uses the same laser – at a higher intensity – inside my mouth; I feel nothing at all, apparently because there are fewer nerve endings inside the cheek than on the outside.

The finale, the fractional laser resurfacing, feels very prickly indeed. After all that, I am amazed to find my skin looked only slightly scorched, as if I've been too long in the sun. The redness subsides the next day, followed by a couple of days of flakiness as the scorched skin sloughs off (my teenage son seizes my jaw and turns my face from side to side, observing, 'Well, that laser certainly worked,'), but by the fifth day my skin is looking much brighter and clearer.

Comfort Level

Mildly to moderately uncomfortable, but not enough to put me off going back.

Verdict

Unusually for me, I manage the whole course of treatment – three sessions, each five or six weeks apart – and keep my skin well protected from UV light all the while. After three treatments, my face looks more even in tone, and noticeably 'lifted' from the inside-and-out skin tightening. The lifting effect even softens my nose-to-mouth lines. My skin is more resilient, too – it bounces back more quickly when pinched, which shows that new collagen and elastin, which give skin its firmness and spring, have formed. Very impressive.

Cost and Location

£580 per treatment with Debbie Thomas, dthomas.com.

Would It Work for You?

Yes, because each treatment is personally tailored to suit your skin's requirements, to get the results you are after.

Potential Problems

Treatment may sting a bit, even with anaesthetic cream, depending on how sensitive you are and the intensity of the treatment. Your skin may be red afterwards, possibly for a few days.

If the laser it used incorrectly, it has the potential to burn the skin. While lasers can reduce pigment in the skin, it is possible that treated areas can afterwards become hyperpigmented (over pigmented).

Heat: Skin Tightening with Tixel

Rather more straightforward than any of the above options, you could also choose to stimulate the production of collagen and elastin in the skin with plain heat, which has the bonus effect of tightening up the skin at the same time – as one dermatologist put it, like shrinking a jumper in the wash: the same fibres just end up a little more tightly packed.

The Tixel device can do this. Its treatment head contains 81 titanium rods which heat up to 400 degrees C, and when they are applied, lightly, to the (anaesthetized) surface of your skin, they create tiny channels of damage into the skin in the way that fractional laser or radiofrequency would. There's a treatment review on page 106 of Tixel around the eyes; the treatment can also be used across the whole face.

THREAD LIFTING

Instant face 'lifting' is done with fine sutures that are threaded through the skin, then pulled tight to hoist saggy parts of the face back into a more aesthetically pleasing position. Thread lifting has become very popular in the past few years, to the consternation of those of us who lived through the first wave of enthusiasm for threads in the early 2000s.

I had great difficulty explaining the concept to my editor at the time (2003), and resorted to drawing him a diagram of the face, with arrows showing where the barbed threads were used – four in a fan over either cheek, starting from an anchor-point in the hairline level with the eye; four in the forehead, running vertically from the hairline down to the eyebrows, four in the neck… When the penny dropped, he looked simply appalled and said, 'But you'd look like Spiderman!' until I explained that the threads were hidden neatly inside the skin. Still, the results of those earlier procedures weren't great – sometimes the threads showed through the skin; sometimes they broke…

So when thread-lifts started reappearing around six years ago, I was surprised and sceptical. However, the new procedures seem to be much more successful. They're very quick, and the immediate results look good.

Potential Problems with Thread Lifting

Having said that, threads are still a divisive issue for doctors. For every practitioner who is mad keen on threads and is hoisting people's faces day in and day out, there is another who feels that threads should be avoided like the plague. Problems with threads include rippling of the skin if the threads are over-tightened, grainy growths called granulomas forming along the threads, and knots or ends of threads sticking out of the skin, though experienced practitioners know how to avoid these.

The most common accusation is that thread lifts don't work as well as they are meant to and don't last as long as the 18 months promised. But each to their own. Here's a treatment review from a woman in her fifties who is very happy with her results.

TREATMENT REVIEW: MIDFACE THREAD LIFT

Thread lifts are quick. They take less than an hour, depending on how many threads are used, and give an instant result.

What It Is

The best-known brand in the thread-lifting market is Silhouette Soft, which uses sutures made of poly-L-lactic acid (it's a substance that's used in dissolvable stitches, so well-proven to be safe). These sutures are threaded through the face just underneath the top layer of the skin, from a starting point in the hairline, down through the cheek. The threads have tiny cone-shaped lumps along them, so as they are pulled tight, they lift the skin tissues and anchor them into a new position. Over the next three months, until they are absorbed by the body, the threads stimulate the production of new collagen in the face to help hold the skin tissues in their new position. The lifting effect should last for up to 18 months.

'Silhouette Soft provides an instant physical lift and stimulates the body to restore the collagen that age has diminished,' says Dr Leah Totton, one of the top Silhouette practitioners in the country. 'The threads can be used in the jowls, the chin, the neck, and the midface, so they are my treatment of choice for patients whose skin has started to sag.'

What It's Like
By Dawn Meggs

Even though I work in the beauty industry, I've never tried any cosmetic procedures before, so it seemed a huge step, and I did lose some sleep over it. I was conscious that my face was starting to sag and I was looking very tired, and I thought this procedure would be better for me than surgery, because I wanted a natural look. I didn't want my face to look radically tighter, just fresher and smoother, particularly along the jawline.

I did my research and chose Dr Leah's clinic because she is one of the top people for this procedure – she trains other doctors in how to do it. She's delightful, too, and has a real passion for what she does.

The actual procedure is very quick. It takes around half an hour to put five threads into my face. I have local anaesthetic where the needles carrying the threads go into the face, so it isn't painful, but it is a really weird feeling as the threads are tugged through the skin. I have one thread along each side of my jaw to tighten my jawline, one thread on my right cheek, to lift it, and two on my left cheek to make my face more symmetrical.

Dr Leah explains that some people can end up quite swollen and bruised after treatment, but I only have minimal swelling and no discomfort, and after a couple of days I look normal and just much better. I'm really happy with the way it has made my face look fresher and plumper. I now have a lovely defined jaw and a great set of cheeks.

You get an instant lift from the way the threads tighten the tissues of the face, then a second, firming effect over the next few months as the threads are absorbed into the skin, stimulating it to make more collagen, which keeps it firm.

Comfort Level

Minimal discomfort. It feels strange, but not painful, thanks to the local anaesthetic.

Verdict

This was completely worth it. I'm over the moon and I boast about it all the time.

Cost and Location

The cost of a Silhouette Soft thread lift depends on how many threads are used. The average four-thread lift costs £1,500. Dawn's lift was done by specialist cosmetic doctor Dr Leah Totton at her clinic in Essex, www.drleah.co.uk; for other clinics offering Silhouette Soft, take a look at www.sinclairpharma.com or my website, www.thetweakmentsguide.com.

Would It Work for You?

The sort of result you could get very much depends on what your face is like and how much loose skin there is in which areas. Get a proper consultation with an experienced practitioner before deciding to go ahead.

Potential Problems

Asymmetry if threads are tightened more on one side than the other, and rippling or puckering of the skin if the threads are pulled too tight. Bruising is possible, as is lumpiness if granulomas (tissue growths) form around the threads.

JOWLS AND DOUBLE CHINS

These two don't need much introduction or explanation, do they? Both are an unfortunate combination of fat around the jaw going south with the years and gathering beneath the jawline, made worse by the way underused neck muscles weaken and sag, and older skin being less resilient, so it stretches and pouches to accommodate the extra fat. If you are overweight, your chances of a double chin rise rapidly. Genetics play a part here too – if your parents had jowly necks, you may be heading that way, too.

Exercises for Your Neck

Skincare really isn't going to help shore up a sagging under-the-chin, but it might be worth putting some effort into targeted neck exercises, the sort of things on offer from Danielle Collins (faceyogaexpert.com), Eva Fraser (evafraser.com), or Pilates expert Carme Ferre (studiocarme.co.uk), all of whom promise that their exercises will give good results as long as you learn them properly and practice them consistently.

I have never managed to learn or continue with any of these exercises in a systematic way, but I do remember meeting a woman who worked with Eva Fraser who had managed to avoid the droopy neck, the sort that travels straight from chin to collarbone, that plagued the rest of her family (she showed me pictures) and give herself a lovely jawline simply by doing these exercises religiously. I also thought that she looked like one of the older mothers from the school gates – say, in her late forties – and was amazed to find she was well over 60. All of which gave me a healthy respect for what facial exercises can do, as long as you can discipline yourself to do them.

Tweakments for the Chin and Jowl

There are two key ways to tackle the fat under the chin: you can have it frozen, a procedure that kills off around 20-30 per cent of the fat in the treated area and takes about 12 weeks to show results, or you can have it injected with a substance that dissolves the fat, which is then gradually expelled from your body. Intrigued? Then read on.

FAT FREEZING WITH COOLSCULPTING

Freezing fat sounds a mighty bizarre way to try to reduce fat – until you learn that if living fat cells are chilled to around 4 degrees C, they die. It's a scientific observation that was made years ago and dubbed 'the popsicle effect' (popsicle panniculitis is its technical name) when it was noted that children who spent a long time sucking on iced lollies (popsicles, if you're in the States) could develop dents in the fat inside their cheeks. There is also an often cited case of a woman who rode her horse, naked, in freezing cold weather (why?) and reported losing fat in her inner thighs. Presumably because the saddle was freezing. (If she'd ridden bareback, the horse would surely have kept her thighs warm).

The process of freezing fat to get rid of it is called cryolipolysis (cryo – freezing, and lipolysis – fat destruction), and its great attraction is that, once those fat cells have died, they are gone from the body. This is unlike many non-surgical fat-busting treatments, where the fat cells release their contents and shrink, but stay in place.

You'll find various machines with various names that offer fat-freezing treatments. The one brand that has FDA clearance is Coolsculpting, which is worth knowing because every clinic that offers a different type of fat-freezing machine will say 'Oh, they're all the same.' This is true up to a point, but none of the other brands can offer the safety and efficacy data which Coolsculpting has built up over the years and with which they were able to persuade the regulators at the FDA that their treatment was a good and effective one.

POTENTIAL PROBLEMS WITH FAT-FREEZING

Mostly, fat-freezing is pretty straightforward. There are a few panic-making minutes as the device suctions the area of fat that it is treating into the chilling chamber and the intense cold starts to bite, then it all goes numb (I've tried it on the body, rather than under the chin). When released from the chilling chamber, the almost-frozen lump of fat is massaged, which it is intensely painful – and that's it. But some people experience bruising from where the cooling device has fastened on to their skin, and have sharp pain in the tissue that was frozen, for a week or two after treatment. Others find that the shape of the cooling head, which sucks up a chunk of fat, means the fat loss looks more like a dent than a smooth reduction, though a good practitioner will know how to avoid this with by planning overlapping treatments either side of the central treatment area.

Cryolipolysis is mainly performed on the body, on areas of stubborn fat such as the love handles on the flanks, and the stomach. But now that smaller treatment heads are available, it can be used to great effect beneath the chin.

And if you're thinking, 'Great, but it won't do anything for the sagging under the jowl, will it?' there's good news: CoolSculpting is also FDA-approved for tightening the skin in the treated area.

TREATMENT REVIEW: UNDER-THE-CHIN FAT-FREEZING WITH COOLSCULPTING

The new 'CoolMini' treatment head means that the Coolsculpting machine can be used to reduce pouches of fat beneath the jawline.

What It Is

Tackling the jowls is a tad tricky. Because of the angle between the chin and the neck, it is hard to position the CoolMini device centrally, so two cycles of treatment are usually involved, coming at this fat from either side, with an overlapping area in the centre which is treated twice. First the fatty tissue is suctioned into the treatment head, then it is cooled rapidly for 25 minutes, then the almost-frozen fat is massaged vigorously. The fat cells destroyed by this process are then eliminated from the body over the next 12 weeks.

What It's Like
By Lisa Littlehales

I had a small lump of fat under my chin, so I didn't have a very clearly defined profile. I'd had a mini face lift seven years ago, which made a difference to my nose-to-mouth lines, but didn't improve my profile at all.

I'm an aesthetic nurse and have been giving CoolSculpting treatments for a while, and I know it works, so when the under-the-chin treatment came out, I was really excited to try it. I was a bit nervous – even though I'm a nurse, I'm always nervous before procedures. It's one thing doing treatments, it's quite another one having them, and some of my patients have said that the treatment is really uncomfortable.

When the treatment head sucks up the fat and began the cooling, it feels impossibly uncomfortable, the sort of cold that feels like it is freezing you through to your bones, so it's not the nicest thing to do. It feels awful for 10 minutes, then it goes numb. You can't talk during the treatment, or the device head will pop off the treatment area. When the device is removed and the frozen area is massaged, it is seriously uncomfortable, but it lasts only for a couple of minutes. It feels like some bizarre out-of-body experience, because the fat is numb, yet painful, and it makes me feel a bit sick.

The treated area is numb and tender for the best part of a week afterwards. But the good thing about the chin is that you tend to see results more quickly than on the rest of the body – so even after only five weeks, I can see how well it is working, as my jawline becomes a bit sharper.

Comfort Level

The initial freezing hurts, as does the massage, but the rest is comfortably numb. And it only takes 25 minutes.

Verdict

Brilliant. People can tell I look a bit different, but the funny thing is they don't know what the difference is. Some people ask if I've done something new with my hair; others think I've lost weight – I haven't – but because my jawline looks sharper, it looks as if I have. My profile is just so much better defined. The bit under my chin that was drooping down before now isn't, and the skin has tightened up, too, which is helpful.

Cost and Location

CoolSculpting, from £750 a cycle at the Cavendish Clinic, www.cavendishclinic.co.uk. For other clinics around the UK, see uk.coolsculpting.com or www.thetweakmentsguide.com.

Would It Work for You?

Yes, though exactly how well it will work, and how much fat will die off with each cycle, can vary from patient to patient.

Potential Problems

See the sidebar 'Potential Problems with Fat-Freezing' on page 283.

Treating Jowls with Fat-Dissolving Injections

Having troublesome pockets of fat just dissolved sounds like an ideal solution. If only it were that easy! Well, it is and it isn't. In the Noughties, a treatment known as the 'flab-jab' was popular for this, but because it involved an off-label (ie not officially approved) use of the product, it was eventually withdrawn.

Since then, a couple of new injectable, fat-dissolving treatments have arrived on the market, both of which use a form of deoxycholic acid, a substance which occurs naturally in our bodies and helps us break down fat in our diet. In a more concentrated form in an injection, deoxycholic acid will munch through fat and other tissue in its path, so it needs to be used with great care.

One of these treatments, Aqualyx, comes from an Italian company, and the person who is using it most in London is Dr Sach Mohan at Revere Clinics. He gets remarkable results with it, which you can see on his website, www.revereclinics.com; the treatment costs from £1,500 upward.

The other treatment is called Belkyra, which has achieved FDA approval for using the treatment to tackle fat under the chin, and which is shortly becoming available in the UK. Belkyra is now owned by Allergan, so we will be hearing a good deal more about this once it starts rolling out into UK clinics.

Friends who have tried these treatments say that they can be effective, but you need to be ready for a significant amount of discomfort. The treatment involves dozens of injections into the fatty tissue that you'd like to have reduced, and a few hours after the treatment, the treated area will swell up ('basically, I looked like a bullfrog,' said one) and take weeks to go back to normal.

POTENTIAL PROBLEMS WITH FAT-DISSOLVING INJECTIONS

Concentrated deoxycholic acid is powerful stuff and can dissolve other facial tissues besides fat, so it needs to be used with care and precision by someone who knows what they are doing with it. The treated area will swell and be uncomfortable, and this swelling may persist for some time.

CHAPTER 12

What About the Neck and Décolletage?

Ah yes – what indeed? The best thing you can do for your neck and décolletage is to use the same skincare on it that you use on your face, and to give it the same amount of UV protection. And to have started doing this when you were a teenager. But when I was younger, I simply didn't know that, not until a helpful dermatologist (Dr Nick Lowe) pointed it out to me about 20 years ago, adding that the trouble with the décolletage is that, because of human anatomy, it is slightly tip-tilted at the perfect angle to catch the sun, like our very own solar panel, which means that it is all the more in need of protection.

But somehow most of us manage to forget about all that, and if we do invest in expensive serums and sunscreens, we don't always take them further south than the jaw. Which is fine until you hit your forties, but the older you get, the more annoying it becomes as your neck seems to age faster than your face, and your décolletage gives the game away about every single time it saw too much sun.

WHY DOES THE NECK AGE SO FAST?

Necks just are different. The skin here is thinner than on your face, which means that it collapses more easily into wrinkles and folds, particularly given the way we twist and turn and stretch and compress our necks the whole time. Then there's the fact that there are precious few oil glands in neck skin to keep the skin supple. It all gets much worse when you hit the menopause and, thanks to the reduction in oestrogen, your skin gets drier and loses elasticity.

Does our new fondness for technology make the problem worse? Some skincare companies – ones with neck creams to promote – have claimed that constantly dropping your head forward to look at your phone ages the neck ('Beware of Tech

Neck!' they warn) but I don't really buy that argument. I can see bending your head forward is dire for your posture and exaggerates the folds in the skin, but it's not actually doing anything bad to the skin.

How Skincare Can Help

The right serums and creams can help keep your neck looking better, particularly if you use the same skincare as you use on your face:

* Hydrating hyaluronic acid serums to plump the skin cells
* Antioxidant Vitamin C serum to stimulate the fibroblasts that make collagen and to rein in the activity of the melanocytes that product pigmentation marks
* Retinol or another retinoid for a properly powerful collagen-boosting and skin-smoothing effect.
* And sunscreen. Never forget the sunscreen.

There are many specific neck creams, but here are a couple I can recommend:

* **Prai's Ageless Throat & Décolletage Crème.** This cream costs £19.99 at Boots and Marks & Spencer, so its ingredients aren't rocket-science (though I'm told it does use a kind of technology borrowed from Nasa space mission discoveries – make of that what you will). That said, it does give a very nice cosmetic result and, much to my surprise, when I used it for a week, it made my neck look a whole lot softer and smoother, exactly as it had claimed. I don't know how it did that, because it takes longer than a week to make proper changes in the skin, so it must be a cosmetic effect, but it does the job.
* **Dr Levy Switzerland Décolletage Regenerating Silk.** (£290, drlevyswitzerland.com and www.cultbeauty.co.uk.) If you have money to burn, this is the super-luxe neck cream to try. One of the magic ingredients in here is 'StressCellRepairRM', which claims to be the world's first proven formula to stimulate the dermal stem cells to help repair UV-induced DNA damage. This cream also feels

fabulous on the skin and gives a lovely result, as it should at that price.

The Silicone Chest Pad

There's one entirely non-surgical option worth trying for the décolletage: the self-adhesive silicone chest pad. You can find these on the internet, and all you have to do it stick the pad onto the clean skin of your décolletage overnight. The pad keeps the skin smooth and prevents it creasing up into the usual folds that are created when you curl up and sleep on your side, so your décolletage should look much less creased than usual by the morning. Worth a try.

Tweakments Worth Trying

Beyond skincare, there are several types of tweakments that you can try for the neck. These include radiofrequency or high-intensity focused ultrasound to tighten the skin and moisturising injections to smooth crepiness and 'necklace-line' wrinkles.

TIGHTENING THE SKIN ON THE NECK WITH RADIOFREQUENCY ENERGY

Crepey neck skin will respond as well as the rest of the face to radiofrequency treatments.

TREATMENT REVIEW: VENUS VIVA RADIOFREQUENCY FRACTIONAL SKIN RESURFACING

Most radiofrequency treatments work by heating the lower layers of the skin, but this one uses direct pulses of fractional radiofrequency energy instead.

What It Is

'Fractional' means the radiofrequency energy is delivered through a microgrid, to create micro-channels of damage in the skin in the same way that fractional laser treatment does; the difference is that it is able to trigger this damage-reaction in the lower layers of the skin without harming the skin's surface, which is quite a feat.

Treatment takes 30 minutes, and up to four treatments are recommended. Afterwards, your skin may be red for up to 12 hours, and you shouldn't use makeup or skincare products for 48 hours.

What It's Like

Radiofrequency treatments can become uncomfortably, stabbingly hot when used on the body, so I'm relieved to find that the pulses of the Venus Viva are more in the 'comfortingly warm' range. It feels very strange having my neck treated. It takes less than half an hour to cover the whole neck area, then I'm good to go. My neck and jawline are noticeably tighter and more defined immediately after treatment, though the skin is also a bit red and, as I've been advised not to use make-up on it for 48 hours and hadn't thought to bring a scarf, I have to go home glowing.

Comfort Level

Quite comfortable. It feels almost hot, rather than scorchingly hot.

Verdict

The redness in my neck calms down by the next morning, and the lifting effect lasts for the best part of a week. I know it takes longer for the skin to rebuild collagen (about three months) and also know I'd have a better idea of how this treatment works in the long term if I had gone back to complete the course and had two more rounds of treatment, each a week apart.

Cost and Location

From £200. For clinics, see www.venustreatments.com.

Would It Work for You?

This treatment works best on neck skin that hasn't gone too slack, and you need to commit to the full programme of treatment to see proper results. But it's not painful and not too expensive, compared to some.

Potential Problems

Radiofrequency treatments can range from not-much-more-than-a-facial to seriously intense, and this is treatment at the latter end of the scale. The skin may feel sore and hot afterwards, and may well look red for 24 hours. Don't even think of exposing it to the sun for a month or two after treatment.

TIGHTENING THE SKIN ON THE NECK WITH HIGH-INTENSITY FOCUSED ULTRASOUND

Ultrasound treatment can work well for tautening crepey skin on the neck. Here are a couple of tweakment options.

ULTHERAPY

Making any sort of improvement to sagging skin, whether it's on the face or the neck, is hard to achieve without serious surgery, but Ultherapy offers an FDA-approved new technology to tighten and lift the neck. It does this using a focused beam of ultrasound energy aimed at the collagen in the deeper layers of the skin. This beam can reach 4.5mm below the surface, as deep as the Superficial Muscular Aponeurotic System (SMAS), the layer of muscular tissue in the face that surgeons manipulate when they are performing a face lift.

The focused ultrasound makes the collagen contract and tighten, actually lifting the whole of the treated area, while also stimulating the formation of new collagen and elastin, which further tightens up the skin. (For a review of this treatment on the face, see page 271.)

Treatment takes around half an hour and is a one-off. You'll see a small immediate tightening. The main results will come through over the next three months as the new collagen is formed, and should last for 18 months.

Ultherapy costs from £1,200, at the Cosmetic Skin Clinic, London and Stoke Poges, www.cosmeticskinclinic.com. To find a practitioner in your area, go to www.thetweakmentsguide.com.

ULTRAWON ULTRASOUND TIGHTENING

Ultrawon is another brand of High Intensity Focused Ultrasound (HIFU) which heats the Superficial Muscular Aponeurotic System (SMAS) to tighten the skin, form new collagen, and provide a long-term smoothing and lifting effect. The treatment takes around half an hour, and you are advised to go back for a top-up after six weeks to get the best results, and to repeat the treatment annually.

Ultrawon costs from £600 for neck and décolletage with Dr Sarah Shah, artistryclinic.co.uk. To find a practitioner in your area, go to www.thetweakmentsguide.com.

Would Ultrawon work for you? Dr Shah says that it is good for patients who need overall skin tightening and rejuvenation, whether that's for the face, neck, or décolletage, and that it is less painful than Ultherapy. I'd hazard a guess that that is because it puts less energy into the skin, but she says that the two devices have equivalent results when compared in clinical trials.

SMOOTHING CREPEY SKIN AND 'NECKLACE-LINE' WRINKLES WITH INJECTABLE TREATMENTS

The neck tends to miss out when it comes to tweakments; there aren't so many neck procedures available, and naturally, we always prioritise our faces. But doing that does mean you can get to a point where your neck starts to look a decade older than your face. This is the sort of treatment that helps the neck to keep pace

If you don't know what crepey skin looks like, count yourself lucky; you are probably too young for it. The term comes from skin that is starting to look like crepe paper, which is thin, soft and definitely wrinkly. Necklace lines, the horizontal wrinkles that run around the neck where the skin creases as you bend your head forward, and stay looking creased when you pick your head up, are just as unwelcome. The next treatment can help the appearance of both.

TREATMENT REVIEW: 'THE MOISTURE JAB' – PROFHILO WITH ALIAXIN FOR THE NECK

This injectable treatment involves one skin-conditioning treatment and one filler that work together to improve the look of older necks.

What It Is

Profhilo, which you may have read about on page 149, is a skin-conditioning substance that is injected just under the surface of the skin. Well, it's more than a skin-conditioner; it's what is called a 'biostimulator', as it measurably improves the hydration and elasticity of the skin and encourages the growth of collagen. When you put all of that together and give it eight weeks to go to work, Profhilo leaves the skin firmer, bouncier, and less crepey.

Aliaxin's Shape & Restore, meanwhile, is a very soft and flexible dermal filler made from hyaluronic acid (HA) which is used to fill out the indentations of the 'necklace lines', the horizontal lines that run around the front of the neck.

What It's Like

The Aliaxin injections come first and are challengingly prickly. It's my own fault that I waved away the chance to have anaesthetic cream, thinking I would hardly feel the jabs, but it turns out that my neck is more sensitive than my face, and I can tell that it's a fiddly job for Dr Saira Vasdev, who is doing the treatment, to place small blobs of the product at strategic points along my necklace lines and massage them into place. My neck is very red by the time they are done.

The Profhilo, on the other hand, is a breeze. This is a very runny liquid, and all it takes is five injections on either side of my neck. These each look like swollen insect bites, and I cover them up with a scarf until I get home. Over the next day, these swellings subside as the liquid within them disperses itself throughout my skin. There is some bruising from the Aliaxin, which takes a week to vanish. After four weeks, I go back to the clinic for a second round of both injections, then wait impatiently for another month until the results start to show.

It's a subtle change, but the skin on my neck, reinvigorated and remodelled by the Profhilo, looks smoother and less crepey, even in unkind morning daylight. It also feels more resilient when lifted and pinched, and the Aliaxin has softened my necklace lines but not got rid of them altogether.

Comfort Level

Manageable, but would have been a breeze with numbing cream.

Verdict

Good and noticeable result, but nothing that other people will notice. But I loved this treatment for the way it made my neck look smoother. It is expensive, but a good investment, even if it only lasts for six months.

Cost and Location

Profhilo (£875 for two treatments) and Aliaxin (£400 for 1ml, £700 for 2ml) or £1,450 together, at the Waterhouse Young clinic, Devonshire Street, London; www.waterhouseyoung.com. To find a practitioner in your area, go to www.thetweakmentsguide.com.

Would It Work for You?

Certainly. Maybe leave the Aliaxin for later, and start with the Profhilo, which seems to suit everyone. All the cosmetic clinics I know that are offering it say they are using it on almost all their patients, because regardless of whether patients have come in for Botox, or fillers, or skin-resurfacing laser treatments, the Profhilo helps boost the quality of the skin in a way which offers all-round improvement.

Potential Problems

Few. There is likely to be localised bruising and swelling around the injection sites, just because the neck is a tricky area to inject and tends to react more to injections than, say, the face. The swellings from the Profhilo will disperse under the skin within 24 hours; the lumps from the injections of Aliaxin may take four or five days to settle. But because this is such a flexible type of filler, it is very unlikely to create further lumpiness under the skin.

TREATMENT REVIEW: BOTOX FOR THE NECK

So why would you Botox the neck area when it doesn't have the sort of wrinkles you'd find on the face? Because what Botox can do is soften a stringy-looking neck. You know the sort of older, thinner neck where the tendons stand out like cords? That happens because the platysma muscles on the front of the neck are overly taut. Treat those muscles with Botox, and they will relax, which makes the whole neck look less tense.

What It Is

Injections of Botox placed carefully at the sides of the neck beneath the jaw, and lower down at the sides of the neck, depending on which bits of the platysma are pulling too tightly.

What It's Like

Dr Aamer Khan, who is treating me, asks me to make an exaggerated grimace, widening and dropping my lower jaw to make my neck tighten. As soon as I do that, it's easy to see where the bands of tight muscles stand out. Once he knows where to treat, the injections are quick and easy, and they are only tiny pinpricks, so they really don't hurt.

It's important not to overdo this, says Dr Khan. Too much Botox in this area, and you won't be able to pick your head up off your pillow – and too much around the gullet, and you'll find you won't be able to swallow.

Comfort Level

Very tolerable.

Verdict

Subtle but noticeable. A week after treatment, I can see that my neck looks more relaxed. It's a nice change – not one that anyone else might notice, but it has a really good, softening effect which lasts for four months.

Cost and Location

Botox costs from £199, www.harleystreetskinclinic.com. To find a practitioner in your area, go to www.thetweakmentsguide.com.

Would It Work for You?

It depends on your neck. If you have the sort of neck that tends to look stringy, and where the muscles look very tight, then yes.

Potential Problems

Few, unless your neck muscles were excessively over-treated, in which case you might find it hard to lift your head up off the pillow until the effects began to wear off.

DÉCOLLETAGE

Many of the neck tweakments can be used to good effect on the décolletage:

- Ultherapy can tighten the skin and stimulate the growth of new collagen, which in turn will soften creases in the area. To get an idea of what Ultherapy is like, see page 271 for a treatment review about using it to tighten the skin around the jaw.

- Thermage radiofrequency (see page 265) can also tighten the skin here, and again has a collagen-boosting effect.

- Medical needling, using a small spiky roller, can give great results on the décolletage, though it's not for the fainthearted (see page 133). 'It's a great treatment for this area,' says cosmetic dermatologist Dr Stefanie Williams of eudelo.com, 'though you get even better results if you combine it with injections of hyaluronic acid such as Restylane Vital.'

- Fractional laser treatment such as Fraxel (see page 173) can clear pigmentation on a sun-damaged décolletage.

- IPL treatment (see page 171) can also reduce pigmentation here.

- 'Moisture jab' injections of Profhilo, Volite, or Restylane Skinboosters (see the next treatment review) can hydrate and smooth the skin of the décolletage, reducing wrinkles.

TREATMENT REVIEW: RESTYLANE SKINBOOSTERS TO SOFTEN
A CREPEY DÉCOLLETAGE

The décolletage is a great giveaway of the life you have lived and particularly, how much sun bathing you have done.

What It Is

Restylane's Skinboosters treatment involves having dozens of tiny injections of a runny type of filler gel placed into the top layers of the skin, to provide a layer of moisture that stays actually within the skin itself, in the parts that moisturisers alone can't reach. The gel is made of hyaluronic acid, which holds up to 1,000 times its own weight in water, and which is 'crosslinked' to make it last up to six months in the skin.

What It's Like

Surprisingly easy. I opt to have the treatment without anaesthetic because the injections are made with a very fine needle, and only just into the skin, and sure enough, they hardly hurt. My skin thinks it rather more of a big deal – the décolletage is a delicate area, after all – and swells up in protest around each tiny injection.

By the time the whole thing is done, my décolletage looks as if it has been neatly quilted, like a Chanel handbag. It doesn't hurt at all, so I tuck a silk scarf over it to hide the evidence and carry on with the rest of my day. The quilting effect subsides after a couple of days – so until then, I wear a high-necked top.

Verdict

Very good. I go back for two more rounds of treatment, after which my skin looks healthier and smoother – and it even looks less wrinkled in the mornings. I know that this isn't as noticeable as having a treatment on the face, but it has helped my neglected décolletage look much better.

Cost and Location

Around £800; for clinics, see www.restylane.co.uk.

Would It Work for You?

Yes, absolutely. This is one of those brilliant skin-conditioning moisture-jabs that seems to work well and improve the skin quality and texture for everyone.

Potential Problems

Few. The injections are superficial, so bruising is rare, and the swelling around injection sites will go down in two or three days.

GET MORE INFORMATION – AND REVIEW THIS BOOK

For more information, you can visit this book's website or follow Alice on social media.

And if you have enjoyed this book, please review it online and let others know about it.

Visit This Book's Website

Visit this book's website, www.thetweakmentsguide.com, for further information:

- Explore the tweakment-finder tool to identify which tweakments might be suitable for your specific concerns.
- Narrow your tweakment search with the tweakment-finder tool to identify tweakments and 'facials plus' that work with your budget and your comfort threshold.
- Use the practitioner-finder tool to find a practitioner who offers the tweakments you want in your area.
- Subscribe to Alice's email newsletter.
- Read up-to-date information on the latest tweakments and 'facials plus' on Alice's blog.
- Explore the skincare, supplements, and beauty devices available to boost your home skincare routine.

Follow Alice on Social Media

You can also follow Alice on social media:

- **Instagram:** @alicehartdavis
- **Facebook:** @alicehartdavis
- **YouTube:** AliceHartDavis

Review This Book Online

If you have enjoyed this book and would recommend it to others, please leave a review online. For example, go to Amazon, search for **alice tweakments guide**, and then click the result to get to the book's page.

Printed in Great Britain
by Amazon